NORTH KOREA IN TRANSITION

From Dictatorship to Dynasty

Tai Sung An

Contributions in Political Science, Number 95

GREENWOOD PRESS
Westport, Connecticut • London, England

Library of Congress Cataloging in Publication Data

An, Tai Sung, 1931–
    North Korea in transition.

    (Contributions in political science, ISSN 0147-1066 ;
no. 95)
        Bibliography: p.
        Includes index.
        1. Kim, Il-song, 1912–   —Philosophy.   2. Korea
(North)—Politics and government.   I. Title.
II. Series.
DS934.6. K5A75   1983   320.9'519'3   82-15866
ISBN 0-313-23638-0 (lib. bdg.)

Library of Congress Catalog Card Number: 82-15866
ISBN: 0-313-23638-0
ISSN: 0147-1066

First published in 1983
Greenwood Press
A division of Congressional Information Service, Inc.
88 Post Road West
Westport, Connecticut 06881

Printed in the United States of America

10 9 8 7 6 5 4 3 2 1

For Sihn Ja, Grace, and Jenny

Contents

Tables

Acknowledgments

First of all, a special debt of thanks is due to my wife, Sihn Ja, and my two daughters, Grace and Jenny, for their devoted understanding and constant encouragement while I was preparing this book.

I am also grateful to Geoffrey M. Rogers and Geoffrey R. Garinther, both of whom were my students at Washington College, for their moral support in this project.

Introduction

Karl Marx, the intellectual father of modern communism, died a century ago, and it is just as well that he is not alive to see what happened to his ideas in the lands that pay them lip service.

Since shortly after Marx's death, self-avowed followers of his teachings have been on the march all over the world. In practically no case, however, did history follow Marx's battle plan. The international Communist movement of the present century has established an important precedent that has contradicted some fundamental tenets of Marx's prescriptions and forecasts: instead of taking root in advanced industrial capitalist societies, Marxism has tended to thrive in countries that are economically underdeveloped, socially decaying, and often in or near a state of internal turmoil.

Marx felt that the world proletariat would be victorious against the capitalist enemies only through unity; yet world communism today is more fragmented than ever before in its history. His self-professed disciples are so antagonistic, so split over questions of ideology and other matters. Rival Communists have not only denounced each other for various revisionist and schismatic sins, but they have also gone to war. For example, China and the Soviet Union fought a border war in March-April 1969. Almost ten years later, China invaded Vietnam to "teach it a lesson" for Hanoi's attempt to subjugate Communist Kampuchea. China is currently assisting the Islamic Mujaheddin guerrillas who are fighting against the Soviet occupation forces and the Kremlin's puppet Communist regime in Afghanistan.

Marx foresaw a classless paradise under communism and predicted that the state would become extinct; but world communism seems to have produced just the opposite. The Soviet Union, China, and the other Communist nations are run by a small, self-perpetuating power elite that, while enjoying privileged status, exerts stronger control over the workers than Marx's capitalist villains ever did. Far from dismantling the postrevolutionary state, which Marx had called a temporary "dictatorship of the proletariat," the Communist rulers have, instead, magnified it into an autocratic instrument that, were Marx living under it, would subject his writings to censorship.

In some parts of the Communist world, the rule of a single clique has eventually turned into the despotic, one-man dictatorship of its chief, as exemplified in Russia under Stalin, Albania under Enver Hoxha, North Korea under Kim Il-song, and Romania under Nicolae Ceausescu.

Nepotism and cronyism are not so uncommon in many of the Communist-orbit countries, despite Marxist pretensions to the contrary.[1] The offspring of Communist party leaders are assured the best education, the best jobs, and other special privileges. The result is not merely what Yugoslavia's Communist-turned-critic, Milovan Djilas, denounced twenty-six years ago as a "new class";[2] it is a new aristocracy.

As another, newly developing, and unprecedented case in the history of world communism demonstrating the further adulteration of Marxism, a ruling Communist dynasty has been developing in North Korea (the Democratic People's Republic of Korea, as it is known officially) under its dictatorial leader, Kim Il-song. More specifically, Kim Il-song, who continues to intensify his personality cult and lavishly glorify his family members as true revolutionaries, officially elevated his 40-year-old son, Kim Chong-il, to the status of his future political heir at the Sixth National Congress of the Korean Workers' (Communist) Party held in mid-October 1980. Thus, the DPRK has virtually emerged as the first Communist state to undertake hereditary rule.

In this connection, those interested in North Korean affairs are likely to ask the following questions. Why has the North Korean chieftain taken such an extraordinary measure to make his son his future political successor, clearly in defiance of orthodox Communist practice? What is the DPRK regime's rationale for undertaking dynastic political succession? What manner of man is Kim Il-song? What is Kim Chong-il's personal and political background? What are the leadership styles and techniques of Kim Il-song? What are the meanings, origins, evolution, and symbolic or substantive significance of the senior Kim's political ideology of *chuch'e*, which has now been proclaimed as the sole official ideology of the North Korean political system? What specific functions has the *chuch'e* ideology been performing in North Korean society? How has the *chuch'e* ideology been translated into the DPRK regime's domestic and external policies for the past decades? What is Kim Il-song's "glorious revolutionary tradition" that his son will, as the DPRK mass media solemnly proclaim, "inherit, uphold, and complete" after his death? Would the North Korean Communist dynasty under the Kim clan, along with the senior Kim's militant revolutionary line, survive long after the death of their creator? And, finally, what would be the important implications of the dynastic succession for North Korea's domestic and external politics, at least in the short-term perspective?

This book attempts to answer those questions and to put the DPRK's dynastic political succession in proper perspective by reviewing the process by which both Kim Il-song and his son rose to political prominence, the extravagant cult of the North Korean dictator and his family, and the striking features of the North Korean political system and dynamics.

NOTES

1. For the practice of nepotism and cronyism in some of the Communist countries, see, for example, *New York Times*, November 27, 1979, April 8, 1980, November 9, 1980, and December 21, 1980; and *Washington Post*, April 8, 1980, and December 21, 1980.

2. Milovan Djilas, *The New Class* (New York: Praeger, 1957), pp. 1–214.

North Korea Under Kim Il-Song's Dictatorial Rule

Kim Il-song is the only leader the North Koreans have known since their country's independence in 1948. As such, he is presently one of the longest-tenured Communist rulers, surpassed only by Enver Hoxha of Albania. He is the undisputed supreme leader of North Korea, and is probably the Communist leader least known to the outside world.

The Communist rule in North Korea under Kim Il-song for the past three and a half decades has been distinguished in four ways: (1) the consolidation of his dictatorial power through a series of political purges; (2) his Draconian, highly personalized, extremely nationalistic leadership styles and techniques; (3) an ever intensifying idolization of himself and his family; and (4) his elaborate scheme to forge the world's first Communist family dynasty.

Kim Il-song (his original name was Kim Song-chu) was born on April 15, 1912, in the village of Mankyongdae, near Pyongyang, the present capital of the DPRK. His father, Kim Hyong-jik (1894–1926), was a middle-school teacher in his hometown province, but he reportedly practiced Oriental herb medicine after he and his family emigrated to Manchuria in the late 1910s. Kim Hyong-jik was imprisoned for a while for his anti-Japanese nationalist activities in the Christian-organized *Choson Kungminhoe* (Korean National Association).[1] One secret Japanese police source lists him as an original member of the Korean National Association, although it does not support the allegation of North Korean eulogies that Kim Hyong-jik was the founder of the organization.[2]

In 1919, when Kim Il-song was 7, his family emigrated to South Manchuria, where he was enrolled in a Chinese school.[3] As he was growing into adulthood in Manchuria, he began to take part in anti-Japanese nationalist activities. Contrary to the heroic saga related in North Korea's official hagiographies of Kim Il-song that distort the historical truth,[4] he was not the only "true" or "central" leader of the Korean people's national independence movement against Japan.[5] Many other Koreans were involved in the anti-Japanese liberation struggles in Korea and abroad.[6]

In the early 1930s, Kim Il-song joined the underground Chinese Communist Youth League at the age of 19, and the following year he became the leader of a tiny band of Korean partisans within a Chinese Communist guerrilla army in Manchuria, called the Northeast Anti-Japanese United Army.[7] After 1940, when virtually all the anti-Japanese guerrilla forces, whether Chinese or Koreans, were wiped out by the Japanese army, he and his surviving Korean partisan colleagues retreated into the Soviet Far Eastern provinces, where he was based from 1941 to 1945.

His precise link with the Soviet apparatus during that period has never been clarified. Even official North Korean biographies of Kim's activities in the Soviet Far East from 1941 to 1945 are conspicuously vague, except to mention that he directed small-unit and small-scale hit-and-run campaigns against Japan's mounting antiguerrilla offensives during World War II.[8]

Conflicting information from several sources makes it difficult to verify his actual military responsibilities and achievements. According to one American source, he joined the Soviet Communist party (CPSU) in Siberia,[9] but a Japanese source claims that he was enrolled at the Soviet Military Institute in Khabarovsk for two years.[10] The author of a book published in Japanese in Tokyo in early 1982, allegedly a one-time confidant of the North Korean chieftain who now resides in the Soviet Union in exile under the pseudonym Lim Un, wrote that Kim Il-song served as a captain in the 200-man 88th Special Regiment, a multinational (Russian-Chinese-Korean) reconnaissance unit under the control of the Soviet Far East Forces.[11] According to the author, who claims that he was with Kim Il-song in Khabarovsk in the early 1940s, the 88th Regiment was not a front-line combat outfit; it was merely a unit exclusively engaged in reconnaissance that penetrated into Japanese-controlled areas in

Manchuria.[12] Of the sixty Koreans within the regiment, fewer than twenty were under the direct command of Kim Il-song.[13]

Kim Il-song, along with survivors of his Manchurian partisan group, returned to North Korea in September 1945 as a major in the Soviet army that accepted the surrender of Japanese forces. On October 14, 1945, the 33-year-old Kim appeared at the Pyongyang City Welcoming Rally, where he was introduced by the Soviet occupation authorities as a "hero."

Kim Il-song had played no part in the indigenous Korean Communist movement in the 1920s, which was notorious for its incessant unprincipled, petty factional rivalries. The persistent factionalism in the early Korean Communist movement brought about a severe condemnation, coupled with the expulsion, from the Moscow-controlled Communist International (COMINTERN) in 1928,[14] and virtually ruined the entire movement. The Soviets, who had never forgiven or forgotten the eccentric, disruptive factionalism of the indigenous Korean Communist movement in the past, and who were determined to create a Soviet-oriented satellite in North Korea, turned a cold shoulder toward both the domestic Communist group and the returned Korean Communists from Yenan, China. Instead, they placed subservient and trustworthy Soviet-trained Korean Communists in key positions of power and influence. In short, the birth of the Communist regime in North Korea in 1948 was imposed on the North Korean people by the Soviet Union after World War II.

In 1945, when Kim Il-song returned to North Korea, he lacked a broad-based indigenous organizational structure to consolidate his power. Partly with the backing of the Soviet occupation authorities, partly with the loyal support of his Manchurian partisans, and partly with the speedy build-up of Communist party cells and nuclei, he proceeded to establish a new Communist state in North Korea.[15] He has ruled the country ever since. He consolidated his dictatorial power by eliminating rival factions; and today his Manchurian (Kapsan)[16] faction holds positions of unassailable supremacy in the North Korean power structure.

Joseph Stalin misjudged Kim Il-song to be a pliable puppet when he helped put Kim into power as North Korea's top leader. Since the mid-1950s, Kim has pursued an increasingly nationalistic, independent, and self-reliant policy by skillfully exploiting the Soviet-Chinese rift to enlarge his scope of autonomous action.[17] By doing so, he has managed to shake off his image as a Russian puppet. (Parallel with this move, official North Korean biographers have also obliterated Kim's old connection with the Chinese Communists in Manchuria.)[18] At the same time, the DPRK regime started to downgrade the Soviet role as the "liberator" of Korea and to assert that the Korean people were freed from the thirty-six-year Japanese colonial yoke, not by the Allied forces, but by great leader Comrade Kim Il-song's military victory against the Japanese army. The Soviet Union has apparently been disturbed and displeased by the unfounded allegation of Kim's role as the "liberator" of the Korean people. Each year, on August 15, the Kremlin sends a "congratulatory" cable to Pyongyang in which it reiterates the Soviet role in defeating the Japanese.

Kim Il-song married his first wife, Kim Jung-sook, during his years of exile in Manchuria, where she was a cook at a guerrilla base camp.[19] She bore him two sons and a daughter before dying of tuberculosis on September 22, 1949, at the age of 31. The following year, Kim married his present wife, Kim Song-ae, who had been his secretary. There are five children (two sons and three daughters) by his second marriage.

From the moment of his return to North Korea from Russia in 1945, Kim Il-song demonstrated his predilection for personalized power. Moreover, his passion to dominate—and where he could not dominate, to destroy—was combined with his unscrupulous and strident egotism. It was apparent that he had the ambition to become an individual supreme leader of preeminence in the tradition of Lenin and Stalin before him. As a result, he acted very much like Hobbes's political man who was gripped by a "perpetual and restless desire for power after power."[20] This tendency, reinforced by the demand of the quasi-religious elements of the newly emerging Communist system in North Korea for a single authoritative guide to doctrine and policy, created the potential for personal dictatorship.

Upon Kim's return to North Korea, he had to contend with his Communist and nationalist rivals for power and leadership, many of whom also had impressive anti-Japanese revolutionary records of their own, and they looked askance at his tendency to exaggerate his contribution to the Korean independence struggle against Japan.

Behind his back, they ridiculed Kim as semiliterate, bungling, pretentious, cantankerous, rude, overbearing, ill-tempered, and vainglorious; some of his critics went so far as to call him a "phony" or an "imposter."[21] Such was his insecurity and ambition, his extreme need for recognition and approval, that disparagement of this kind—indeed, any sort of slight—was both unbearable and unforgivable. He probably never forgot the old excruciating ordeal of his wounded and battered pride. Since that time, as evidenced by the cult of his personality that developed after his return (see Chapter 6), he has placed an extraordinarily high premium on public approval and acclaim, as if the memory still pains.

The history of the DPRK repeatedly tells of bloody purges of men with any prominence in their political or military careers who might eclipse Kim's own, whether or not they had actually dared to challenge his leadership. In this process, Kim carried Lenin's favorite maxim, *Kto Kogo?* ("Who compels whom?" or "Who wins against whom?"), into literal practice, not only against outside enemies, but against opponents, both real and imagined, within the ruling hierarchy. Few among the senior Communist revolutionaries, or even his closest comrades from the early days of the Pyongyang regime, were spared in the ruthless series of condemnations. They were stigmatized as "spies for United States imperialists," "factionalists," "revisionists," "flunkeyists," "doctrinaires," and "opportunists," and were removed from the scene one after another.

There are no signs of any opposition likely to challenge Kim Il-song's dictatorial authority. And this has been the situation virtually since the Fourth National Congress of the Korean Workers' Party (KWP) in 1961. It took Kim fifteen years to consolidate his dictatorial rule.

Between 1945 and 1953, Kim Il-song, who was the favorite son of the Soviet military occupation authorities, managed to form a coalition that assured a Communist domination of North Korea. This coalition, under the facade of collective leadership, which Kim had no choice but to tolerate because he was not yet strong enough to dominate single-handedly, was composed of (1) the "domestic" Communists who had survived Japanese repression in Korea and Japan and who were split into North and South Korean factions at that time; (2) the Kapsan, or Manchurian, faction, made up solely of Kim Il-song's Manchurian partisans; (3) the Soviet faction (Soviet-Koreans), composed of Koreans who had lived and studied in the Soviet Union; and (4) the Chinese faction (Yenan-Koreans), consisting of Koreans who had followed Mao Zedong to Yenan and had fought with the Chinese Red Army.

Within this coalition, and indeed even among the foreign-trained Communists, Kim Il-song's Kapsan faction was a minority. Nevertheless, the Russians installed him as North Korea's premier and chairman of the ruling KWP.

From 1945 to 1950, Kim Il-song brought the Soviet and Chinese factions into an alliance to purge the North Korean domestic Communists. Some were put to death, others were sent to prison, and a few fled to South Korea (see Table 1).

In 1953, immediately after the Armistice Agreement on Korea was signed, Kim Il-song used North Korea's failure in the Korean War to eliminate from the party apparatus the South Korean domestic faction led by Pak Hon-yong, who was then the DPRK's deputy premier and foreign minister. In other words, the South Korean domestic faction was made a scapegoat for the poor showing in the Korean War, which was the most disastrous war in Korean history. Kim tried and executed all the South Korean domestic Communists on the grotesque charges of espionage and subversive activities in the service of the U.S. forces during the Korean War (see Table 1).[22]

In the process of consolidating his dictatorial power, Kim Il-song won only a limited victory in 1953. By the rule of politics, a limited victory involves a limited mandate. His unfinished business was to make the victory complete and the mandate unconditional and unconstrained by destroying the remaining rival factions. He succeeded in accomplishing this in 1956, when he launched a second political purge in the midst of the DPRK's preoccupation with reconstruction of the war-torn economy.

Nikita S. Khrushchev's de-Stalinization speech[23] at the Twentieth Congress of the Soviet Communist Party in February 1956 and the subsequent Soviet campaign to downgrade Stalin and Stalinism were critical times for Kim Il-song, who felt the need to defend his own adaptation of Stalinism to North Korean conditions. The opposition to Kim, which surfaced after Khrushchev's de-Stalinization speech and which was led by both the Soviet and Chinese factions within the KWP, hardened into a real campaign of criticism at the

Table 1:
Korean Workers' (Communist) Party Factions, Their Leaders and Key Members, and Purge Data, 1945-1977

Names of Leaders and Key Members	Positions Held	Purge Date	Ultimate Fate
Soviet-Korean Faction			
Ho Ka-i	vice-chmn., KWP CC; lst secy.,. KWP CC; deputy premier	1951	suicide in 1953
Pak Chang-ok	deputy premier; mbre, of Pol. Comm., KWP CC	August 1956	expulsion from KWP, later arrested and deported to Russia in 1958
Pak Ui-wan	mbre. of KWP CC; deputy premier; min. of railroads; min. of light industry; chmn. of State Control Commission	August 1956	expulsion from KWP, arrest
Kim Sung-hwa	mbre. of KWP CC; min. of construction; Principal, Central Party School	August 1956	expulsion from KWP, arrest
Yenan-Korean Faction			
Kim Tu-bong	chmn., SPA; vice-chmn., KWP CC; mbre., KWP CC	August 1956	expulsion from KWP, house arrest
Choe Chang-ik	deputy premier; mbre., Pol. Comm., KWP CC; min. of finance	August 1956	expulsion from KWP, arrest

Table 1: (continued)
Korean Workers' (Communist) Party Factions, Their Leaders and Key Members, and Purge Data, 1945-1977

Names of Leaders and Key Members	Positions Held	Purge Date	Ultimate Fate
Yun Kong-hum	min. of commerce; min. of finance; mbre., KWP CC	August 1956	expulsion from KWP, escape to China
Mu Chong	Army general; vice-chmn., KWP CC; commander of artillery force, KPA	1950	penal servitude, exile to China, where he died
Pak Il-u	mbre., Pol. Comm., KWP CC; min. of internal affairs	April 1955	expulsion from KWP, arrest
Yi Pil-gyu	mbre., KWP CC; bureau chief, cabinet	August 1956	expulsion from KWP, escape to China
So Hwi	mbre., KWP CC; chmn., GFKTU	August 1956	expulsion from KWP, escape to China
Chang Pyong-san	mbre., KWP CC; general, KPA; commander of 4th Corps, KPA	1957	executed
Kim Chang-man	vice-chmn., KWP CC; mbre., Pol. Comm., KWP CC; director, Propaganda Dept., KWP CC; deputy premier	April 1966	expulsion from KWP

North Korean Domestic Faction

Name	Position	Date	Outcome
Hyon Chun-hyok	vice-chmn., Provincial Pol. Comm.	September 1945	assassination
O Ki-sop	mbre., KWP CC; min. of grain purchase	August 1956	expulsion from KWP, arrest
Chu Yong-ha	vice-chmn., KWP CC; mbre., Pol. Comm., KWP CC; min. of transportation	1953	expulsion from KWP

South Korean Domestic Faction

Name	Position	Date	Outcome
Pak Hon-yong	vice-chmn., KWP CC; mbre., Pol. Comm., KWP CC; deputy premier; foreign minister	August 1953	execution in December 1955
Yi Sung-yop	mbre., KWP CC; secy., KWP CC; min. of justice	August 1953	execution
Cho Il-myong	vice-min. of culture and propaganda	August 1953	execution
Yim Wha	vice-chmn., CC; Korean-Russian Cultural Association	August 1953	execution
Pak Sung-won	vice-chmn., Liaison Dept., KWP CC	August 1953	execution
Yi Kang-kook	mbre., KWP CC; president, Commodity Import Company, min. of trade	August 1953	execution
Pae Chol	chief, Liaison Dept., KWP CC	August 1953	execution
Yun Sun-dal	vice-chief, Liaison Dept., KWP CC	August 1953	15 years' imprisonment

Table 1: (continued)
Korean Workers' (Communist) Party Factions, Their Leaders and Key Members, and Purge Data, 1945-1977

Names of Leaders and Key Members	Positions Held	Purge Date	Ultimate Fate
Yi Won-cho	vice-chief, Propaganda and Agitation Dept., KWP CC	August 1953	12 years' imprisonment
Cho Yong-bok	chmn., People's Censorship Comm. staff, min. of home affairs	August 1953	execution
Paik Hyong-bok		August 1953	execution
Sol Chong-sik	seventh mbre., General Political Bureau, supreme command, KPA	August 1953	execution
Kapsan Faction			
Kim Chang-bong	mbre., KWP CC; general of KPA; deputy premier; min. of defense	January 1969	expulsion from KWP, execution
Ho Pong-hak	mbre., KWP CC; general of KPA; chief, Pol. Bureau, KPA; vice-min. of defense	January 1969	expulsion from KWP, execution
*Choe Kwang	mbre., KWP CC; general of KPA; mbre., Pol. Comm., KWP CC; chief of staff, KPA	January 1969	expulsion from KWP, imprisonment

Name	Position	Date	Action
Choe Min-chol	mbre., KWP CC; general of KPA; vice-min. of defense; commander of 1st Corps, KPA	January 1969	expulsion from KWP, imprisonment
Chong Pyong-gap	general of KPA; commander of 3rd Corps, KPA	January 1969	expulsion from KWP, execution
Kim Yang-chun	general of KPA; commander of 7th Corps, KPA	January 1969	expulsion from KWP, imprisonment
Yu Chang-gwon	mbre., KWP CC; vice-admiral, KPA; chief of naval operations, KPA	January 1969	expulsion from KWP, imprisonment
Kim Chong-tae	general of KPA; chief, Intelligence Dept., KPA	January 1969	expulsion from KWP, imprisonment
Kim Kwang-hyop	Brother of Mrs. Kim Il-song (Kim Song-ae); mbre., KWP CC; general of KPA; deputy premier; min. of defense	November 1970	expulsion from KWP
Kim To-man	chief, Propaganda Dept., KWP; mbre., KWP CC Secretariat	April 1967	expulsion from KWP, imprisonment
Sok San	mbre., KWP CC; general of KPA; vice-min. of defense; min. of public security	November 1970	expulsion from KWP
Yi Yong-ho	mbre., KWP CC; general of KPA; vice-min. of defense; ambassador to China	November 1970	expulsion from KWP

Table 1: (continued)
Korean Workers' (Communist) Party Factions, Their Leaders and Key Members, and Purge Data, 1945-1977

Names of Leaders and Key Members	Positions Held	Purge Date	Ultimate Fate
**Yi Ul-sol	mbre., KWP CC; general of KPA; commander of 5th Corps, KPA	February 1974	expulsion from KWP
Yi Yong-mu	mbre., Pol. Comm., KWP CC; general of KPA; director of General Pol. Bureau, KPA	October 1977	expulsion from KWP penal servitude
Pak Kum-chol	mbre., Pol. Comm., KWP CC; director, Organization Dept., KWP CC; general of KPA; vice-chmn., CPUF	April 1967	expulsion from KWP, penal servitude
Yi Hyo-sun	mbre., Pol. Comm., KWP CC; vice-chmn., KWP CC; director, Liaison Dept., KWP CC	April 1967	expulsion from KWP penal servitude

*Rehabilitated in 1977. **Rehabilitated in 1979.

Abbreviations:

CC: Central Committee
Chmn.:   Chairman
Comm.:   Committee
CPUF: Committee for the Peaceful Unification of the Fatherland

Dept.:   Department
GFKTU: General Federation of Korean Trade Unions
KPA: Korean People's Army
KWP: Korean Workers' Party

Mbre.:   Member
Min.:   Minister
Pol.:   Political
Secy.:   Secretary
SPA: Supreme People's Assembly

KWP Central Committee plenum in August 1956 against his ever growing personality cult and other Stalinist tendencies. After this plenum struggle, which was the first and most serious challenge to Kim's leadership since 1945, both the Soviet-Koreans and the Yenan-Koreans were outwitted and expelled from the party as "reactionary and anti-party elements" (see Table 1).[24]

After the August incident, both Moscow and Beijing (Peking) interceded on behalf of the Soviet-Koreans and the Yenan-Koreans by sending Soviet Deputy Premier Anastas Mikoyan and Chinese Defense Minister Peng Dehuai to North Korea. The two men advised Kim Il-song not to consider the August dissidents as "anti-party factionalists" and to reinstate them in the KWP as loyal critics of party policy.[25] As a result of this advice, a few of those who had been expelled were reinstated in the KWP as a token gesture, but both the Soviet-Koreans and the Yenan-Koreans were eventually eliminated by 1958 as the last intraparty factions. At the same time, the hunting down and purging of all those suspected of sympathy with the anti-Kim attack continued with ruthless vigor.[26].

Khrushchev's de-Stalinization campaign was obviously distasteful to Kim Il-song, who was at that time following in Stalin's footsteps. In fact, he and the DPRK regime have hitherto refused to practice de-Stalinization seriously. In November 1961, five years after the August 1956 incident, Kim declared de-Stalinization to be purely an "internal problem of the Soviet Communist Party" and without any relevance whatever for North Korea.[27] Almost two years after that declaration, *Nodong Sinmun (Workers' News)*, the KWP daily organ, asserted: "It is more impermissible to try to force the 'antipersonality cult' campaign on other parties, and behind this smokescreen interfere in the internal affairs of brother Parties and even scheme to overthrow their Party leadership."[28]

During the 1960s and the 1970s, Kim Il-song had staged minor political purges of other remaining dissidents and of unruly members of the Kapsan faction (see Table 1).

Kim Il-song and his Kapsan faction emerged dominant at the KWP's Fourth National Congress in 1961; by then, they had succeeded in eliminating from the KWP leadership all the domestically bred Communists, from the north and the south, and all the foreign-trained Communists, both from Russia and China. He was then ready to set in motion the campaign to consolidate his dictatorial power and to intensify his own idolization.

After destroying all his active opposition, Kim Il-song became dazzled by power and glory and lived up to his concept of his own prestige, his dictatorial form of power. Without doubt, Kim has been the most extravagant Communist ruler of his time. Pomp and pretense have been indispensable to him. For example, his living quarters on the outskirts of Pyongyang are the most sumptuous in Asia.[29] Always, and in everything, he has cared most intensely about his image, his prestige, and his singularity, even through the exaggeration or distortion of self-evident historical truths.

The first step toward the intense glorification of the DPRK chieftain was to rewrite Korean history in the form of excessive adulation of his and his family's contributions to the anti-Japanese national liberation cause, totally denying the contributions made by other patriotic Korean leaders. (It should be noted in this connection that the ruling Communist regimes in the Soviet Union, East Europe and Asia have taken it upon themselves to create historical truths to the detriment of actual events in order to glorify their leaders in power.) His North Korean official biographers have competitively manufactured more and more heroic sagas and legends about his anti-Japanese revolutionary struggle in Manchuria, partly for political myth-making and partly to justify the legitimacy of his rule. The North Korean people have constantly been urged to uphold and emulate their leader's "glorious revolutionary tradition" in Manchuria. This religion-like Kim Il-song cult has been reinforced by the well-established tradition of idolatry toward the ruler in the orient and in the Korean monarchical politics. The result has been one of the most extravagant personality cults accorded any Communist leader, living or dead (see Chapter 6).

The campaign to intensify Kim Il-song's personality cult in the early 1960s was carried out simultaneously with the promotion of his political ideology, the core of which is the concept of *chuch'e* ("self-identity" or "national identity"),[30] which will be discussed shortly. At the fifth plenary session of the Fourth KWP Central Committee in December 1962, Kim Il-song-*chui* ("Kimilsongism"), similar to "Mao Zedong Thought" in China, was upheld by the ruling party apparatus as having "creatively applied Marxism-Leninism into the unique and specific conditions of North Korea and, in so doing, made a great, new, and original contribution to the political thoughts of communism".[31] At the same time, it was adopted and hailed as the one and only ideological system *(yuil han sasang ch'ege)*[32] of the country, and Kim was called "a great Marxist-Leninist theoretician and leader of our times," thus elevating him to a rank equal to that of Lenin and Mao.[33]

Kim Il-song explicitly expounded the idea of *chuch'e* as early as 1955 (see Chapter 2). The concept of *chuch'e*, which will be discussed in detail in Chapters 2 through 5, can be translated into more specific programs of developing and preserving political and ideological independence, economic self-reliance and self-sufficiency, and independent defense capability "to the fullest extent possible."[34] Kim explained:

> Establishing *chuch'e* means, in a nutshell, being the master of revolution and reconstruction in one's own country. This means holding fast to an independent position, rejecting dependence on others, using one's own brains, believing in one's own strength, displaying the revolutionary spirit of self-reliance, and thus solving one's own problems for oneself on one's own responsibility under all circumstances. And it means adhering to the creative position of opposing dogmatism and applying the universal principles of Marxism-Leninism and the experience of other countries to suit the historical conditions and national peculiarities of one's own country.[35]

According to the DPRK regime, the basic premise of *chuch'e* is in full accord with the universal principles of Marxism-Leninism, and the *chuch'e* idea has come into existence as a reflection of a new stage in the international Communist movement. Moreover, North Korean leaders and scholars assert that "Kimilsongism," with the *chuch'e* idea as its backbone, is not merely a modernized version of Marxism-Leninism in the context of changes in time and circumstance; rather, it is a completely original theory based on an independent viewpoint and methodology that is fundamentally different from Marxism-Leninism.

Since the mid-1960s, the DPRK has embarked on a frenzied campaign to institutionalize the *chuch'e* idea as the foundation of North Korea's unique brand of communism and as the cornerstone of all of its domestic and international policies,[36] and the DPRK has begun referring to Kim Il-song as the "Great Leader" (*widaehan chido-ja*). Simultaneously, Kim Il-song's *chuch'e* ideology has been enshrined as a secular national religion that is more sacred, in many ways, than the canons of Marxism-Leninism. For example, Kim's idea of *chuch'e* was codified in Article 4 of the newly revised DPRK Constitution of 1972, as well as in the Preamble of the KWP Charter revised at the Fifth KWP Congress held in November 1970.[37] In the last analysis, the *chuch'e* ideology represents the DPRK's sacrosanct, unchallengeable dogma to rationalize and reinforce all policies and actions—political, economic, military, and diplomatic. Today, the DPRK regime asserts that the *chuch'e* ideology represents the supreme value and the noblest virtue that all North Koreans must aspire to and adopt.

The DPRK under Kim Il-song today is a garrison state, with all the restrictions and austerity that this term implies. A vast apparatus is in place to control the thoughts and behavior of the entire populace. In terms of control mechanisms, North Korea today is reminiscent of the Soviet Union during the Stalin era, and they share the following characteristics: (1) a one-man rule; (2) the excessive deification of the supreme party leader; (3) an officially sanctioned orthodox political ideology that tolerates no challenge, ruling out the existence of an opposing view or argument; (4) a one-party system tightly controlled by a dictator; (5) a pervasive police control system operated by the ruling party and the secret police in order to crush the enemy of the regime and make the party loyal to the dictator; (6) a near-perfect monopolistic control over mass communications; (7) a monopoly of all arms needed for armed conflicts, coupled with the maintenance of highly politicized military forces; and (8) a highly centralized government control over the economy and other aspects of society.[38] In fact, North Korean society is perhaps the most highly regimented, controlled, and mobilized in the world today, within the framework of a clearly defined set of purposes and goals.

The North Korean people are subjected to very rigid control measures, notwithstanding the fact that internal dissidence seems minimal. Every day the North Korean people are subjected to intensive indoctrination on Kim Il-song's political ideology of *chuch'e* that interferes with their private leisure. North Korea vies only with

Stalinist Albania in being the world's most closed society. The DPRK regime prevents North Koreans from eavesdropping on the bourgeois South Korean radio programs by having North Korean radio dials altered so that they can be tuned only to government broadcasts. Life in South Korea and in Western capitalist countries is depicted in the blackest terms.

Persons who fail to cooperate with the regime face imprisonment, confiscation of property, or enforced removal to remote, desolate villages. Those who will not repent are subjected to humiliating abuse. Informers are so prevalent that the average citizen is distrustful of even his close associates. The limits on personal freedom—to travel, to choose one's place of work, and to venture to a big city from the countryside to improve one's life—are all severe. Trips to foreign countries, even Communist allies, are prohibited for the common citizens but are reserved only for trustworthy officials. Emigration is simply not discussed or is unthinkable. "Who would want to leave paradise?" the regime asks.

North Korea under Kim Il-song is a xenophobic, perhaps paranoid, nation. The DPRK regime is notoriously suspicious of all foreigners—including its "fraternal" Communist comrades—and it works very hard to maintain a policy of maximum insulation from the outside world. It is fearful that openness to foreign ideas may subvert the country's official ideology and transform the North Korean people's attitudes and life-styles. The regime tends to see conspiracies everywhere, and Kim Il-song has been quick to discard aides who seemed susceptible to outside ideas and influences. Most parts of the country, including the Demilitarized Zone (DMZ), the 1953 cease-fire line near South Korea, and the northern districts along the borders with China and the Soviet Union, are virtually off limits to foreigners.

George Orwell's fantasy *1984*, depicting the nightmare of a totalitarian society, is close to reality in North Korea. Everything is planned and organized in North Korea. Nothing simply "happens"; everything must be induced to "happen," or, if something has "happened," it must be explained, brought under control, and induced to serve the objectives of the leadership. North Korea is the People's Paradise,[39] so nothing in the world can make the North Koreans envious. Everyone is disciplined, obedient, and happy under the wing of the Beloved and Respected Superman-like Leader who has a panacea for all ills and problesm.[40] The North Korean Ministry of Truth informs, or feels compelled to remind, its privileged citizens that even the birds sing his praise and the animals dance in appreciation of his benevolence, grace, and wisdom. Kim Il-song is the most perfect being, the Emperor of the Kingdom of Happiness, the Omnipotent, and the Omniscient, who has attained divine majesty. His *chuch'e* idea functions as the Holy Scripture.[41]

The DPRK regime under Kim Il-song is highly bureaucratized, and the North Korean bureaucracy is one of the most politicized in the modern world. It seeks a union of the twin priorities of being both "Red" and "expert" in every individual—that is to say, both politically and ideologically loyal and technically competent. In the event of conflict between both demands of being "Red" (political dogma or faith) and "expert" (science and technology), politics takes command.[42] In the quasi-religious atmosphere of the North Korean political system, the DPRK regime strives to deepen the degree of revolutionary dynamism, which explains the need for the chronic mass mobilization that perpetuates the commitment to the politics-takes-command principle. Technical expertise per se may have been tolerated on practical grounds, and "Redness" is proclaimed to be the only source of the right to rule and lead. Kimist political loyalists or priests currently control both the party and the government, with key personnel holding concurrent positions in both organizations in the form of interlocking directorates.

Kim Il-song has converted the ruling Communist party apparatus into a reflection of his personal will. He tolerates no derogation of his own authority, permits no opposition to raise its head within the ruling KWP, and insists that the KWP functions as a unit in executing his will, in pursuit of total mobilization, total control, and total influence. Elsewhere, he monopolizes the mass media with party propaganda and permits no outlet for political programs that challenge his own.

A careful assessment of Kim Il-song's personality and achievements indicates that he is not an especially philosophical or intellectual man, as will be elaborated in Chapter 3. Contrary to the DPRK regime's exaggerated propaganda claims that Kim is the most "brilliant revolutionary theoretician the world has ever produced," he is hardly an original thinker or a foremost creative theorist. For example, his writings and speeches do not reflect the kind of subtle, sophisticated, and deeper consideration given by Mao Zedong to Marxist-Leninist ideology and to the art of revolution. The intellectual quality of Kim's writings and speeches, which are usually tireless but boring repetitions of a few simple, central themes previously expounded, is mediocre in its conceptualization—that is to say, pedestrian or homespun or even catechetical. In addition to the lack of an acute, analytical mind, he is not a gifted orator, and he usually speaks in monotone.

The essence of Kim Il-song's political skill is the manipulation of ideas—usually other people's ideas. He certainly has known how to use them, adapt them, and adjust them, although he may not have been able to invent new ideas. In so doing, moreover, he has replaced complexity with a new kind of simplistic, hyped-up, and practical form.

Kim Il-song is an activist with a keen instinct for survival and power, as well as a doer with great political energy and willpower. Luck and the disunity of his opponents account for some of Kim's success, but the fact remains that he is a man of iron will and indomitable energy who combines fanatical faith in his revolutionary movement and its cause with the same degree of faith in himself. In 1945, he began his political career with only the support of the Soviet occupation authorities. He had neither a substantial indigenous power base nor the prestige of a Lenin, a Mao Zedong, or a Ho Chi Minh. He had to rely heavily on his own dynamism and skill. For the past several decades since then, he has been remarkably successful in effectively using these qualities by gradually and firmly establishing his personal power and influence, which now function as the symbol of North Korean political institutions. Moreover, he has succeeded in transforming uninitiated and disinterested masses into highly disciplined, regimented, and indoctrinated people through a single-minded dedication to his version of a new order in his country and his prescription for attaining that goal.

To achieve what he has done, Kim Il-song needed—and possessed—extraordinary political talents, however autocratic or oppressive their fruits. Without them, he would possibly have been ousted from his position, no matter how strong his Soviet support, in the power and policy struggles of the immediate post-1945 period. His abilities have been demonstrated in the past: his mastery of the irrational factors in politics; his insight into the weaknesses of his opponents; his quick and adroit response and adaptability to changing power relationships at home and abroad; his gift for simplification and pomp; his sense of timing; his formidable resourcefulness; his unscrupulous resoluteness; and his willingness to take risks.

The lesson Kim Il-song draws from his skillful survival as the only leader of the DPRK since 1948 is not, as one might expect from very devout Christian zealots, that destiny is predetermined. Instead, his remarkable survival record for the past several decades has made him something of a loner, confident of his own skill, and wary of trusting his fate to others, at least to other mortals. He is extremely self-confident and arrogant, and he does things his own way. His critics may call these qualities stubborn prejudice and self-righteous combativeness. As a self-made man who has a megalomaniacal estimate of the importance of his undertakings, he has become an evangelist for his beliefs, and he considers his *chuch'e* dogma cardinal principles for which he is determined to fight at any political cost.

As the state president, party chief, and commander-in-chief of the armed forces, Kim Il-song presently has in his hands all the strings of power. As such, he is the acknowledged individual supreme leader of preeminence in North Korea, and he exercises the most pervasive authority over the entire North Korean society. If the French king Louis XIV could say, *L'etat c'est moi*, Kim Il-song, without putting it into words, always has the feeling, *L'etat c'est moi*—that, in him, the national destiny of his country and the will of the continuing movement of socialist revolution and construction in North Korea are concentrated in one man.

Kim Il-song knows that wealth may not always be accompanied by splendor but that power always is. He has yearned, not for the power of law, but for the law of power. Everybody in North Korea is marshalled to join a movement of political dedication requiring total "surrender of souls" to him—a form of spiritual enslavement. In the modern history of despotism, he has had more than a few rivals, yet he remains, so far, one of the most remarkable of those who have used modern techniques to apply the classic formula of tyranny. He has acknowledged no masters or superiors, and until now, he has exercised arbitrary rule over North Korea to a degree rarely, if ever, equaled in a modern society.

Contrary to some views widely held in the West, Kim Il-song is not impulsive, mad, irrational, and reckless. As a hard-boiled realist, he would not rashly jump into risky adventures. His leadership has been based on a realistic calculation of his self-interest, as well as of his country's national interests. In point of fact, his *chuch'e* ideology places the greatest emphasis on self-preservation; Kim and his colleagues are vigorously intent on survival.

An opportunist to some extent, Kim Il-song has shown remarkable consistency in pursuing his objective of unifying the entire Korean peninsula under Communist domination. In fact, the whole nature of North Korean society has been founded on Kim's claim to be the nationalist hero seeking to reunite his divided country in the face of U.S. opposition. He has sought to go down in history as the great unifier of Korea, an ambition that chills South Koreans. (For one thing, the move to make Kim Chong-il his future political successor may reveal the elder Kim's growing realization that his long-held dream may not be fulfilled in his own lifetime. His son will have to pursue this goal persistently after Kim's death.)

Like other self-centered, sanctimonious politicians of the world, Kim Il-song has not been immune to charges of indulging in self-contradiction, double-talk, and double standards. For example, he has repeatedly condemned individual "heroism" as the symptom of bourgeois romanticism while accepting and even encouraging his own extravagant personality cult. He has strongly attacked religion as the opiate of the people while promoting the nationwide quasi-religious worship of himself as a messiah or demigod. He has assailed individualism, parochialism, clannishness, and nepotism, but he glorifies almost all the members of his family, dead and alive, as true revolutionaries and retains his relatives, his Manchurian guerrilla colleagues, and their kinfolk in high party and government positions. In essence, politics in North Korea today has become a highly personalized family affair built around his personality cult. He has often castigated revisionists, dogmatists, and other types of factionalists, but he has turned a blind eye to his own factional activities and revisionist ideas.

Although Kim Il-song is one of the few Communist leaders in the world with long tenure, he clearly does not possess authority and prestige in the Communist world which Mao Zedong and Ho Chi Minh commanded. As far as is known, his international reputation or prestige does not measure up to what he and the DPRK regime think it is or ought to be, as several of the following incidents demonstrate.

In September 1977, when the DPRK sponsored an international seminar on the *chuch'e* philosophy in Pyongyang in order to draw worldwide attention to "Kimilsongism," nongovernmental delegates from seventy-three countries (mostly from the Third World) and four regional organizations participated.[43] Significantly, none of the Communist-orbit countries, except for Yugoslavia, sent representatives. (Yugoslavia sent very low-level nongovernmental delegates to the seminar, probably not because it was impressed by the doctrinal quality of Kim's *chuch'e* ideology, but because it simply wanted to render moral support to Kim's policy of positive independence in Communist-bloc affairs—the same nationalistic posture that Belgrade has been maintaining persistently and diligently since 1948.)

The Beijing regime has publicly praised Kim Il-song by calling him a great leader. However, according to Enver Hoxha of Albania, who had maintained close relations with China from 1961 to 1977, the Chinese Communist leaders privately told him and other Albanians: "He has no value at all; he has been a corporal in the Chinese [Communist guerrilla] army [in Manchuria in the 1930s]."[44]

A Chinese attack against Kim Il-song was made publicly and directly during the hectic days of the Cultural Revolution. In early 1967, wall posters of the Red Guards in Beijing called him a "fat revisionist."[45] In a speech during the same disruptive phase of the Cultural Revolution, Chinese Premier Zhou Enlai's reference to the North Koreans as belonging to China's enemies in the "revisionist" camp obviously did not exclude the DPRK chieftain from this category.[46]

It is apparent that the Kremlin, in early 1982, did not try to dissuade a former Korean guerrilla colleague of Kim Il-song in Manchuria, now in exile in the Soviet Union under Moscow's protective custody, from publishing a Japanese-language book that is designed primarily to smear the DPRK dictator personally and politically by washing Kim's dirty linen in public.[47]

Enver Hoxha, the long-time Stalinist Communist leader of Albania, publicly called Kim Il-song "a pseudo-Marxist and a vacillating, revisionist megalomaniac," in his book published in late 1979.[48]

Kim Il-song still seeks to build himself as a leading figure of the Third World,[49] and for years, he has been portrayed in North Korean propaganda as a senior statesman of the nonaligned world. (A high point in North Korea's worldwide diplomatic campaign was its entry to the nonaligned Third World at the conference of foreign ministers of eighty nonaligned states in Lima, Peru, in August 1975. South Korea's membership application was rejected.) Kim has established many pro-Pyongyang organizations in the Third World that have preached his *chuch'e* ideology. He is now known to consider himself a successor to the late President Tito of Yugoslavia as a father figure for the nonaligned world.[50] But there are clear indications that this ambition has not been warmly received by the political leaders of the Third World countries. Several examples can be cited in support of this hypothesis.

The DPRK's decision to support Iran against Iraq in the Persian Gulf war between the two countries that began in 1980 seemed to have done more harm than good to Kim Il-song's ambition for leadership in the Third World. (During the fall of 1980, North Korea was selling ammunition for small arms and artillery to Iran in its war against Iraq. There seemed to be no particular ideological reason for Pyongyang to aid Iran. Rather, the DPRK regime probably wanted hard currency that Iran could supply. In retaliation, Iraq broke off diplomatic ties with North Korea in mid-October 1980.)[51]

At the nonaligned foreign ministers' conference held in New Delhi in mid-February 1981, the DPRK suffered a major diplomatic setback when its demand to include the Korean unification question on the conference agenda was ignored or even rejected ignominiously by the conference participants.[52] India's Prime Minister Indira Gandhi was believed to have played a major role in this event.

During late 1981, the International Olympic Committee awarded the 1988 Summer Olympic Games to South Korea, and the 1986 Asian Games were also given to South Korea after an Asian Games Federation delegation found the rival facilities offered by North Korea "poor" and "outdated."[53] South Korea's successful bids for both events raised the prospect of a flood of visitors from the Third World and vast publicity for Seoul, and it was a bitter disappointment for Kim Il-song and his regime. The awarding of both sets of games to South Korea clearly represented a dramatic gesture to bolster its legitimacy internationally to counteract North Korea's tirades against the "puppet regime" in Seoul.

At the age of 70, Kim Il-song nears his twilight. The approaching post-Kim era poses many uncertainties about the future of the DPRK. Whatever the nature of the Pyongyang regime and the direction of its internal and external policies in the post-Kim period ahead, it must be remembered that Kim Il-song is a man of many significant revolutionary achievements in his own lifetime. Under his leadership, North Korea has a rejuvenated national confidence, a spirit of national identity and unity, and a sense of national purpose. It has acquired a commitment and a dedication to self-discipline and self-reliance based on hard work and on collective efforts to solve the country's urgent and difficult problems of underdevelopment. Kim Il-song will undoubtedly go down in the long history of Korea as one of its revolutionary leaders, which should be enough for the ambition of any man. It is clear, however, that he is not satisfied with these lifetime accomplishments; he wants more. He would wish to go down in history as the man who expounded and prescribed an immortal guiding philosophy for the future of his country.

At the same time, Kim Il-song appears to be keenly aware of the ultimate fate of both Stalinism and Maoism in the hands of posterity. In a way, he is a lonely and restless man who is obsessed with the immortality of his militant revolutionary line but who is simultaneously unsure of the survival of his own brand of radical revolutionary orthodoxy after his death.

In this connection, incidentally, a striking contrast to Kim Il-song is Ho Chi Minh, Vietnam's unique, outstanding revolutionary leader of truly international status, for whom even the bitterest opponents could not help feeling grudging respect. Ho was always modest, reserved, and unpretentious in his outward mannerisms,[54] but he felt extremely secure and self-confident about his achievements and place in history and the eventual reunification of the whole Vietnam under Communist domination. He knew that events in history were transitory or ephemeral, so he never sought the immortality of his ideas and actions. He firmly refused to be idolized and deified by his people, asserting that "deification of a leader will lower the position of the masses of people and even the leader himself."[55] He criticized Mao Zedong as a "leader cut off from the people" and a Don Quixote tilting at ideological windmills, when the extravagant personality cult of the late Chinese Communist leader climaxed during the Cultural Revolution.[56]

NOTES

1. See, for example, Sung Chul Yang, "The Kim Il-song Cult in North Korea," *Korea and World Affairs* (Seoul), Spring 1980, p. 164.

2. Kang Tok-sang, ed., *Chosen* [Korea] 1 (Vol. XXV of *Gendaishi shiryo* [Sources of Contemporary History]) (Tokyo: Misuzu Shobo, 1976), pp. 35–38, cited in Yong-ho Ch'oe, "Reinterpreting Traditional History in North Korea," *Journal of Asian Studies,* May 1981, p. 520.

3. Na Yung-yi, *Choson Minjok Haebang Tujangsa* [The History of Korean People's Liberation Struggle] (Pyongyang: Choson Nodong-dang Ch'ulpsansa, 1958), p. 337.

4. For North Korea's officially sanctioned biographies of Kim Il-song, see, for example, *Brief History of the Revolutionary Activities of Comrade Kim Il-song* (Pyongyang: Foreign Languages Publishing House, 1969), pp. 1–295; Baik Bong, *Kim Il-song Biography: From Birth to Triumphant Return to Homeland* (New York: The Guardian, 1969), I: 1–571, II: 1–623, and III: 1–674; and Han Im-hyok, *Kim Il-song Tongji Uihan Choson Kongsangdang Ch'ang-gon* [The Founding of the Korean Communist Party by Comrade Kim Il-song] (Pyongyang: Nodong-dang Ch'ulpansa, 1961), pp. 1–56. See also a list of the DPRK-published, Korean-language books in the Bibliography, which are related to the extravagant personality cult of Kim Il-song.

5. For a more accurate description of Kim Il-song's controversial life in Manchuria and the Soviet Union, see, for example, Dae-Sook Suh, *The Korean Communist Movement 1918–1948* (Princeton: Princeton University Press, 1967), pp. 253–93.

6. For a detailed study of the anti-Japanese Korean independence movements in Korea and abroad up to 1945, see Chong-sik Lee, *The Politics of Korean Nationalism* (Berkeley and Los Angeles: University of California Press, 1963), pp. 1–327.

7. Suh, *Korean Communist Movement,* pp. 275–82.

8. See note 4 of this chapter.

9. Robert A. Scalapino, "Foreign Policy of North Korea," *China Quarterly,* April–June 1963, p. 44.

10. Tsuboe Senji, *Hokusen no Kaiho Junen* [Ten-Year History of North Korea] (Tokyo: Mikkan Rodo Sushinsha, 1955), p. 19.

11. The title of this book is *The Secrets of the North Korean Dynasty: True Biography of Kim Il-song.* See excerpts of this book in *Korea Herald* (Seoul), April 4 and 5, 1982; and in *Dong-A Ilbo* (Seoul), March 26, 1982.

12. Ibid.

13. Ibid.

14. For the details of notorious factionalism in the Korean Communist movement in the 1920s, see Robert A. Scalapino and Chong-sik Lee, "The Origins of the Korean Communist Movement," *Journal of Asian Studies,* November 1960, pp. 9–31, and February 1961, pp. 149–67; and Suh, *Korean Communist Movement,* pp. 1–338.

15. For a detailed study of the process of Communist takeover in North Korea under Kim Il-song, see U.S., Department of State, *North Korea: A Case Study in the Techniques of Takeover* (Washington, D.C., 1961), pp. 1–121.

16. Kapsan is the name of the place in North Korea near the Manchurian border where Kim Il-song's Korean Communist guerrillas had headquarters before escaping to the Soviet Far Eastern provinces in 1940.

17. For the details, see Chin O. Chung, *Pyongyang Between Peking and Moscow: North Korea's Involvement in the Sino-Soviet Dispute, 1958–1975* (University, Alabama: University of Alabama Press, 1978), pp. 1–224.

18. See note 4 of this chapter.

19. Kim Jung-sook was born in Haeryong, North Hamgyong Province, on December 24, 1917, as the second daughter to Mr. Kim Chun-song, her father, and Mrs. O Pok-tong, her mother. She had two brothers, Kim Ki-song and Kim Ki-chun.

20. Quoted from Thomas Hobbes, *Leviathan* (New York: Dutton, 1950), pp. 79–80.

21. Oh Young-jin, *Sso Goonjung Hahei Bukhan: Hahna ei Jeungun* [North Korea Under Soviet Occupation: An Eyewitness] (Seoul: Joongang Moonhwa-sa, 1952), pp. 141–43.

22. *Nodong Sinmun*, August 5, 6, and 7, 1953; *New York Times*, December 19, 1955; and Kim Il-song, *Kim Il-song Sonjip* [Selected Works of Kim Il-song] (Pyongyang: Choson Nodong-dang Ch'ulpansa, 1960–1966), IV:192.

23. For the full text of Khrushchev's de-Stalinization speech, see *Khrushchev Remembers*, translated and edited by Strobe Talbott (Boston: Little, Brown and Co., 1970), pp. 559–618.

24. For the details, see Kim Chang-sun, *Pukhan Sibonyon Sa: 1945 nyon 8 wol— 1961 nyon 1 wol* [Fifteen-Year History of North Korea: From August 1945–January 1961] (Seoul: Chimungkak, 1961), pp. 1–283; and Lee Chol-chu, "The North Korean Communist Party," *Sin Tong A* [New East Asia] (Seoul), May 1965, pp. 260–97.

25. Kim Chang-sun, *Pukhan Sibonyon Sa*, pp. 57–58] and Glenn D. Paige and Dong Jung Lee, "The Post-War Politics of Communist Korea," *China Quarterly*, April–June 1963, pp. 25–26.

26. Han Jae-duk, "Communist Life in North Korea," *Korea Journal* (Seoul), November 1963; p. 13.

27. *Nodong Sinmun*, November 28, 1961.

28. "Let Us Defend the Socialist Camp!" *Nodong Sinmun*, October 28, 1963. This editorial was perhaps the severest of all the indictments directed at the Soviet Union by the North Korean leadership.

29. An Egyptian columnist for the Egyptian daily "Al Akhbar" [The News] in Cairo, Maha Abdel Fattah, who accompanied Egyptian Foreign Minister Kamal Hassan Ali on his trip to North Korea in September 1981, said: "We have visited the countries of the world and seen the palaces of the kings of Europe and entered the [American] White House but nowhere have we seen the splendor and magnificence of Kim's palace." *Al Akhbar*, October 11, 1981, cited in *Korea Herald* (Seoul), October 18, 1981.

30. Literally, *chuch'e* means "subjective core." In the DPRK lexicon, it has its identical meaning of "national identity" or "self-reliance."

31. Nam In-hyok, *Widaehan Suryong Kim Il-song Tongchi ui Yongdo mit'ae Sungilhan Minchok Haepang Inmin Minchuchi Hyokmyong Kyongham* [The Expe-

rience of National Liberation and People's Democratic Revolution Under the Leadership of the Great Leader Kim Il-song] (Pyongyang: Humanistic Sciences Press, 1972), pp. 1–65; and "For a Correct Understanding of Chuch'e," *Nodong Sinmun*, July 21, 1956.

32. Literally, *yuil han* means "the one and only," and *sasang ch'ege* means "ideological system." Then, *yuil han sasang ch'ege* means "the one and only, or sole, ideological system"—that is to say, the sacrosanct and unchallengeable dogma.

33. See, for example, Ch'oe Yong-kon, "The Great Leader Kim Il-song Is the Originator of Our Party's Revolutionary Tradition," *Nodong Sinmun*, April 1, 1972; and *Nodong Sinmun*, October 21, 1972.

34. Kim Il-song, "The Present Situation and the Tasks Confronting Our Party," report delivered at the Conference of the Korean Workers' Party on October 5, 1966 (Central Committee of the General Association of Korean Residents in Japan, October 1966), p. 38.

35. Kim Il-song, "On Immediate Political and Economic Policies of the Democratic People's Republic of Korea and Some International Problems," answers to questions raised by newsmen of the Japanese daily *Yomiuri Shimbun*, January 10, 1972.

36. Kim Il-song, *On Some Problems of Our Party's Chuch'e Idea and the Government of the Republic's Internal and External Policies*, answers to the questions raised by journalists of the Japanese newspaper "Mainichi Shimbun," September 17, 1972 (Pyongyang: Foreign Languages Publishing House, 1972), pp. 14–15.

37. See Dae-Sook Suh, *Korean Communism 1945–1980* (Honolulu, Hawaii: University of Hawaii Press, 1981), pp. 502, 524.

38. See, for example, Merle Fainsod, *How Russia Is Ruled* (Cambridge, Mass.: Harvard University Press, 1953), pp. 3–545; and Robert A. Scalapino and Chong-sik Lee, *Communism in Korea* (Berkeley and Los Angeles: University of California Press (1972), 2: 686–1533.

39. North Korea was officially declared "paradise" in the late 1970s. See Chapter 6.

40. Ibid.

41. Ibid.

42. Ilpyong J. Kim, "The Mobilization System in North Korean Politics," *Journal of Korean Affairs*, April 1972, pp. 3–15.

43. For the details of this seminar, see An Chang-su and Pak In-su, *Chuch'e-ae Songka* [The Song of the Chuch'e Idea] (Pyongyang: Samhaksa, 1977), pp. 1–543.

44. Enver Hoxha, *Reflections on China* (Tirana, Albania: The "8" Nentori Publishing House, 1979), 1: 579.

45. Chin O. Chung, *Pyongyang Between Peking and Moscow*, p. 130; and *China Quarterly*, April–June 1967, p. 247.

46. Cited in Chien Yu-shen, *China's Fading Revolution: Army Dissent and Military Division, 1967–1968* (Hong Kong: Center of Contemporary Chinese Studies, 1969), p. 322.

47. See note 11 of this chapter.

48. Enver Hoxha, *Reflections*, II: 520–21, 548, 592–93.

49. For the expression of this ambition, see "Our People Will Continue to Advance Upholding the Banner of Nonalignment, the Banner of Independence," *Nodong Sinmun*, August 24, 1980; and "The Nonaligned Movement Is an

Antiwar, Peace Force," *Nodong Sinmun*, September 17, 1980.

50. According to Japanese correspondent Schiozima in Beijing, at his meeting with a Japanese Socialist party delegation, Kim Il-song expressed the notion that he would like to play a leading role in the nonaligned movement following the death of Tito. *Foreign Broadcast Information Service*, Asia and Pacific, September 29, 1980, pp. D3-D4. In recent years, Kim Il-song has been a staunch supporter of the Tito thesis that the nonaligned movement of the Third World must remain "an autonomous political force outside power blocs." See *Le Monde* (Paris), August 2, 3, and 4, 1979.

51. *New York Times*, October 9, 1980; and *Korea Herald*, October 10, 11, 12, and 26, 1980.

53. *Korea Herald*, November 27, 1981.

54. Ho Chi Minh died on September 3, 1969. When a foreign visitor asked him if he planned to publish articles or books, as did Mao Zedong, he replied modestly and even sarcastically, "If there is a subject Chairman Mao has not written about, tell me and I will try to fill in the gap." Jean Lacouture, *Ho Chi Minh: A Political Biography*, translated by Peter Wiles; translation edited by Jane Clark Seitz (New York: Random House, 1968), p. 247.

55. Hong Chuong (pseudonym presumably for Ho Chi Minh), "Leaders and the Masses," *Hoc Tap*, Hanoi, May 1967.

56. Ibid.

2

The Historical Roots and Development of the *Chuch'e* Ideology

The Korean nation, with its national existence of more than 2,000 years and with a homogeneous population of 57 million (north and south combined), is one of the oldest countries in the world. Until its partition into the two antagonistic political entities at the end of World War II, Korea, a small peninsula in Northeast Asia, had waged persistent struggles to retain its national independence and identity against powerful, often expansionist neighbors. From the centuries-old struggles against foreign domination, the tradition of strong nationalism has developed among the Korean people. Even today, three and a half decades after the partition of Korea, national-ism continues to play an important role in South and North Korea.

The tradition of strong nationalism among the Korean people in the pre-1945 period coexisted with another tradition of *sadaechuii* ("rely on or emulate superior foreign powers," or competition for foreign support through "flunkeyism" or sycophancy) that was preva-lent and notorious among the Confucian-educated imperial power elite (palace officials) of the last imperial Yi dynasty (1392–1910). It also existed among an educated elite group of antimonarchist, progressive-minded Koreans, particularly in the late nineteenth and early twentieth centuries, before the Japanese colonization of Korea in 1910.[1] Different factions within these ruling and nonruling elite groups were eager to make their own bid for political and cultural collaboration with their favorite foreign powers who were bent on dominating Korea.[2]

The intensified emphasis on nationalism is an outstanding characteristic of North Korean politics under Kim Il-song. This has been reflected in his economic, diplomatic, military, and other policies—all of which are embodied in his ideology of *chuch'e* (see Chapters 4 and 5). In a fundamental sense, Kim's *chuch'e* ideology represents his reaction to the *sadaechuii* tradition of slave mentality in old Korea, thereby conveying his yearning for national pride, self-identity, and independence. Kim defines *chuch'e* as follows:

> By the establishment of *chuch'e* we mean holding to the principle of solving for oneself all the problems of the revolution and construction in conformity with the actual conditions at home, and mainly by one's own efforts . . . This is an independent, self-reliant policy of solving one's own affairs by oneself under all circumstances.[3]

In other words, the *chuch'e* ideology is based on the conviction that the management of both domestic and international affairs of the country should be handled by the North Koreans, independent of foreign interference, through the policy of self-reliance "to the fullest extent possible."[4] In short, Kim has combined the ingrown elements of Korea's nationalistic heritage with Marxism-Leninism within the ideological framework of *chuch'e*. (In the process, as will be seen in Chapter 4, the Marxist-Leninist elements in his *chuch'e* ideology have suffered a progressive symbolic and substantive slippage.)

The idea of *chuch'e* did not emerge full-grown overnight with the establishment of the North Korean Communist regime in September 1948. Kim Il-song's *chuch'e* ideology is based on his revolutionary experiences over several decades.

The historical origins can be traced back to Kim Il-song's early anti-Japanese guerrilla experiences in Manchuria in the 1930s. In fact, an official North Korean biographer dates the origin of *chuch'e* as far back as the 1930s, when this symbol was said to have been "established for the first time" in his long revolutionary career.[5] During this period of extremely difficult and arduous guerrilla resistance, Kim realized that he could count on nobody but himself, his trusted Korean partisan colleagues, and his kinfolk. While in Manchuria, moreover, Kim and his Korean Communist guerrilla unit heard about the Min-sheng-t'uan Incident of 1933–1936[6] in which the Chinese Communists displayed heavy-handed anti-Korean bias.[7]

While in exile in the Soviet Far East, he was believed to have developed deep personal antipathies for the Soviet Union based on its racist mistreatment of the Korean minority in the Soviet Far East during the pre-1945 period.[8] It is quite possible that Kim himself felt pressured to accept an inferior racial status toward his Russian hosts because he, as Moscow's client, had to function under their "benevolent" hospitality and paternalistic guidance. During the preliberation days, by and large, a deep-rooted xenophobia, in the form of intense nationalism, had steadily grown in Kim Il-song's mind. And it eventually developed into the present form of his *chuch'e* ideology after his return to North Korea.

It is not accurate to say that Kim Il-song alone originated the idea of *chuch'e* since other prominent anti-Japanese Korean revolutionaries, both Communist and nationalist, also advocated the same idea (if not by name) of independence, self-identity, or self-reliance in the immediate postliberation period. But Kim Il-song was the only Korean political leader of that time who succeeded in elaborating the idea and in developing its full political potential, in response to a succession of various circumstances at home and abroad after the establishment of the DPRK in 1948.

After Kim Il-song's return to North Korea in 1945, he quickly began manifesting his reaction against Korea's pre-1945 political and cultural tradition of *sadaechuii*, although he had started his political career as a Soviet puppet. In the late 1940s, his *chuch'e* idea was slowly but obliquely developing into an embryonic, low-key form under the watchful eyes of the Soviet occupation authorities.[9] In September 1948, for example, the Pyongyang regime initiated the language reform of officially banning the century-old use of Chinese characters (*hancha*), inaugurating a nationalistic process of the exclusive use of the pure Korean alphabet (*hangul*).

Between 1945 and 1950, when North Korea was virtually a Soviet satellite, the Soviet model of development as the "universal truth" was applied to almost every aspect of North Korean society in a highly mechanized fashion. During this period, Kim Il-song was apparently disturbed by the striking similarity between the Soviet and the Japanese economic exploitation of North Korea.[10]

Pyongyang's own sources help to confirm this fact, as will be discussed later. (It is well known now that, in the immediate post-1945 period, Stalin tyrannized the Soviet-occupied territories in Eastern Europe and Asia, exploited their resources, and looted them in the short-term national interests of the Soviet Union. For the rest of the world, he was content to exploit revolutionary attitudes and moods in a purely negative way.)

Kim must have recognized then that powerful and often expansionist neighbors had never dealt kindly with Korea, and that however much they had wrung their hands in anguish about trying to help Korea, they had shown very little real benevolence and a great tendency to be patronizing and oppressive toward Korea and Koreans. (One of the earliest encounters between Russia and Korea came in Mongol times when Russian recruits were included in an expeditionary force sent to crush Korean uprisings.)

In a rebuttal to a polemical *Pravda* article reminding the North Koreans not to forget the Soviet aid shortly after 1945, *Nodong Sinmun*, in September 1964, unleashed a scathing attack against the Soviet leadership, accusing it of having taken away during the late 1940s "several tens of tons of gold and huge quantities of precious metals and raw materials at prices much lower than international market prices."[11] The KWP organ also charged that the Soviet Union was less than fraternal since North Korea had to pay for the equipment, stainless plate, and other materials provided by Moscow "at prices much higher than international prices as part of the so-called aid."[12]

The April 1963 issue of *Kulloja* (*Workers*), the theoretical monthly journal of the KWP Central Committee, pointedly alluded to the fact that as early as 1947, Kim Il-song had given serious thought to the question of economic independence. He was quoted as having said at that time: "We must by all means build our own self-reliant economic foundation . . . Without a self-sustaining economic foundation, we cannot be independent, build a nation, nor even survive."[13] This was his first manifestation of *chuch'e* in the economic domain. In retrospect, it is apparent that in the early 1950s, Kim Il-song began to argue that economic independence was a precondition for political independence and for the construction of a modern, industrialized economy, particularly in an excolonial, underdeveloped nation like North Korea.[14]

Apart from the economic grievances, Kim Il-song's disastrous Korean War experience,[15] during which the Soviet Union proved to be an unreliable ally, had also powerfully stimulated his quest for self-reliance. Undoubtedly, the war left Kim feeling bitter because he believed he would have conquered and thus reunified the entire Korean peninsula under Communist control if he had a little extra aid from Stalin when the advancing Russian-armed North Korean forces were stopped almost within reach of Taegue and Pusan only because of the air superiority of the United States. Available evidence confirms that Kim did not get that extra military help from Moscow during the critical hour before his forward columns were encircled and cut to pieces following General MacArthur's landing at Inchon. Khrushchev's memoirs leave the impression that Stalin apparently did not approve Kim's request for more direct Soviet military aid, probably in the form of air coverage by the Soviet air force, because of Stalin's fear of a direct Soviet military confrontation with the United States.[16]

North Korea's exclusive economic and military reliance on the Soviet Union came to an end after the Korean War, and China clearly emerged as Russia's principal rival for influence in North Korea. However, the primacy of Soviet influence in the DPRK continued a while longer.

On the political level, Kim Il-song's efforts to assert *chuch'e* had begun even before the Korean War ended. For him, the idea of *chuch'e* served the dual purpose of appealing to the traditionally nationalistic Korean people for their support and of undercutting the position of his domestic rivals, whom he was to denounce and purge in the 1950s as being oriented toward foreign countries— namely, the Soviet Union and China—by their advocacy of the Soviet or the Chinese way of solving domestic problems.[17]

Kim Il-song's parallel strategy was to bolster his political prestige and stature by exalting his revolutionary credentials as a genuine national hero through the development of his personality cult campaign (see Chapter 6). Thus, both the *chuch'e* idea and the personality cult campaign were utilized as devices to rationalize and legitimize Kim Il-song's consolidation of power at home, in addition to eradicating the Russian influence in his country.

Kim Il-song deeply resented the Soviet determination to keep him and his regime under fairly tight control. The Soviet attempt to interfere with the domestic affairs of the DPRK in the 1950s undoubtedly helped to accelerate the drive for *chuch'e*. On October 28, 1963, for example, *Nodong Sinmun* angrily denounced Soviet meddling in North Korea in the late 1940s and early 1950s in a 28,000-word editorial entitled "Upholding the Socialist Camp." It declared that the Soviet Union, "assuming the arrogance of a suzerain nation, wanted to have everything its own way. Soviet interference even extended to supervision of methods of studying Communist party history and the Russian language, and to the inspection of how well Soviet films were shown."

In the early 1950s, Kim Il-song was already searching discreetly for ways to minimize Soviet interference in North Korea's domestic affairs and to maximize the scope of his political independence and freedom in domestic and external affairs. During this period, it clearly dawned on him that subservience and reliance on an ideological rationale framed in the foreign (Russian) language of Marxism-Leninism were more a liability than an asset.[18] Thus, he favored allowing significant national variations in the application of Marxism-Leninism in his country. He had to look for a readily comprehensible symbol to rationalize the policy shift from "Learn from the Soviet Union" to self-reliance, and he found it in the idea of *chuch'e*. In the early 1950s, the domestic political implications of *chuch'e* were, by and large, clearly visible. (The foreign policy implications of *chuch'e* were barely visible but became more obvious as the linkage between the two policies grew closer over the years.)

In December 1952, Kim Il-song told the KWP Central Committee to accelerate their ideological efforts with a view to applying creatively the Marxist-Leninist theory to the actual conditions of North Korea.[19] At the same time, in his drive to replace the Soviet and Chinese models with an indigenous role model, he reorganized North Korea's educational system in order to stress Korean language, culture, and history.[20] The theme of Koreanization in every aspect of North Korean life was again stressed at the KWP Central Committee's plenums in April and December 1955, but in a subdued manner so as not to arouse suspicion or ill will in Moscow and Beijing. In 1956, the first volume of *Choson T'ongsa*, the general history of Korea, was published, giving special attention to "the history of Korean revolutionary movements since the modern era."[21] A research institute on the history of the KWP, especially the "glorious revolutionary tradition" of Kim Il-song's anti-Japanese Korean partisans in Manchuria, was also created directly under the KWP Central Committee's control. In short, these efforts signaled the beginning of a carefully orchestrated transition from dependency to independence.

When North Korea was faced with the colossal task of postwar rehabilitation and reconstruction after the 1953 cease-fire, Moscow attempted to interfere with the domestic economic affairs of the DPRK, stressing the development of light industry and agriculture.[22] (The Soviet Union also ridiculed the DPRK's first five-year economic plan from 1957 to 1961 as "a fantasy.")[23] But Kim Il-song doggedly persisted in his policy of developing heavy (that is, machine-building) industry at all costs and at the expense of other economic sectors, thereby incurring the wrath of the Soviet leadership and antagonizing his domestic Soviet-Korean and Yenan-Korean critics as well.[24] In the mid-1950s, what was worse, the Soviets exerted strong economic pressure, in the form of sharp reductions in economic aid, against the North Koreans in an effort to make them adhere to the Soviet line. But this pressure tactic failed, spurring Kim's resolve to rely as far as possible on indigenous sources, both economic and human, to achieve economic reconstruction and development.[25]

The participation of the Chinese Communist "volunteer" army in the Korean War in 1950, and its subsequent stationing in North Korea for eight years, increased Beijing's influence over the DPRK, resulting in a steady decline in Moscow's control over Pyongyang's political, military, and diplomatic affairs. Toward the end of 1955, when Kim Il-song introduced his *chuch'e* ideology by name for the first time, the Chinese and the Soviet influence in North Korea were in near balance. With the relative authority of the two major Communist powers balanced, this enabled the DPRK regime to reduce its exclusive subservience to either of them and to pursue a relatively independent and self-reliant policy in both domestic and foreign affairs.

Kim Il-song was keenly aware that laying the groundwork for the new *chuch'e* policy of self-reliance required psychological preparation as well as ideological indoctrination. To prepare the

North Koreans psychologically for the new policy of *chuch'e*, the DPRK regime, in late December 1955, had already begun to promulgate and put into practice thereafter the doctrine of *chuch'e* as North Korea's single ideological system.

The first official introduction and elaboration of the ideology of *chuch'e* occurred in his December 28, 1955, speech to KWP propagandists and agitators, "On Eliminating Dogmatism and Formalism and Establishing *Chuch'e* in Ideological Works,"[26] which was perhaps one of Kim's most important speeches to date. The purpose of the speech was to call on the ruling KWP apparatus to promote and uphold the *chuch'e* ideology as the DPRK's unitary ideological norm. To carry out a Korean revolution properly, Kim called for the independent, creative application of Marxism-Leninism to North Korea's unique and specific conditions instead of blindly copying the experiences of the Soviet Union and China without alteration. "Those from the Soviet Union insisted upon the Soviet method and those from China stuck to the Chinese method. So they quarreled, some advocating the Soviet fashion and others the Chinese way." He firmly rejected as a chronic ailment the elements of "flunkeyism" or subservience to big foreign powers that had historically developed in Korea: "There can be no set rule that we must follow the Soviet pattern. Some advocate the Soviet way and others the Chinese, but is it not high time to work out our own?"[27] He lashed out against these domestic opponents as "revisionists," "doctrinaires," and "flunkeyists."[28] He emphasized the strict observance of the norm of *chuch'e* by the entire North Korean population, insisting on nationalistic pride.

Seen in this context, underlying much of Kim Il-song's *chuch'e* ideology is the belief that a small and strategically located state such as North Korea will become dominated by its powerful neighbors if it becomes unduly reliant on them, with the consequent danger of the country's being "de-Koreanized" and losing control over its own national destiny. (Incidentally, some scholars on Asian communism can notice the striking resemblances between the arguments in Kim's December 28, 1955, speech on the *chuch'e* idea and the statements by Mao Zedong during his Rectification Campaign of 1942–1944 on the need to "Sinify" Marxism-Leninism and stop mechanical, institutional imitation of the Soviet model as the "universal truth."[29] In fact, Kim Il-song publicly acknowledged this point in 1958.)[30]

The campaign to establish the *chuch'e* ideology solidly within North Korea was greatly accelerated by the new de-Stalinization policy of the Soviet Union, Khrushchev's formula of "different roads to socialism" at the Twentieth Congress of the Soviet Communist Party in February 1956,[31] and by the subsequent "thaw" in Communist-bloc affairs. Such a liberalized atmosphere in the Communist bloc emboldened Kim Il-song to turn to an independent course more firmly than before. At the same time, he quickly and adroitly grasped the situation by establishing the DPRK's ideological and political independence within the Communist bloc by laying down the ground rules for reconciling "national roads" to communism with the requirements of solidarity within the entire camp.[32] Thereupon, a new policy line of independence in politics and ideology, as well as self-reliance in economy and defense, began to develop steadily and openly as the DPRK's policy line.

The foreign policy of a nation-state, either Communist or non-Communist, is a vital extension of domestic political priorities, values, and institutions.[33] Therefore, the internal momentum for *chuch'e* was bound to spill over into the domain of external relations. This occurred in 1956, though in guarded terms, with respect to Khrushchev's new, more flexible "peaceful coexistence" line expounded at the Twentieth Congress of the CPSU. From 1956 through 1959, the DPRK regime continued to endorse the peaceful coexistence policy of the Soviet Union,[34] but Kim Il-song also wanted it known that it was not to be forced on him as a matter of universal application. In other words, Kim was not ready to accept the application of Khrushchev's new policy to the Korean situation, thereby intensifying hostility against the United States and South Korea. He said that there were some who extended the policy of peaceful coexistence of the two world camps to Korea and who wrongly concluded that the two separate Koreas could coexist. But the principle of peaceful coexistence was, he continued, impossible to apply to Korea because it was "a view obstructing our efforts for unification."[35]

The broadening of international perspectives, interacting with the muted but tenacious longing for *chuch'e*, was to be paralleled by a changing North Korean attitude toward the norm of relations between the Communist-orbit countries and among the Communist parties of the world. Friendship, solidarity, and equality were no longer viewed by the DPRK as an adequate basis for these mutual relations of the Communist states and parties. Thus, in November 1956, the Pyongyang regime began to assert that the mutual relations of the Communist countries and parties of the world, large and small, must be governed by the principles of "complete equality, noninterference in each other's domestic affairs, and mutual respect and reciprocity."[36]

Kim Il-song was probably disillusioned with, and became increasingly uneasy about, the Khrushchev line of peaceful coexistence in 1958,[37] when the Soviet leader failed to give Mao's China full military support in its test of nerves with John Foster Dulles during his "brinkmanship" policy in the Taiwan Strait crisis.[38]

A bolder note of divergence with the Kremlin was struck in September 1959, when, despite an earlier Soviet declaration of neutrality in the Sino-Indian border dispute, the DPRK publicly stated a position that was tantamount to an expression of moral support for the Chinese.[39]

When the bitter Sino-Soviet rift became full-blown and public in 1960, Kim Il-song grasped the situation by taking a posture of strict neutrality and independence and playing off Moscow against Beijing while tightening his internal political control. "We shall not take any side," Kim asserted. "Should anyone ask us which 'side' we are on, we would answer that we are on the 'side' of Marxism, on the 'side' of the revolution. Communists should not be too inquisitive about that."[40]

North Korea's most forthright statement of independence from both China and the Soviet Union came on the occasion of the twenty-first-anniversary celebration of its liberation from Japan. On August 12, 1966, *Nodong Sinmun* carried an editorial entitled "Let Us Defend Independence." The paper asserted that Pyongyang, not Beijing or Moscow, was the best judge of how Communist doctrine should be applied to North Korea's problems. "The Communists," the editorial declared, "should always do their own thinking and act independently, maintaining their own identity." It also rejected "big-nation chauvinism": "There are big parties and small parties but there can be no superior party or inferior party, not a party that gives guidance and a party that receives guidance." Since there "is no privileged party" in the Communist bloc, the editorial stressed the principles of complete equality, sovereignty, noninterference in each other's internal affairs, and mutual respect.

North Korea's posture of strict neutrality in the Sino-Soviet conflict and its efforts to maneuver and mediate the dispute in the early 1960s began with the signing of two separate treaties of friendship and mutual military assistance with the Soviet Union (July 6, 1961) and with China (July 11, 1961).[41] In other words, even the leadership of a small nation like North Korea has acquired, as a result of the Moscow-Beijing schism, the capacity to maneuver between the two major Communist powers and to engage in diplomacy for its nation's security and best possible interests—the full degree of political independence and the inflow of tangible economic, technical, and military benefits from both countries.

Seen in this context, one aspect of Kim Il-song's *chuch'e* ideology, which theoretically calls for the DPRK to develop under its own resources, means a fine balancing between the two major Communist powers, with the goal of playing off Moscow against Beijing for Pyongyang's maximum advantage. Kim Il-song has proven himself a true master at balancing in the disputes between the Communist giants and neighbors. In point of fact, both Moscow and Beijing have been deferential to the DPRK's wishes, particularly in their treatment of the Korean question in international diplomacy. In this case, they have largely bent to Kim's dictate, recognizing Pyongyang as the only legitimate government on the Korean peninsula and supporting the North Korean formula for reunification.

Until the Sino-Soviet rift became overt, *chuch'e* was not asserted in national defense as much as in other matters because Kim Il-song obviously could not afford to divert his limited internal resources to defense. His strategy was, first, to establish and preserve the DPRK's independence in political, economic, and diplomatic affairs while relying on the Soviet Union and China to provide protective military cover for North Korea. Of necessity, he tended to equate the security of the DPRK with the degree to which the Communist bloc's fraternal unity was perceived to be either strong or weak.[42] When unity with Moscow and Beijing, in particular, was considered firm, he tended to feel very confident and secure, and he concentrated on domestic economic construction. When the unity was believed to be fragile, he reacted apprehensively and accelerated his efforts to bolster defense.

Kim Il-song's concern about the ominous implications of the Sino-Soviet disunity was accentuated in October 1962, when the Soviet Union decided to support India against China in the Sino-Indian border conflict.[43] Kim's insecurity was further heightened after Khrushchev abandoned Castro by capitulating to American military power in the Cuban missile crisis of October 1962. As he perceived it, Khrushchev's act to blink first in this crisis was nothing but a sign of weakness and an indication that the Kremlin could not be counted upon, as Moscow's unreliability had been demonstrated during the Korean War.[44] For Kim, China's extremely cautious behavior toward the escalating Vietnam War in the midst of the intensifying Sino-Soviet schism in the mid-1960s[45] also meant that the DPRK might not be able to count on China's support in the event of a renewed major military conflict in the Korean peninsula.[46]

Faced with crucial changes in international affairs during the first half of the 1960s such as the ascension to power of military generals in a South Korean coup, the Cuban missile crisis, the Sino-Indian border conflict, the escalation of the Vietnam War, the normalization of South Korean-Japanese relations, and, above all, the hopeless prospect of reconciliation between Moscow and Beijing, Kim Il-song in December 1962 proclaimed his grim determination to strengthen defense, even though economic development might suffer as a result. At the same time, the DPRK announced its four-point military policy of promoting all troops to leading officers, modernizing arms, arming the entire people, and fortifying the entire nation.[47] (This policy of increasing defense expenditures[48] at the expense of economic development brought about a split in the KWP's leadership.[49] Kim Il-song admitted in early 1965 that the defense requirements slowed the progress of the 1961–1967 seven-year plan somewhat.)[50]

By the mid-1960s, the policy implications of the *chuch'e* ideology had, by and large, been fully implemented into the realms of politics, ideology, economy, diplomacy, and defense; that is to say, the *chuch'e* concept had firmly crystallized into a comprehensive, full-fledged political ideology. This process of institutionalizing the *chuch'e* ideology in a comprehensive form was already in full swing when Kim Il-song made his speech "Let Us Defend the Revolutionary Spirit of Independence, Self-Reliance, and Self-Defense More Thoroughly in All Fields of State Activities" to the Supreme People's Assembly (the DPRK's unicameral legislative branch) on December 16, 1967.[51] This speech later formed the basis of the ten-point political program of the DPRK. The comprehensive formulation of the *chuch'e* ideology, referring to politics, ideology, economy, diplomacy, and defense, has remained consistent from then to the present.[52]

Because of Kim Il-song's immense personal pride in the *chuch'e* ideology, he has never felt constrained from extolling its validity and inner strength, even when addressing a foreign audience, as can be seen in the following passage from his article in *Pravda* (April 16, 1970):

> Our Party has firmly adhered to the *chuch'e* line which consists of ensuring that the general principles of Marxism-Leninism and the experience of other countries creatively applied in accordance with our historical conditions and national features and that the Party always answers its own questions itself and resolves them independently by displaying the revolutionary spirit of reliance on one's own forces; the Party thereby achieved great victories and successes in the Socialist revolution and Socialist construction. Our country has now become a Socialist state with the full right to political self-determination and a stable independent national economy, flourishing national culture, and powerful defense forces.

While attending the tenth-anniversary celebration of the Bandung Conference in Djakarta, Indonesia, in April 1965 (Kim Il-song's first trip to the non-Communist world as head of the DPRK), Kim sought to give maximum worldwide publicity to his *chuch'e* ideology.[53] In effect, he used the forum to publicize his *chuch'e* ideology as an appropriate application to other small countries that shared similarly backward, colonial, and semifeudal backgrounds.[54] (In time, the DPRK was to assert: "Our country is called by the world people the 'fatherland of *chuch'e*' and 'a model of social-

ism.' "⁵⁵ "The *chuch'e* idea is exercising a great influence over people's ideological and political life and the revolutionary development of the world."⁵⁶)

In 1972, the concept of *chuch'e* and the achievements allegedly
based on it were given considerable international publicity by the
DPRK, apparently to improve its image, to win friends, and to gain
international acceptance. This was done partly by inviting a
number of foreign journalists to North Korea (with traveling
expenses paid in most cases) and by placing advertisements in
foreign newspapers.

In concluding the historical evolution of the *chuch'e* ideology,
one important point must be clarified: Kim Il-song's *chuch'e* ideology
does not imply or advocate North Korea's total or complete isolation
from Moscow, Beijing, or any other nations or power blocs.
Needless to say, Kim and other DPRK leaders fully realize that
total isolation would be suicidal in the present age of interdependence.
Despite North Korea's persistent and consistent pursuit of the
chuch'e policy, the nature of North Korea's geopolitical position
and domestic resource conditions, both human and material, leaves
the DPRK no alternative but to rely, to some extent, on outside
powers for economic, military, and other support⁵⁷ and to be
dependent on the policies and attitudes of its neighbors such as
China and the Soviet Union. Kim Il-song can never forget, even for
a moment, that the DPRK is confronted by a socially dynamic,
economically superior, militarily well-armed, diplomatically
active, very hostile neighbor to the south.⁵⁸

In point of fact, Kim Il-song stated clearly in 1972 that the DPRK
was pursuing, developing, and preserving his *chuch'e* policy "to the
fullest extent possible."⁵⁹ A special article in the June 7, 1982, issue
of *Nodong Sinmun*, which lauded Kim Chong-il's recent treatise on
the *chuch'e* idea,⁶⁰ said: "The problems of the revolution and
construction must be solved by the people's own efforts based on
the principle of self-reliance. The help of others can be accepted in
revolution and construction. However, what is most important is
people's own efforts."⁶¹

In other words, the DPRK continues to favor interaction with the
outside world only to the extent that such a move or action would
benefit North Korea while at the same time trying to utilize as much
indigenous resources as circumstances permit. More specifically,
the foreign policy implications of the *chuch'e* ideology in interna-

tional relations are that if there are opportunities to win advantages from normal diplomatic relations, negotiations, and compromises without sacrificing principle, then these would be appropriate. If there are opportunities to exploit rivalries between or among big powers, then these should be pursued and utilized. Limited tactical alliances with one big power or group of powers against others are in order, as long as the DPRK does not rely heavily on foreign help or cling to one big-power bloc or another. The DPRK's primary concern in this tactical framework, in short, has been to maintain its independence and security without antagonizing allies and neutrals or provoking adversaries.

The overall evaluation of the historical evolution of Kim Il-song's *chuch'e* ideology suggests that his policy of self-reliance has been derived more from pragmatic needs than from a derivation or projection of his already-well-developed ideology. (That is to say, the development of the *chuch'e* ideology's theoretical framework in a coherent form came after the DPRK regime began to implement its *chuch'e*-oriented policy programs.) The *chuch'e* policy has necessarily been a defensive exercise, more or less ordained by his adverse circumstances in the past, as some scholars on North Korean affairs correctly observe.[62] In the process, it has become a philosophy of sorts with a pretention as to its ability to turn weakness into strength. It has a certain psychological appeal as a rationale for coping with adversity.

The preceding evaluation does not cover all aspects of the *chuch'e* ideology, however. It is important to point out that Kim Il-song's *chuch'e* ideology has been both offensive and defensive in function and in effect, as will be seen in Chapters 3 through 5. As one seasoned observer of North Korean affairs points out,[63] the *chuch'e* ideology has performed a number of vital or positive functions in North Korean society since the establishment of the DPRK in 1948. To cite a few examples: it has accelerated the radical transformation of the traditional political culture based on Confucian ethics into a new socialist political culture; generated a sense of patriotic nationalism among the North Korean people by eradicating from their society the chronic, historical ill of *sadaechuii;* fostered a sense of participation in the great cause of building a new socialist state; elicited positive responses from the masses of people to the task of socialist revolution and construction; and instilled in the minds of the entire North Korean population national pride, self-reliance, self-confidence, and their positive role in society. All in all, the functions of Kim Il-song's *chuch'e* ideology have taken on idiosyncratic and singularly dynamic forms in North Korea. Indeed, it has become the essential tool both in forging revolution in the unique North Korean environment and in building and sustaining revolutionary fervor in a once economically backward, culturally conservative land. Above all, it has shaped much of post-1945 North Korea's distinctive history, functioning as the supreme value firmly institutionalized in the country's political system.

NOTES

1. For the discussion of *sadaechuii,* see Yung-hwan Jo, ed., *Korea's Response to the West* (Kalamazoo, Mich.: The Korean Research and Publications, 1971), pp. 1–14, 141–62; and C. I. Eugene Kim and Han-kyo Kim, *Korea and the Politics of Imperialism 1876–1910* (Berkeley and Los Angeles: University of California Press, 1968), pp. 1–260.

2. See references in note 1 of this chapter.

3. Baik Bong, *Kim Il-song Biography: From Birth to Triumphant Return to Homeland* (New York: The Guardian, 1969), 1:129.

4. See note 34 of Chapter 1.

5. Baik Bong, *Kim Il-song Biography,* p. 552.

6. For the details of this incident, see Chong-sik Lee, "Witch Hunt Among the Guerrillas: The Min-Sheng-T'uan Incident," *China Quarterly,* April–June 1966, pp. 107–17.

7. For the references made by Kim Il-song and his former Manchurian guerrilla colleagues about the Min-sheng-t'uan incident, see, for example, *Kim Il-song Sonjip* [Selected Works of Kim Il-song] (Pyongyang: Choson Nodong-dang Ch'ulpansa, 1960), p. 351; and Yim Chun-chu, *Hangil Mujang Shiki rul Hoesang hayo* [Recollecting the Period of Anti-Japanese Armed Struggle] (Pyongyang: Choson Nodong-dang Ch'ulpansa, 1960), p. 97.

8. For a study of the Soviet Communist treatment of the Korean minority in the Soviet Far East in the pre-1945 period, see Walter Kolarz, *The Peoples of the Soviet Far East* (New York: Praeger, 1954), pp. 36–42.

9. Kim Il-song, "Report to the Second Congress of the Workers' Party of North Korea on the Work of the Central Committee," March 28, 1948, *Selected Works* (Pyongyang: Foreign Languages Publishing House, 1965), 1:256; and Kim Il-song, "On the Eve of the Historical Democratic Election," November 1, 1946, ibid., 1:125.

10. For Moscow's economic squeeze of North Korea in the lat 1940s, see U.S., Department of State, *North Korea: A Case Study in the Techniques of Takeover* (Washington, D.C.: U.S. Government Printing Office, 1961), pp. 105, 120.

11. *Nodong Sinmun,* September 7, 1964.

12. Ibid. For the events leading to this accusation, see Byung Chul Koh, *The Foreign Policy of North Korea* (New York: Praeger, 1969), pp. 77–79.

13. "The Construction of Self-Reliant Economy Is the Path to the Unification, Independence, and Prosperity of the Fatherland," *Kulloja,* April 1963, p. 19.

14. Editorial Department, *Nodong Sinmun, Self-Reliance and Independent National Economic Construction,* June 12, 1963 (Peking: Foreign Languages Press, 1963), pp. 7–8; and *Nodong Sinmun,* October 28, 1963.

15. According to the Khrushchev memoirs, the Korean War was not Stalin's idea, "but Kim Il-song's. Kim was an initiator. Stalin, of course, did not try to dissuade him. . . ." *Khrushchev Remembers,* p. 370.

16. Ibid. The Khrushchev memoirs relate that "when Kim Il-song was preparing for his march," Stalin apparently withdrew all Soviet advisers from North Korea. Stalin is quoted as saying: "It's too dangerous to keep our advisers there. They might be taken prisoner. We don't want there to be evidence for accusing us of taking part in this business. It's all Kim Il-song's affair." Khrushchev opines, "If we hadn't refused him aid in qualified personnel to assess the distribution of forces and to direct operations, there is no doubt that North Korea would have been victorious. I think if Kim had received just one tank corps, or two at the most, he could have accelerated his advance south and occupied Pusan on the march."

17. Kim Il-song, *Selected Works* (Pyongyang: Foreign Languages Publishing House, 1965), 1:587; and "Let Us Defend Our Independence!" *Nodong Sinmun,* August 12, 1966.

18. In the early 1950s, Kim Il-song criticized mechanical imitation of Soviet or Chinese forms. Kim Il-song, *Selected Works,* 1:591–92.

19. Kim Il-song, "The Party's Organizational and Ideological Strengthening Is the Foundation of Our Victory," *Kim Il-song Chojak Sonjip* [Selected Writings of Kim Il-song] (Pyongyang: Choson Nodong-dang Ch'ulpansa, 1967), 1:390–91.

20. Kim Il-song, *Selected Works* (Pyongyang: Foreign Languages Publishing House, 1965), 1:25–26, and II:64–101. See also Hyang-chan Kim, "Ideology and Indoctrination in the Development of North Korean Education," *Asian Survey,* November 1969, p. 833.

21. "The Path Followed by the Korean Historical Academic World Since the August 15 Liberation," *Yoksa Kwahak* [Historical Science] (Pyongyang), no. 4 (1960), pp. 8–9.

22. *Nodong Sinmun,* October 28, 1963; Kim Il-song, "The Korean People's Army Is the Successor to the Anti-Japanese Armed Struggle," speech delivered on February 8, 1958, in *Kim Il-song Sonjip* [Kim Il-song's Selected Works] (Pyongyang: Choson Nodong-dang Ch'ulpansa, 1960), II:82–83; and Joungwon Alexander Kim, "Soviet Policy in North Korea," *World Politics,* January 1970, p. 245.

23. See references in note 22 of this chapter. See also *Third Congress of the Workers' Party of Korea: Documents and Materials,* April 23–29, 1956 (Pyongyang: Foreign Languages Publishing House, 1956), pp. 44–45, 424.

24. Kim Il-song, "On Socialist Construction in the DPRK and the South Korean Revolution," April 14, 1965, *Selected Works* (Pyongyang: Foreign Languages Publishing House, 1971), IV:206.

25. Kim Il-song, "To Give Full Play to the Great Vitality of the Unified and Detailed Planning of the National Economy," September 23, 1965, *Selected Works,* IV:288.

26. Kim Il-song, "On Exterminating Dogmatism and Formalism and Establishing Independence in Ideological Work," in *Kim Il-song Sonjip,* IV:325–54; and in *Selected Works,* I:582–606.

27. See references in note 26 of this chapter.

28. According to the lexicon of the KWP, "doctrinairism" means falling into flunkeyism with no regard for specific conditions of the nation or state, while "revisionism" means negation of the general relevance of socialist revolution and construction as a result of preoccupation with the particular nature of a nation. Kim Il-song, *Selected Works* (Pyongyang: Foreign Languages Publishing House, 1972), V; 504–505.

29. See, for example, Mao Tse-tung, "The Reconstruction of Our Studies," February 1, 1942, translated in Boyd Compton, ed., *Mao's China: Party Reform Documents, 1942–1944* (Seattle, Wash.: University of Washington Press, 1966), pp. 62–63.

30. In a speech at the mass rally to welcome the Chinese delegation led by Premier Zhou Enlai on February 14, 1958, Kim Il-song claimed that the real contribution of the Chinese Communists to Marxism-Leninism "is the creative application of Marxism-Leninism to the specific conditions of China, which the people in North Korea must not only admire and praise but also learn," in order to build socialism in North Korea. See *Wei-le Chao-hsien ti ho-p'ingt'ung-i* [For the Peaceful Reunification of Korea] (Peking: Shih-chieh chih-shih ch'u-pan in she, 1958), pp. 19–26.

31. For the full text of Khrushchev's speech at the Twentieth Congress of the CPSU, see *Pravda*, February 15, 1956, pp. 1–11, in the *Current Digest of the Soviet Press* VIII, no. 4 (March 7, 1956): 3–12.

32. "For the Victory of Marxism-Leninism!" *Nodong Sinmun*, December 7, 1960.

33. For a study of this theoretical point, see Melvin Gurtov and Byong-Moo Hwang, *China Under Threat* (Baltimore: Johns Hopkins University Press, 1980), pp. 1–336.

34. *Nodong Sinmun*, November 9, 1957, October 27, 1959; *Korea Today* (Pyongyang), no. 34 (1959), p. 37; and Korean Central News Agency, Pyongyang, January 30, 1959.

35. Kim Il-song, *Selected Works* (Pyongyang: Foreign Languages Publishing House, 1971), IV:189, 343; and *Kulloja*, December 25, 1957, p. 27.

36. "Under the Invincible Living Banner of Proletarian Internationalism," *Kulloja*, November 25, 1956, p. 6; and *Nodong Sinmun*, October 28, 1958.

37. *Nodong Sinmun*, January 18, 1960; and Korean Central News Agency, January 19, 1960. See also John Bradbury, "Sino-Soviet Competition in North Korea," *China Quarterly*, April–June 1961, p. 24.

38. For the details of the Taiwan Strait crisis of 1958, see Tang Tsou, "Mao's Limited War with the Taiwan Strait," *Orbis*, Fall 1959, pp. 332–50; John R. Thomas, "Soviet Behavior in the Quemoy Crisis of 1958," *Orbis*, Spring 1962, pp. 38–64; and Alice Langley Hsieh, *Communist China's Strategy in the Nuclear Era* (Englewood Cliffs, N.J.: Prentice-Hall, 1962), pp. 119–30.

39. Bradbury, "Sino-Soviet Competition," p. 24.

40. Kim Il-song, "The Present Situation and the Task Confronting Our Party," report to the conference of the KWP on October 5, 1966 (Central Standing Committee of the General Association of Korean Residents in Japan, Tokyo, 1966), p. 38.

41. For the full texts of these two treaties, see *Pravda* and *Izvestia*, July 7, 1961, in the *Current Digest of the Soviet Press* XIII, no. 27 (August 21, 1961): 23–24; *Peking Review*, July 14, 1961, pp. 5–6; and *Choson Chungang Nyomgam 1962* [North

Korean Yearbook 1962] (Pyongyang: Choson Chungang T'ongsinsa, 1962), pp. 157–58.

42. For the North Korean tendency to equate strength with the unity of the Communist bloc, see *Nodong Sinmun,* October 28, 1963.

43. For the expression of this concern, see *Nodong Sinmun,* October 28, 1963; and Kim Il-song, "Immediate Tasks of the Government of the Democratic People's Republic of Korea," *Selected Works* (Pyongyang: Foreign Languages Publishing House, 1965), II:370.

44. Kim Il-song, "The Present Situation and the Task Confronting Our Party," report to the conference of the Workers' Party of Korea, October 5, 1966, *Kim Il-song Shosaku-shu* [Collected Works of Kim Il-song] (Tokyo: Miraisha, 1971), IV:100–87.

45. See, for example, Tai Sung An, "The Sino-Soviet Dispute and Vietnam," *Orbis,* Summer 1965, pp. 426–36.

46. See note 44 of this chapter.

47. *Nodong Sinmun,* December 7, 1962.

48. An estimated 15 percent to 20 percent of North Korea's gross national product (GNP) was spent on the military in the 1960s and an even higher percentage in the 1970s. See Young Ho Lee, "Military Balance and Peace in the Korean Peninsula," *Asian Survey,* August 1981, pp. 852–64.

49. Ilpyong J. Kim, *Communist Politics in North Korea* (New York: Praeger, 1975), pp. 73–76.

50. In his New Year message for 1965, Kim Il-song said: "It is true that the economic development of our country has been delayed somewhat compared with what was expected, because we had to direct great efforts to further increasing the defense capability in the last two or three years." As cited in *Pukhan Ch'onggam, 1945–1968* [General Survey of North Korea, 1945–1968] (Seoul: Kongsankwon Munjeyonguso, 1968), p. 323.

51. Kim Il-song, *Selected Works* (Pyongyang: Foreign Languages Publishing House, 1971), IV:546–610.

52. Kim Il-song, "Report to the Fifth Congress of the Workers' Party of Korea on the Work of the Central Committee," November 2, 1970, *Selected Works,* V:408–526; and Kim Il-song, "On Some Problems of Our Party's *Chuch'e* Idea and the Government of the Republic's Internal and External Policies," *For the Independent Peaceful Reunification of Korea* (New York: International Publishers, 1975), pp. 173–200.

53. *Nodong Sinmun,* April 17, 1965.

54. Ibid.

55. Korean Central News Agency, Pyongyang, July 29, 1968.

56. "The *Chuch'e* Idea Is the Great Guiding Ideology of Revolution Based on the Demands of a New Era and the Experience in the Revolutionary Struggle," *Nodong Sinmun,* May 31, 1982.

57. For example, Kim Il-song said in 1971 that the victory of the North Korean people's struggle and construction would depend "in large measure on the strengthening of solidarity with the international revolutionary forces as well as on the consolidation and development of the revolutionary forces in North and South Korea." Kim Il-song, *Report on Work of Central Committee to the 5th Congress Workers' Party of Korea* (London: Africa-Magazine Ltd., 1971), p. 67.

58. For a detailed study of South Korea's growing national strength vis-a-vis North Korea, see, for example, U.S., Central Intelligence Agency, National Foreign Assessment Center, *Korea: The Economic Race Between the North and the South* (a research paper), January 1978, pp. 1–16; Henry Scott Stokes, "Competition Between the Two Koreas Pays Off in Greater Prosperity for Both," *New York Times*, August 11, 1980, p. 10; and Richard L. Sneider, "Prospects for Korean Security," in *Asian Security in the 1980s: Problems and Policies for a Time of Transition* edited by Richard H. Solomon (Santa Monica, Calif.: Rand Corporation, November 1979), pp. 109–147.

59. See note 34 of Chapter 1.

60. A treatise on the *chuch'e* idea was reportedly written by Kim Chong-il in recent weeks. According to *Nodong Sinmun* on April 1, 1982, the young Kim's thesis was read by KWP Central Committee Secretary Kim Yong-nam at the closed session of the national forum on the *chuch'e* ideology held on March 25–31, 1982, to mark the elder Kim's 70th birthday.

61. "The *Chuch'e* Idea Is a Great Ideology Which Has Elucidated Afresh the Basic Principles of Social Movement and Revolutionary Movement," *Nodong Sinmun*, June 7, 1982.

62. Robert A. Scalapino and Chong-sik Lee, *Communism in Korea*, I:499–504, and II:1313; and Joseph Sang-hoon Chung, *The North Korean Economy: Structure and Development* (Stanford, Calif.: Hoover Institution Press, 1974), pp. 92–93.

63. Byung Chul Koh, "Ideology and Political Control in North Korea," *Journal of Politics*, August 1970, p. 656.

3

The Theoretical Contents and Functions of the *Chuch'e* Ideology

As was already mentioned, the core of Kim Il-song's political ideology is the idea of *chuch'e*, which serves as the sole state ideology for socialist revolution and construction in North Korea. For the past two decades, the DPRK regime has been asserting that Kim Il-song, through his *chuch'e* idea, has added his creative and original idea to Marxism-Leninism and developed it into a universal truth to suit the contemporary situation. "Starting from the interests of the Korean revolution and the world revolution," *Kulloja*, the KWP monthly journal, wrote, "Comrade Kim Il-song has most accurately defined the character of modern times, and has explicated Marxist-Leninist themes and policies in line with the development of global revolution in the current era."[1] As such, Kim has been hailed as "a revolutionary strategist of genius," one who has made "a priceless contribution to the treasure of Marxism-Leninism." Such eulogies are now commonplace in all DPRK publications.

In evaluating the *chuch'e* ideology, three important questions are raised. What are the theoretical contents of Kim Il-song's *chuch'e* ideology? Has Kim really made any significantly new and original contributions to Marxism-Leninism? And, if the answer to the second question is negative, is the *chuch'e* doctrine just another version or imitation of other Communist doctrines or even some Western political theories?

Those questions will be addressed in this chapter. The discussion of the functions of the *chuch'e* ideology in North Korean society will follow thereafter.

On the question of what the *chuch'e* ideology is, Kim Il-song
gave the following definition:

> To establish *chuch'e*, in short, is to have an attitude of a
> master toward the revolution and construction of one's
> own country. Abandon dependence on others, and
> think with your own head. We should be responsible for
> resolving our own problems with a self-reliant posture and
> in the spirit of revolution for self-rehabilitation. Doctri-
> nairism is rejected, while the general principles of Marx-
> ism-Leninism and the experience of other countries will
> be applied in a way that would suit the historical condi-
> tions and national idiosyncracies of one's own nation.
> Maintaining such a creative position means *chuch'e*.[2]

Kim Il-song places special emphasis on applying the truth of Marxism-Leninism in the most appropriate way to the historical
conditions, characteristics, and realities of each socialist country.
Expanding further on the theme that the truth of Marxism-Leninism
should be effectively applied to different environmental conditions,
he insists that every Marxist-Leninist must be able to adjust his
environment as he sees fit, instead of simply falling prey to
circumstances and environments.[3]

Kim Il-song is very complacent about the significance of his
chuch'e ideology: "It is a very strong force enabling man to recognize
and transform the world by scientifically explaining his standing
and role in the world and providing humanity with a correct vision
of nature and society."[4] This self-praise or self-flattery further
contends that his *chuch'e* is an immortal revolutionary theory that
originates a man-centered world view. This "man-is-a-mighty-
creator-of-historical-progress" theory explains man's position in
the material world and his role in the task of change and development
in the material world. When men are collectively organized into the
revolutionary working class, they can shape the world anew or
transform it radically, Kim believes.

More specifically, Kim Il-song's theory of "man-is-a-mighty-
creator-of-historical-progress" is based on the following
propositions:[5] (1) "man is the master of all things and man decides
everything"; (2) self-reliance is the soul of human existence; (3) "all

behaviors of man in historical development are decided by his ideological consciousness," and only when the masses of the working class people are guided by ideological consciousness can they become the masters of their destinies and the mighty creators of history; (4) the masses of the working class are the prime movers of revolution and construction; (5) revolution in one's country should be central to the thinking and revolutionary action of all men; and (6) the masses of the working class people should take a masterly attitude with regard to revolution and construction because they are the masters.

According to the *chuch'e* ideology, in short, it is the masses of the working class who create and develop history. But they are neither homogeneous nor immune to self-doubt, passivity, or internal friction. To put it another way, they lack the self-generating ability to organize spontaneously, to unite, and to guide themselves for the heroic revolutionary struggle. The masses of the working class can become the main force of the revolution, the powerful driving force for social development, and the rewarding creators of a new history *only if and when* they are imbued with revolutionary consciousness and are mobilized to the revolutionary struggle under the guidance of an exceptionally brilliant and outstanding leader *(kajang kolchulhan chidoja)* who is carefully and correctly selected.[6] (Accordingly, an irreducible element of authoritarianism is inherent in the *chuch'e* ideology. Particularly noteworthy is the fact that the DPRK's pronouncements of the *chuch'e* ideology concerning this aspect of a hierarchical elitism and a highly personalized leader have, in some measure, been low-key and brief, with a strong emphasis on the participatory aspects of the masses of the working class in the revolutionary struggle. Thus, the DPRK regime is able to make full use of the wide range of democratic symbolism and terminology for propaganda purposes.)

This superman-like individual leader (what Ellen Brun and Jacques Hersh call "the supreme organ for proletarian dictatorship"),[7] with the assistance of the revolutionary vanguard institutionalized in the form of a Communist party, which functions as his general staff of the revolution,[8] fully arouses the ideological consciousness of the masses of the working class as the masters of their revolutionary movement, enabling them to unleash and exhibit an unlimited revolutionary zeal and creative talent to solve all problems arising in revolution and construction. This exceptionally qualified, preeminent individual educates and remolds the masses of the working class, the masters of the revolution, and rallies them around him to strengthen the ranks of revolution politically and ideologically, which enables them to discover the right direction of historical development. Thus, the respect and veneration shown to such a single great leader of special mold is a spontaneous and simultaneous way of uniting the masses around a coherent political line and of mobilizing them to carry it out successfully.

This exceptionally outstanding leader of the revolutionary masses, who is the leader of the working class and the brain of the people, is the heart of the people and the center of the unity that gives the people ideology, strategy, and tactics. He is the banner of unity enabling the revolutionary masses to rise up in the struggle and victoriously pioneer their destinies. He can perform "miracles" in the revolutionary cause, and only through him is victory possible. Without him, the masses of the working class would be powerless and even suffocate. The greatness of a nation rests with the greatness of its leader; the greatness of the leader is the source of the nation's greatness. In short, to recognize and uphold the role of the superman-like leader correctly and faithfully constitutes a supreme duty of the Communists. *Nodong Sinmun* wrote candidly and bluntly on April 12, 1972, that "to think independently and creatively is to think in keeping with the thought and will of the leader."

The DPRK mass media constantly warn the North Korean people that because of the antirevolutionary plots of the "revisionists" in the international Communist movement in the past several decades (as happened in the Soviet Union after Stalin and in China after Mao), the movement faces a grave crisis today.[9] The twists, turns, and travails experienced today in the international Communist movement demonstrate that the question of a revolutionary successor in North Korea has become very serious and crucial.[10]

At the same time, these same media ceaselessly stress that the North Korean people face the great "noble" task of carrying through, generation after generation, the North Korean chieftain's revolutionary cause and that only the "sole" and "correct" successor will play the decisive role in this continuing revolution. Kim's successor should and will be a distinguished individual who is infinitely loyal to him and who was born with his revolutionary idea, the excellent art of leadership, and a lofty Communist character. The successor also should and will devote himself to defending firmly and implementing thoroughly Kim Il-song's revolutionary ideology in a difficult and arduous struggle, regarding the completion of the senior Kim's cause as his lifelong task. In this way, he can credibly inherit and develop the North Korean chieftain's cause generation after generation.

It is obvious that the DPRK regime believes that Kim Il-song's 43-year-old son, Kim Chong-il, surely possesses all these brilliant, outstanding, and noble leadership qualities as the "sole" and "correct" successor and the future supreme leader of North Korea. A DPRK spokesman insists that Kim Chong-il has been chosen as his father's future political heir, not because of his bloodline, but because of his truly exceptional ability and achievements.[11]

The Pyongyang regime also asserts that the junior Kim's hereditary succession is a cornerstone of the *chuch'e* ideology. It is against this background that the regime claims, and even brags, that Kim Il-song's *chuch'e* ideology has scientifically clarified the question of political succession in the Communist countries for the first time in the history of world communism and that Communist political succession has brilliantly reached epochal fruition in the fatherland of *chuch'e*. This achievement, it says, is to the utmost honor and praise of the DPRK.

Since the birth of the DPRK in 1948, Kim Il-song has converted North Korea into his personal fief. The KWP, his political ideology, and the people are, in the final analysis, only a means to realize himself and his one-man mandate during his lifetime, as well as to ensure the immortality of his revolutionary ideas and heritage after his death. He clearly believes that the entire course of history often depends on a single great leader ("genius"). It seems obvious that he has himself in mind. (As will be seen in Chapter 6, this is one of the important reasons for his extravagant personality cult campaign.) The great political leader must expound and interpret doctrine in his own way. The philosophical rationale for Kim Chong-il's hereditary succession is based on the theory of the single superman-like leader.

Kim Il-song's ideology of *chuch'e* is based essentially on his experiences during the anti-Japanese guerrilla campaign in Manchuria in the 1930s (what the DPRK regime calls Kim's "glorious revolutionary tradition" that the North Korean people must inherit and uphold).[12] During that long, bitter, and arduous struggle for Korean national liberation and independence, Kim observed that the key to survival and victory lay in such spiritual qualities as indomitable human will, iron discipline, personal dedication, self-reliance, self-sacrifice, and austerity rather than in such materialistic factors as professional expertise and sophisticated weapons.

To Kim Il-song (as it was to Mao Zedong),[13] his notion of guerrilla warfare is not solely a military strategy, but a broader conceptual frame of reference for political, economic, and social mobilization. Just as he regarded the Manchurian battlefield as his country in microcosm while he was there, so he later came to consider North Korea his Manchurian battle theater in macrocosm, as he sought to apply the basic features of guerrilla warfare to industry and agriculture on a national scale.[14] Armed with superior political morale, will, and revolutionary consciousness, he insists that the 19 million North Korean people can and will perform economic, military, or any kind of miracles, overcoming all technical and physical limits.

A romantic revolutionary (like Mao Zedong),[15] Kim Il-song believes in the superiority of politics, ideology, and manpower over technology, specialization, machines, and weapons. Since the establishment of the DPRK in 1948, he has sought to build a "true" Communist state based on egalitarianism, proclaiming that his ideas are the panacea for virtually all the problems of North Korean society. He has long contended that spiritual force and ideological incentives can transform human nature; so, too, his "glorious anti-Japanese revolutionary tradition" can inspire and induce North Korea's 19 million people to perform all sorts of miracles.[16] The central thesis of Kim's *chuch'e* ideology is that the force of the spirit can be transformed into tremendous material strength or that, as Stuart R. Schram succinctly describes the essence of Maoism, "the subjective can create the objective."[17] One of the Kimist myths stemming from this notion of "voluntarism" is that Kim Il-song's guerrilla-warfare strategy overcame many insurmountable obstacles and achieved a victory against the far superior Japanese army by relying on the "human or subjective factors"—that is, brilliant and "correct" leadership, conscious and dedicated activism, moral rectitude and austerity, and *esprit de corps*.

In evaluating the theoretical structure of Kim Il-song's *chuch'e* ideology, it is not difficult to see whether it is as original and scientific as his followers in North Korea claim or whether it is just a replica or a changed version of Marxism-Leninism or even a radical departure from traditional Communist doctrines.

First, the two basic philosophical propositions of the *chuch'e* ideology—that "man is the master of all things and man decides everything" and that "all behaviors of man in historical development are decided by his ideological consciousness"—directly or fundamentally contradict Karl Marx's philosophy of "economic or material determinism." Marx's view of dialectical and historical materialism makes room for the role of the proletariat, but, according to him, man does not make history as he wants it, or man makes history under given limitations.[18] This means that Marx did not estimate too highly the role of man in history. Marx said that the personal qualities of historical individual figures could only affect individual features of events, not the general trend.[19] In other words, individuals could make a mark on history by accelerating the socioeconomically predetermined course of human development.[20]

Then, how does Kim Il-song's argument that man's ideological consciousness determines all actions of man relate to Marx's theory? Marx insisted on the superiority of the material conditions over man's economic life. According to him, society's upper structure ("superstructure") is affected by its "infrastructure." Marx said:

> The mode of production in material life determines the general character of the social, political, and spiritual processes of life. It is not the consciousness of men that determines their existence, but, on the contrary, their social existence determines their consciousness.[21]

In this connection, it is important to note that Marx did not say that man was not a conscious being. In fact, he allowed that spirit did influence the development of man. But he held that circumstances would largely define a man's consciousness, while at the same time man may reform his circumstances under certain conditions.

Kim Il-song's view also represents a departure from the Leninist emphasis on the primacy of the educating and organizing functions of a revolutionary vanguard elite in historical development.[22] Lenin subscribed to the great-man ("hero") theory in the historical process of radical revolutionary movement. In other words, Lenin, like many Russian populist revolutionaries of the 1870s such as Alexeyev, Myshkin, Khalturin, Zhelyabov, and Lavrov, accepted a theory of "hero and crowd" according to which historical progress issued from the impingement of outstanding individuals' thoughts on the minds of the uncreative mass of humanity.[23] But, unlike Kim, Lenin advocated the party of individual heroes (a nucleus of committed, energetic, and enlightened leaders) in the form of a dictatorship of the revolutionary elite on behalf of the proletariat (that is, a Communist party). Meanwhile, Kim subscribes to, and has created, the theory of a leader-oriented revolutionary movement. In short, Kim Il-song refuses to see history in terms of the most basic teachings of Karl Marx and Vladimir Lenin.

This divergence is also true between some aspects of Kim's *chuch'e* ideology and Maoism. Like Kim, Mao Zedong often upheld the importance of human elements and the necessity of remaking man's mind.[24] But the Maoist conception that the masses are the basic and decisive elements in historical process[25] clearly deviates from Kim's *chuch'e* ideology concerning the role of men in history. Mao said: "The people, and the people alone, are the motive force in the making of world history. Humble people are the most intelligent and prominent people are the most idiotic."[26]

The basic postulate of the *chuch'e* ideology is to apply Marxism-Leninism to any socialist country in a creative manner that would best suit its historical conditions, its political characteristics, and its realities. This necessity, or Khrushchev's thesis of "different roads to socialism," was often stressed by Mao Zedong[27] and other Communist leaders of Eastern Europe.[28] Accordingly, there is nothing new or original about Kim Il-song's assertion about the North Korean road to socialism.

In this connection, it is important to note that Mao Zedong's political thought and actions influenced the development of the DPRK's political institutions and process considerably in the past, particularly in the late 1940s and the 1950s. These two Asian Communist countries have several important factors in common: the timing of their revolutions; their historically backward and predominantly agrarian societies; and their approaches to identical problems of creating new values and institutions to replace old ones. Accordingly, Kim Il-song followed the Maoist policy line with keen and enlightening interest, and Maoist policies had not infrequently influenced his own. One example of such a parallel development, not necessarily a mechanical emulation, was the North Korean strategy of manpower mobilization (the mass line) in the late 1950s, which was symbolized by Kim's *Chollima Undong* ("one thousand-ri-racing-horse movement").[29] There is good reason to believe that this movement was inspired by Mao Zedong's Great Leap Forward movement of 1958–1960.

But Kim Il-song has been reluctant to acknowledge publicly his debt to Mao, with respect to either theoretical or practical insights of great merit, especially since the DPRK regime firmly institutionalized Kim's *chuch'e* ideology as the country's unitary ideological system in the early 1960s. Kim's aversion probably stems from a conscious or unconscious manifestation of fierce North Korean nationalism symbolized by the *chuch'e* ideology; moreover, he is too proud and egotistic to accept the implications of being inferior to Mao.

Of course, China and North Korea are also different from each other in many other aspects. Out of these dissimilarities have come divergent policy actions and ideological perspectives.

There is nothing new or original about the *chuch'e* ideology's philosophical proposition on the role of the single great leader in history, whose role in history-making has been recognized as a fundamental element in social transformation throughout the history of world civilization. "Western theorists from Plato to Rousseau, [Hegel, Nietzsche,] Marx, Weber, and Lenin," as Richard M. Pfeffer asserts quite correctly, "have all recognized that a great leader or vanguard is essential to radically transforming existing society."[30]

Particularly noteworthy are the striking resemblances between Kim Il-song's thesis on the individual superman-like leader's role in radical revolutionary change and Max Weber's theory of a "charismatic leader." It is difficult to tell whether Kim borrowed extensively from Weber's theory in expounding his own doctrine or whether the two theories were independently established and merely represent a concurrent, similar conceptual approach to an identical issue.

Charismatic authority, which Max Weber contrasts with "traditional" and "rational-legal" types of leadership, is described as repudiating the past and representing a new revolutionary force in pursuit of profound change.[31] According to Weber, charismatic authority occurs in the context of a radical social movement, whether of religious, political, cultural, or some other complexion. These movements typically require and attract a charismatic leader of extraordinary human quality in whom the promise of ultimate success is embodied. Such a leader possesses a definite messianic quality, with inspirational power, and is capable of playing the role of messiah by performing "miracles" in the revolutionary cause. Accordingly, the masses of people respond spontaneously with passionate devotion to his banner, accepting his leadership freely and unconditionally. The ardent emotional bond that grows up in these circumstances may find expression, either during his lifetime or after his death, in a cult of the leader. Indeed, according to Weber, a personality cult is one of the characteristic signs of charisma.

By and large, a detailed, careful study of Kim Il-song's *chuch'e* ideology suggests that, whether viewed from a Marxist-Leninist approach or from some other perspective, Kim has advanced neither new nor original ideas. He cannot be called a theorist in any sense, let alone "a foremost creative theorist." In some basic way, Kim's *chuch'e* ideology is even incompatible with Marxism, Leninism, and Maoism, and he has made no new addition to Marxism-Leninism. Meanwhile, many of Kim's pronouncements on such subjects as class struggle, the mass line, the dictatorship of the proletariat, contradiction, anti-imperialism, nonalignment, the united-front strategy, and Communist political institutions are rooted in Soviet, Chinese, and even Yugoslav[32] theories.

The central core of the *chuch'e* ideology—self-reliance, or national identity—can easily be regarded as a straightforward, orthodox form of nationalism; it is hardly original, albeit emotionally very effective. Placing *chuch'e* at the center of Kim Il-song's theoretical thinking means simply that, just like other contemporary Communist leaders of the world, he has put nationalism in the central position of his own revolutionary movement. Like Mao Zedong and Ho Chi Minh, Kim is one of Asia's supremely skillful practitioners of the art of blending nationalism with communism. North Korean nationalism under Kim Il-song has an unmistakable tendency of being militant and messianic in tone.

In general, Kim Il-song's *chuch'e* ideology contains neither theoretical contents of great merit nor any original additions. It has merely tampered with, or even perverted, Marxism, Leninism, and Maoism, partly because of the imperatives of the specific, unique conditions of his revolutionary movement and partly to rationalize and legitimize his own peculiar leadership styles and techniques. In other words, it represents a curiously coarse mixture of Marxism, Leninism, Maoism, Titoism, nationalism, and Western political theories.

In a way, Kim Il-song's *chuch'e* ideology is the natural and inevitable phenomenon in the present age of national communism. Different Communist doctrines have emerged from the decentralized world Communist movement. They were born out of the divergent traditions, conditions, experiences, and vested interests of the ruling power elites in the contemporary setting of the world Communist movement. Despite their charges and countercharges of "revisionism" and other forms of heresy in recent years, all Communists, including Kim Il-song, are revisionists today.

Although the theoretical level of Kim Il-song's *chuch'e* ideology is simple, eclectic, mediocre, and pedestrian, the amazing fact is that it fulfills a number of useful and positive functions in the political life of North Korea. First, the *chuch'e* ideology provides a set of political symbols—beliefs, emotions, or values—by which the DPRK regime justifies, rationalizes, and legitimizes Kim Il-song's one-man dictatorial rule, his deification campaign, and his family's succession to power.[33] It also serves as the practical guideline for every state activity of North Korea at home and abroad.

Another important function of the *chuch'e* ideology is to organize and mobilize the masses fully in the service of Kim Il-song's goals on socialist revolution and construction. The *chuch'e* ideology also reflects the desire of Kim and his regime to eradicate the unhealthy, old legacy of *sadaechuii* and thus to accelerate the process of Koreanizing every aspect of life in North Korea.[34] Kim constantly reminds the North Koreans that their country should maintain its self-respect and self-confidence, that it never goes hat in hand to big powers for essentials. North Korea has received economic, technical, and military aid from the Soviet Union, China, and Eastern Europe in the past,[35] but this fact is largely de-emphasized. In the ongoing process of transforming the traditional political culture into a new socialist culture, the *chuch'e* ideology inculcates the new attitudes, beliefs, values, and skills of the DPRK leadership among the North Korean people.

All in all, Kim Il-song has instilled in the North Korean people an impassioned nationalism and the intrinsic worth of all things Korean. He has harped on the *chuch'e* philosophy to evoke nationalist sentiment among the North Korean people, to unify the country and the people behind his leadership, and to justify his emphasis on frugality, self-reliance, hard work, and internal unity. Moreover, the theme of *chuch'e* can develop a high degree of social cohesiveness among the North Korean people, bring national pride, and unlock the energy and the creativity of his people.

NOTES

1. "The Revolutionary Task of Our People Under the Wise Leadership of the Great Leader Comrade Kim Il-song Is Invincible," *Kulloja*, April 15, 1969, p. 9.

2. Kim Il-song, *Selected Works* (Pyongyang: Foreign Languages Publishing House, 1972), V:504–505; and Kim Il-song, *Revolution and Socialist Construction* (New York: International Publishers, 1971), p. 87.

3. Kim Il-song, *The Nonalignment Movement Is a Mighty Anti-Imperialist Revolutionary Force of Our Times* (Pyongyang: Foreign Languages Publishing House, 1978), p. 284.

4. Ibid.

5. The exposition of the *chuch'e* ideology is taken from the following sources, unless indicated otherwise. Kim Il-song, "On Exterminating Dogmatism and Formalism and Establishing Independence in Ideological Work," *Selected Works* (Pyongyang: Foreign Languages Publishing House, 1965), I:582–606; "Independence and Proletarian Internationalism," *Kulloja*, July 1, 1969; Hwang Chang-yop, "The Chuch'e Idea—Scientific, Revolutionary World Outlook Regarding Man as the Central Factor," *Study of the Chuch'e Idea* 1, no. 3 (1972): 30–38; Kim Il-song, "On Some Problems of Our Party's *Chuch'e* Idea and the Government of the Republic's Internal and External Policies," answers to the questions raised by journalists of the Japanese newspaper, *Mainichi Shimbun*, September 17, 1972, in *For the Independent Peaceful Reunification of Korea* (New York: International Publishers, 1975), pp. 173–200; *On Chuch'e in Our Revolution*, 2 vols. (Pyongyang: Foreign Languages Publishing House, 1975); "Let Us More Firmly Arm Ourselves with the *Chuch'e* Idea of Our Party," *Nodong Sinmun*, May 3, 1982; "The *Chuch'e* Torch Will Ablaze Forever," *Nodong Sinmun*, May 9, 1982; "The *Chuch'e* Idea Is the Great Guiding Ideology of Revolution Based on the Demands of a New Era and the Experience in the Revolutionary Struggle," *Nodong Sinmun*, May 31, 1982; and "The *Chuch'e* Idea Is a Great Ideology Which Has Elucidated Afresh the Basic Principles of Social Movement and Revolutionary Movement," *Nodong Sinmun*, June 7, 1982.

6. The part of the *chuch'e* ideology concerning the single superman-like leader in historical progress is taken from the following sources, unless indicated otherwise. Kim Il-song, "Report on the Work of the Central Committee to the Fifth Congress of

the Workers' Party of Korea," *Pyongyang Times,* November 3, 1970; "The Great Leader Comrade Kim Il-song Is the Founder and Leader of the First State of Proletarian Dictatorship in Our Country," *Minchu Choson,* January 10, 1972; "The People Praise Their Leader," *Nodong Sinmun,* December 12, 1980; "Blood Ties with the Masses Is the Source of the Boundless Might of Our Party," *Nodong Sinmun,* February 3, 1981; "The Respected and Beloved Leader Comrade Kim Il-song Is the Great Leader Who Brilliantly Pioneered Our People's Fate," *Nodong Sinmun,* April 10, 1981; "The *Chuch'e* Idea Is the Great Guiding Ideology of Revolution Based on the Demands of a New Era and the Experience in the Revolutionary Struggle," *Nodong Sinmun,* May 31, 1982; "The *Chuch'e* Idea Is a Great Ideology Which Has Elucidated Afresh the Basic Principles of Social Movement and Revolutionary Movement," *Nodong Sinmun,* June 7, 1982; *Foreign Broadcast Information Service* (FBIS), Asia and Pacific, April 14, 1980, p. D1; April 30, 1980, pp. D12–D14; June 9, 1980, pp. D6–D8; June 30, 1980, pp. D11–D12; July 10, 1980, pp. D4–D7; July 11, 1980, pp. D5–D7; July 14, 1980, pp. D1–D3; July 17, 1980, pp. D1–D3; August 4, 1980, pp. D11–D12; August 8, 1980, pp. D1–D2; August 13, 1980, pp. D7–D9; October 14, 1980, pp. D33–D36; November 18, 1980, pp. D8–D9; and December 31, 1980, pp. D3–D9.

7. Ellen Brun and Jacques Hersh, *Socialist Korea* (New York and London: Monthly Review Press, 1976), p. 415.

8. According to Ellen Brun and Jacques Hersh, who had visited the DPRK a couple of times in the past, North Korean scholars asserted that "the unity and smooth functioning of collective leadership may very well depend on the individual leader, who commands a respect that transcends any temporary disagreements." Brun and Hersh, *Socialist Korea,* p. 412.

Kim Il-song, reviewing Stalin's accomplishments and weaknesses, said: "We Communists criticize Stalin for his violation of Leninist collective leadership and Marxist-Leninist ideology. This does not mean that we deny the role of the individual in history. Marxism-Leninism recognizes the important role of [individual] leaders in history." *Nodong Sinmun,* May 31, 1956.

9. See, for example, "To Protect and Complete the Revolutionary Task Launched by the Great Leader Is the Firm Resolve and the Revolutionary Creed of Our Party," *Kulloja,* February 1977; and "We Must Arm Our Society with the Idea of *Chuch'e* to Fulfill Our Historical Revolution," *Kulloja,* February 1977.

10. See references in note 9 of this chapter.

11. *Foreign Broadcast Information Service,* Asia and Pacific, April 19, 1982, p. D26.

12. In an article to commemorate Kim Il-song's 60th birthday in April 1972, "The Great Leader Kim Il-song Is the Originator of Our Party's Revolutionary Tradition," Choe Yong-kon, then chairman of the Supreme People's Assembly's Standing Committee, who was also a member of the anti-Japanese Korean guerrilla band in Manchuria in the 1930s, said that the *chuch'e* had now been institutionalized as the monolithic ideology (*yuil sasang*) of the KWP, the government, and the people of North Korea, because "we have now inherited the revoltuionary tradition, which means that we have accepted the ideological system of the anti-Japanese guerrilla units and applied their method and style of work to solve our problems of revolution and construction." *Nodong Sinmun,* April 7, 1972.

The KWP action program, adopted by the Fourth Congress of the KWP in 1961, stressed, among other things, the preservation of the revolutionary tradition acquired in the anti-Japanese armed struggle in Manchuria and the attainment of a complete victory of socialism in North Korea on the basis of this tradition. See *Documents of the Fourth Congress of the Workers' Party of Korea* (Pyongyang: Foreign Languages Publishing House, 1961).

13. *Peking Review*, October 21, 1966, pp. 21–25; and October 28, 1966, pp. 32–35.

14. Kim Il-song, "Let Us Develop the Chollima Workteam Movement in Depth," in *Kim Il-song Sonjip* [Selected Works of Kim Il-song] (Pyongyang: Choson Nodong-dang Ch'ulpansa, 1960), V:56; and *Choson Inminhui Jayu wa Haepang* [The Freedom and Liberation of the Korean People]: *Records of the Anti-Japanese Armed Struggles*, compiled by the KWP's Institute of Party History, no date, p. 470.

15. *Chieh-fang-chun Pao*, August 1, 1966; *Peking Review*, August 5, 1966, pp. 1–10; *Jen-min Jih-pao*, August 1, 1967, and November 3, 1967; Tai Sung An, *Mao Tse-tung's Cultural Revolution* (New York: Pegasus, Bobbs-Merrill Co., 1972), p. 11; Stuart R. Schram, *The Political Thought of Mao Tse-tung* (New York: Praeger, 1960), pp. 1–330; Rene Goldman, "Mao, Maoism and Mao-ology: A Review Article," *Pacific Affairs*, Winter 1968–1969, pp. 560–74; and "What Is Maoism? A Symposium," *Problems of Communism*, September–October 1966, pp. 1–30.

16. In 1969, Kim Il-song stressed, in his answers to questions concerning economic growth in North Korea, the idea that "the ideological and cultural revoltuion to remold the consciousness of the people and enhance their technical and cultural levels" was still an essential part of his strategy of development. Kim Il-song, "On Some Theoretical Problems of the Socialist Economy," answers to questions raised by scientific and educational workers on March 1, 1969, in *Juche: The Speeches and Writings of Kim Il-song* (New York: Grossman Publishers, 1972), p. 133.

In the same year, Kim Il-song again stressed that "the determining factor in the development of productive forces in the socialist society is certainly the higher revolutionary consciousness of the people rather than the improvement of management techniques by adopting the market mechanism or the material incentives of the capitalist system." Kim Il-song, "On Some Theoretical Problems of Socialist Economy," *Nodong Sinmun*, March 1, 1969.

17. Schram, *Political Thought of Mao Tse-tung*, p. 80.

18. Robert C. Tucker, ed., *The Marx-Engels Reader* (New York: W. W. Norton, 1972), p. xxi; George H. Sabine and Thomas L. Thorson, *A History of Political Theory*, 4th ed. (Hinsdale, Ill.: Dryden Press, 1973), p. 682; Edwin R. A. Seligman, *The Economic Interpretation of History* (New York: Columbia University Press, 1902), p. 142; and Karl Marx, *A Contribution to the Critique of Political Economy*, translated and edited by Nahum Isaac Stone (Chicago: Charles Kerr and Co., 1918), p. 11.

19. The historical role of individuals was one of the subjects of the earlier controversy among anti-Czarist, Marxist revolutionary thinkers during the late nineteenth century. This Marxist thesis on the historical role of man in society was further elaborated by G. V. Plekhanov in his book *The Role of Individuals in History*, translated by J. Fineberg (Moscow: Foreign Languages Publishing House, 1946), pp. 1–56.

20. Ibid.

21. Cited in Sabine and Thorson, *History of Political Theory*, p. 698; and Tucker, *Marx-Engels Reader*, p. 4.

22. See Vladimir Lenin, *Selected Works* (New York: International Publishers, 1943), II:27–192.

23. Tucker, *Marx-Engels Reader*, pp. xl–xli.

24. See note 15 of this chapter.

25. For the Maoist conception of the historical role and functions of the masses, see, for example, *Selected Works of Mao Zedong* (Beijing: Foreign Languages Press, 1955), III:118–257; and "Notes from Chairman Mao's Talks with Leading Comrades on Inspection Trips," reprinted in *Studies on Chinese Communism* (Taipei, Taiwan), September 1972, pp. 18–24.

26. See references in note 25 of this chapter.

27. See note 29 of Chapter 2.

28. Zbigniew K. Brzezinski, *The Soviet Bloc* (Cambridge, Mass.: Harvard University Press, 1960), pp. 153–410.

29. The *Chollima* movement will be discussed in Chapter 4.

30. Quoted from Richard M. Pfeffer, "Serving the People and Continuing the Revolution," *China Quarterly*, October–December 1972, p. 620.

31. Max Weber, *The Theory of Social and Economic Organization*, translated by A. M. Henderson and Talcott Parsons, edited with an introduction by Talcott Parsons (Glencoe, Ill.: Free Press, 1947), pp. 359–62; Max Weber, *Essays in Sociology*, edited by H. H. Gerth and C. Wright Mill (New York: Oxford University Press, 1958), p. 52; Robert C. Tucker, ed., *The Lenin Anthology* (New York: W. W. Norton, 1975), pp. xliii–xliv; and Robert C. Tucker, "The Theory of Charismatic Leadership," *Daedalus*, Summer 1968, pp. 731–56.

32. For the influence of the Titoist thesis on the nonalignment of the Third World on Kim Il-song's *chuch'e* ideology, see note 50 of Chapter 1. See also Kim Il-song's speech to the Sixth National Congress of the KWP in October 1980, in *Foreign Broadcast Information Service*, Asia and Pacific, October 15, 1980, pp. D11–D18.

33. As mentioned previously in this chapter, the DPRK puts great emphasis on the *chuch'e* ideology with regard to the hereditary leadership movement, probably to fend off the possible scorn of the Soviets, Chinese, or other Communists. It asserts that the North Korean-style hereditary leadership movement is justifiable in terms of the *chuch'e* ideology. See note 9 of this chapter. See also "Respected and Beloved Leader Comrade Kim Il-song Is the Great Leader Directing the Cause of *Chuch'e* to Shining Victory," *Nodong Sinmun*, November 19, 1980; "Modeling the Whole Society on the *Chuch'e* Idea Is the General Task of Our Revolution," *Nodong Sinmun*, November 24, 1980; and "Great Programmatic Work Indicating the Way to Brilliantly Accomplish Our Cause Under the Banner of the *Chuch'e* Idea," *Nodong Sinmun*, October 20, 1980.

34. Kim Il-song, "Against Passivism and Conservatism in Socialist Construction," September 16, 1958, *Selected Works* (Pyongyang: Foreign Languages Publishing House, 1965), II:241–42.

35. The total amount of foreign economic aid and loans received by North Korea from the Communist-bloc nations during the period from 1949 to 1962 is estimated at about US$1.37 billion. Of this total, US$577 million, or nearly 41 percent, reportedly came from the Soviet Union. China provided approximately US$517

million, or about 38 percent; Eastern European nations contributed US$296 million, or 21 percent of the total.

The U.S. Arms Control and Disarmament Agency estimates that during the period from 1967 to 1976, arms transferred to North Korea from China and the Soviet Union amounted to a total of US$771 million. According to U.S. Defense Department figures declassified in August 1977, North Korea had received US$180 million in various forms of military aid from the Chinese and US$145 million from the Soviet Union during 1974–1977. See U.S., Arms Control and Disarmament Agency, *World Military Expenditures and Arms Transfers, 1967–1976* (Washington, D.C.: July 1978), p. 158; *Washington Post*, August 9, 1977; Ilpyong J. Kim, *Communist Politics in North Korea*, pp. 99, 109; Joseph S. Chung, *The North Korean Economy: Structure and Development* (Stanford, Calif.: Hoover Institution Press, 1974), pp. 21–23; *New York Times*, November 24, 1953; Alexander Eckstein, *Communist China's Economic Growth and Foreign Trade: Implications for U.S. Policy* (New York: McGraw-Hill, 1966), p. 163; and *Choson Chungang Yongam* [Korean Central Yearbook] (Pyongyang: Korean Central News Agency, 1961), p. 136.

4

The Policy Aspects of the
Chuch'e Ideology: Mass Mobili-
zation and the Economy

THE POLITICS OF MASS MOBILIZATION

Every aspect of life in North Korea is pervaded by Kim Il-song's efforts
to build a modern socialist country by restructuring the traditional
social order in compliance with his *chuch'e* ideology. The domestic
development of the DPRK, since its inception in 1948, has focused
on building new political culture[1] and institutions to replace old
ones, modernizing the economy to implement socialist industrialization, and creating a new socialist culture.

As was mentioned earlier, the *chuch'e* ideology mandates the
policy of self-reliance, which was fully implemented beginning in
1957.[2] The goal of self-reliance is to mobilize the domestic resources
and human energy of its own people in order to minimize dependence
on outside countries, just as the Chinese Communists had done in
line with Mao Zedong's revolutionary concept of mass line.[3]
Furthermore, the DPRK regime wants to build a highly motivated,
well-disciplined, increasingly efficient, and politically committed
work force. The campaign to glorify Kim Il-song's "glorious anti-
Japanese revolutionary tradition" in Manchuria is designed partly
to inculcate the spirit of self-reliance in the general population. Kim
said very bluntly in 1972 that the North Koreans would never want
foreigners to carry out their socialist revolution and construction
on their behalf.[4]

The DPRK policy of self-reliance stresses that the leadership and
the masses are to be closely linked on the domestic front in carrying
out the task of building a modern, proud, dynamic, and self-

supporting socialist state.[5] In point of fact, the DPRK is today the most extensively mobilized state, with strict guidance and control from the top, and it demands of every citizen extraordinary loyalty, commitment, dedication, and sacrifice in support of a clearly defined set of purposes and goals.[6] Indeed, active participation in the politics of mass mobilization is mandatory, and it represents a North Korean Communist style of so-called participatory democracy, which is imposed from above through the mixture of persuasion and coercion. The rationale of the mass-mobilization theory is that through active participation in the mass political movement, every North Korean citizen comes to appreciate the true meaning of socialist revolution and construction and his own particular place and role in the revolutionary transformation of North Korean society. At the same time, the individual becomes imbued with political and ideological consciousness, which, in turn, determines correct political attitudes, sound and efficient organizational behavior, and total allegiance and commitment.[7]

The politics of mass mobilization is closely linked to the triple revolution of technology, ideology, and culture—the North Korean version of modernization and development—which aims at accelerating the sweeping changes in every aspect of North Korean life more smoothly and efficiently.[8] In the late 1960s, Kim Il-song asserted that "unless we cast away the old system, old ideas, old methods of work, and old customs of life that stand in the way of progress, we cannot build a new, socialist society."[9] The triple revolution has been formulated and implemented as the prerequisite for the successful construction of socialism in North Korea.[10]

The technical revolution includes a major emphasis on the advancement of science and technology for social, especially economic, progress toward modernity. The DPRK regime has been attempting to achieve this objective in several ways: by promoting the popularization of compulsory technical education even at the high-school level; by rapidly increasing the number of scientists, technicians, and other types of specialists with both tertiary and higher-level qualifications; and by improving the quality and facilities of the overall technical-education program. According to Article 25 of the DPRK Constitution adopted in 1972, the technical revoluton ultimately aims, through the mechanization of industrial and agricultural facilities, to eliminate the distinctions between heavy and light labor, between agricultural and industrial labor, between physical and mental labor, and between cities and rural areas.

political consciousness of the masses of the working class, as well as to bring about new attitudes, beliefs, behavioral patterns, and institutions, through the indoctrination program based on the *chuch'e* ideology. Among the several components of the triple revolution, the ideological and cultural transformations of the North Korean people have priority over the technological transformation.[11] The Pyongyang regime wants to arouse the enthusiasm, creativity, and productivity of the masses of the people by emphasizing political and ideological stimulation rather than materialistic incentives.

The cultural revolution is designed to replace the traditional political culture based on Confucian ethics with a new socialist culture that emphasizes remolding individual personalities into New Socialist Men who are willing to work enthusiastically and selflessly for collective objectives through collective efforts. In pursuit of this objective, the DPRK regime has been committed to improve the educational level of the people, to strengthen the public-health and medical-welfare systems, and to develop the new socialist cultural activities of every citizen.

The organizational technique adopted by the Pyongyang regime in implementing the politics of mass mobilization is the mass line approach, which calls on party workers (cadres) to go to the masses with general policies and principles, grasp their views and problems, integrate them into policy execution, and then mobilize the people to carry out enthusiastically the requisite tasks of socialist revolution and construction.[12] (In effect, the DPRK mass line, like the Maoist mass line, is based on paternal authoritarianism.) In other words, the mass line policy is designed to forge a close link between the leadership and the people in order to mobilize the broadest possible support for Kim Il-song's policies.

During the 1950s and 1960s, the DPRK mass line policy was specifically translated into such mass political actions as the *Chollima* movement, the *Chongsan-ni* method, and the *Taean* system. (The *Chollima* movement and the *Chongsan-ni* method paralleled Chinese procedures developed during the Great Leap Forward in the late 1950s.)

Chollima means, literally, "one thousand-ri horse," and is officially called "Flying Horse." It refers to the legendary Chinese horse said to have galloped a phenomenal distance in a single day. The *Chollima* movement was adopted at the 1956 plenum of the KWP Central Committee to fulfill the first five-year economic plan from 1958 to 1963. Starting in 1958, it was used by the DPRK regime to designate its rapid, mass-production drive in industry and agriculture, especially its priority for developing heavy industry.[13] Moralistic fervor and ideological appeal rather than materialistic incentives were used to maintain maximum productivity.

Chongsan-ni is the name of a village in Kangso County, South Pyongan Province. The *Chongsan-ni* method was normally identified with the managerial-guidance system for rural areas as a whole. This method was said to have been first demonstrated by Kim Il-song in February 1960, when he personally went down to a rural, backward village, *Chongsan-ni*, to show that agricultural production could be much improved if party and government cadres actually mingled with and guided the peasants instead of issuing directives from above.[14] A synthesis of ideological indoctrination and material incentives was used in this method to stimulate the peasant population to increase productivity.

The *Taean* system was an application of the *Chongsan-ni* method to industrial factory enterprises. Inaugurated in December 1961 at the Taean Electric Appliance Factory by Kim Il-song, the *Taean* system was described as one in which "superior agencies would assist lower agencies and superiors would assist inferiors" in managerial and ideological matters.[15] Apart from features designed to maximize industrial productivity, new KWP committees were set up in industrial factories in order to ensure the "primacy of politics over economy." This system was also characterized by the introduction of a collective leadership system into industrial management by which the ordinary workers participated in the planning and decision-making processes through party committees and the concept of decentralization in the industrial sector.

NORTH KOREAN ECONOMY

The most extreme form of nationalism, economic as well as polit-ical, is found in North Korea. Kim Il-song has been determined to transform his backward, agrarian society into a modern industrial-ized state, fully utilizing domestic resources and techniques of development such as the mass line, self-reliance, and the labor-intensive method of production.[16] The goal of socialist industrialization is to turn North Korea into a socialist industrial state with modern industry and highly developed agriculture.

Chuch'e in economy means self-reliance and autarky to the fullest extent possible; that is to say, the DPRK wants to build the healthy and comfortable material foundation of a socialist state "by its own efforts," with minimum reliance on external sources of capital, investment, and technology.[17] The regime argues that the policy of economic independence is a precondition for political independence and for the construction of an integrated economy, particularly in an excolonial nation where industry was weak.[18]

The DPRK acquired observer status at the Moscow-dominated COMECON (Council for Mutual Economic Assistance)[19] in 1957, but it is not a member. North Korea has been opposed to the COMECON principles of international division of labor and comparative advantage in trade, for it believes that these policies will help big powers dominate small nations economically and may hinder the independent and comprehensive economic development of the latter.[20] Foreign machines and technology are likely to generate a *sadaechuii* mentality. Economic cooperation among nations is necessary, but it should be achieved, not through assistance, but through direct trade based on the principles of independence and equality.[21]

The North Korean economic system is based on a highly centralized and socialized pattern of command economy; it is organized into state-owned and cooperative-owned sectors, with the private sector as minimal as possible. State ownership and control of industrial enterprises were completed in 1958, along with all other sectors of the economy such as agriculture, internal commerce, foreign trade, banking, transportation, and communications. The most important state agency for economic planning is the State Planning Commission, which functions under the supervision of the KWP, and all major economic decisions made by this agency are carried out by the various governmental ministries.

Material incentives to increase labor productivity are minimally employed, and moral or ideological stimuli are used extensively.[22] Pragmatic economic thinking and methods—"economism" that gives predominance to economics at the expense of politics in the sphere of social relations—have no room for survival,[23] despite the fact that Marxism defines economy as the basic foundation of a society and politics as its superstructure.

When the Korean peninsula was partitioned in 1945, North Korea was left with the bulk of the peninsula's mineral and hydroelectric resources and most of the existing heavy industrial base,[24] but it had only one-third of the work force. In 1945, approximately 69 percent of the peninsula's light industry, 63 percent of its agriculture, and 82 percent of its commerce were in the south.[25]

Since its birth in 1948, the DPRK has pursued the consolidation of a self-supporting and nationalistic economy as its foremost goal. This policy has been more vigorously developed and pursued since the early 1960s, when the Pyongyang regime put forward its ideology of *chuch'e*. The primary emphasis on self-help has been the chief momentum in the search for economic growth. Although North Korea originally relied heavily on Soviet advice, techniques, institutional models, and aid, the Pyongyang hierarchy has adopted its own development model, which aims at modernizing the economy with its own resources and skills in a way that would best suit the conditions of the country. In so doing, Kim Il-song has envisaged that the primary orientation of the North Korean economy would shift from agro-forestry to industry.[26]

During the past three and a half decades, the DPRK regime has instituted eight distinctive plans for economic growth.

1. one-year plan, 1947
2. one-year plan, 1948
3. two-year plan, 1949–1950
4. three-year plan, 1954–1956
5. five-year plan, 1957–1961(60)—(a de facto four-year plan, due to the fulfillment of the plan a year ahead of schedule)
6. seven-year plan, 1961–1967(70)—(a de facto ten-year plan, due to the three-year extension for the completion of the plan)
7. six-year plan, 1971–1976(77)—(a de facto seven-year plan, due to the one-year extension for "supplement-

ing" the plan and easing strains formed in some fields
in the course of implementing the plan)

8. seven-year plan, 1978–1984

Although general trends can be perceived, detailed knowledge of
the state of North Korean economy is difficult to obtain because
North Korea is one of the most secretive countries in the world; it
releases only fragmentary economic data, and the small amount of
information available is often ambiguous. Since 1966, the DPRK
regime has not made public the annual economic statistics usually
released in mid-January. Economic information published since
1966 has been limited to the achievements of individual production
units. Moreover, the few statistics issued appear to have been carefully selected for propaganda purposes and thus are believed to present an exaggerated picture of economic performance.

Since 1948, the DPRK has made every effort to accomplish rapid
economic development. Although most of the economic data deriv-
ing from the Pyongyang regime are better suited for propaganda
purposes than for economic studies, it cannot be denied that North
Korea has achieved substantial economic growth during the postwar decades. Within the cradle-to-grave system implemented by
Kim Il-song, the nation has, in less than three decades, rebuilt itself
from virtual ruin at the end of the Korean War in 1953 to a point
where it provides its 19 million citizens with the basic necessities of
food, shelter, and clothing—almost all produced locally—while
also achieving a high degree of industrialization.

The DPRK regime has been assisted in these efforts by economic
and technical aid from other Communist countries, notably the
Soviet Union and China.[27] This aid was particularly beneficial and
effective in the years immediately following the Korean War, when
the economy experienced a high rate of growth.[28]

The foreign aid during the immediate postwar period was
desperately needed, but it was also used to build the basis for self-
reliance for the future.[29] The important of foreign aid from Communist countries gradually declined over the decade after the Korean cease-fire of July 1953—more specifically, after the five-year
economic plan from 1957 to 1961 was launched.[30] During the
1960s, when Pyongyang had deteriorating relations alternately
with both Moscow and Beijing, foreign-aid levels dropped sharply

and became unreliable, with the result that foreign aid ceased to be an important factor in North Korea's economic development.

INDUSTRIAL PROGRESS

Endowed with the greater part of the Korean peninsula's natural resources and having inherited the heavy industries installed by the Japanese before 1945,[31] the DPRK has made impressive gains in its goal of industrialization and economic viability.[32] (A Communist-style command economy demonstrates its greatest strength in initial industrialization.) From the beginning, the priority has been on developing heavy industry, particularly the machine-building industry, as the key to mechanization of the economy and development of economic independence,[33] while moving to redress weakness in agriculture. As a result, North Korea has become a nation of heavy industry, mining, steel, metals, machinery, and chemicals, and there has been a dramatic and fundamental shift in the composition of its national output, reflecting the transformation of the North Korean economy from an agricultural base to an industrial one. From 1945 to 1965, agriculture's share of the GNP declined from 59.1 percent to 19.3 percent while industry's share increased from 23.2 percent to 62.3 percent. During the same period, the percentage of the labor force in industry increased from 12 percent to 42 percent while the proportion in agriculture decreased from 75 percent to 42.8 percent.

North Korea's development strategy in allocating priority to heavy industry has resulted in the lagging growth of both light industry (consumer goods) and agriculture. In budgetary appropriations, the central government is responsible for investing in both heavy and military-related industries. On the other hand, local governments are largely responsible for tapping financial resources to develop light industries. After 1968, in fact, local industry was given greater responsibility for consumer-goods production, and, in the mid-1960s, more than half of all consumer goods were produced by locally operated enterprises. The DPRK regime argues that consumer products must still be restricted or sacrificed to allow investment in the capital goods necessary to provide the basis for comprehensive industrialization, national self-reliance, and rapid growth potential. Strict state control over consumption allows consumer prices to be controlled: necessities are kept cheap, and luxuries are expensive.

Industrial growth was rapid in the first postwar decade. From 1954 (the first year of the three-year economic plan) through 1965 (the midpoint of the seven-year plan), an average annual growth rate of 28.1 percent was claimed. (The DPRK regime also announced that industry had grown at an average annual rate of 22.6 percent during the period from 1953 to 1973.) Its gross industrial product in 1965 was reportedly 4,200 percent of the 1946 total. Discounting these officially announced growth rates for statistical inflation would still leave an impressive industrialization rate. (See Table 2 for North Korea's probable production figures of selected products, 1946–1979, estimates made by non-Korean outside experts on Korean affairs.)

More specifically, during the three-year economic plan (1954–1956), gross industrial output grew at an average annual rate of 41.8 percent; and under the five-year plan (1957–1961), at an average of 36.6 percent. After reaching a peak in 1960, however, the industrial growth rate slowed considerably during the seven-year economic plan (1961–1967), averaging 14.3 percent annually from 1961 through 1965, and the North Korean economy has not yet recovered its former momentum since then. (The DPRK's industrial growth rate registered 12.8 percent annually during the 1960s). In October 1967, the Pyongyang regime's ambitious seven-year plan was extended for three years because of the urgent need for "greater defense efforts." The six-year economic plan for 1971–1976 was launched in November 1970, but it required an additional year for completion.

During the 1950s and the 1960s, meanwhile, the composition of North Korea's industrial products changed significantly. In 1956, for example, ore mining, metallurgy, timber-related products, and marine industries accounted for 23.9 percent of the gross industrial product, and in 1960, the last year of the five-year economic plan, their combined share decreased to 15.8 percent. By contrast, the share of the machine-building and metalworking industries in the gross industrial output rose from 17.2 percent in 1956 to 21.3 percent in 1960, and to 31.4 percent in 1967, the original completion date of the seven-year plan. By 1967, industry was reported to be meeting almost all domestic needs, relying mainly on domestic raw

Table 2:
Probable Production Figures of Selected Industrial Products in North Korea During 1946-1979
(Estimated by Non-Korean Outside Experts on Korean Affairs)

	Units	1946	1949	1956	1961	1965	1970	1976	1979
Electric power	billion	3.9	5.9	5.1	10.4	13.0	16.5	28.0	40.0
Coal	million metric tons	1.3	4.0	3.9	11.5	17.8	27.5	49.5	65.0
Iron ore	million metric tons	n.a.	0.68	0.68	3.2	3.8	n.a.	n.a.	n.a.
Pig iron	million metric tons	0.03	0.17	0.23	0.85	1.3	2.2	3.3	n.a.
Crude steel	million metric tons	0.005	0.144	0.19	0.64	1.2	2.2	4.0	4.9
Fertilizer	million metric tons	0.156	0.401	0.195	0.57	0.71	1.5	2.8	4.5
Cement	million metric tons	0.103	0.537	0.597	2.3	2.4	4.0	8.0	8.8
Textiles	million linear meters	2.7	12.9	77.1	191.1	227.3	400.0	600.0	n.a.
Refined petroleum products	million metric tons	n.a.	n.a.	n.a.	n.a.	n.a.	0.09	1.0	n.a.
Marine products catch	million metric tons	n.a.	n.a.	n.a.	0.595	0.643	0.7	1.6	2.7
Machine tools	thousand units	n.a.	n.a.	n.a.	n.a.	n.a.	10.0	24.0	n.a.
Trucks	thousand units	n.a	n.a.	n.a.	3.2	4.0	4.5	10.0	24.5
Zinc	thousand metric tons	n.a.	20.0	n.a.	90.0	105.0	88.0	125.0	n.a.
Lead	thousand metric tons	n.a.	21.0	n.a.	50.0	60.0	61.0	80.0	n.a.
Television sets	thousand units	none	none	none	negl.	negl.	negl.	100.0	n.a.

NOTES: n.a.: not available
negl.: negligible

SOURCES: U.S., Central Intelligence Agency, National Foreign Assessment Center, *Korea: The Economic Race Between the North and the South* (a research paper), ER 78-10008 (Washington, D.C., January 1978), p. 11; *Far Eastern Economic Review*, May 15, 1981, p. 49; Foreign Area Studies, American University (Shinn, Rinn-sup, and others), *Area Handbook for North Korea* (Washington, D.C.: U.S. Government Printing Office, 1969), pp. 316, 330, 332; and Robert A. Scalapino and Lee Chong-sik, *Communism in Korea* (Berkely and Los Angeles: University of California Press, 1972), II: 1210, 1223, 1244, 1263.

materials.[34] (one of the important tasks of the seven-year economic plan from 1971 to 1976 was to base North Korea's industrial expansion on 65 to 70 percent self-reliance in raw materials.)[35]

The textile industry's share in the gross industrial product also increased significantly during the 1950s and 1960s: in 1946, it was 6.0 percent of the total; in 1963, an estimated 18.6 percent. Similarly, the processed-food industry's share rose from 7.8 percent in 1946 to an estimated 13.7 percent in 1963. The chemical industry, such as synthetic fibers, resins, rubber (these products were manufactured as synthetic import-substitutes to reduce dependence on imported raw materials) and fertilizers (to increase agricultural production and promote self-sufficiency in food grain), had also become a significant element in North Korea's industrial output.

There are a number of reasons why North Korea's GNP and industrial production have slowed down since the mid-1960s. First, there have been indications that, as with economic development in many developing nations, a period of diminishing returns in the form of a moderated growth rate may have been reached after the North Korean economy passed an initial period of rapid growth. Another key reason is Pyongyang's overriding commitment of resources to the military and military-related industries at the expense of the civilian economy. Although no reliable data are available, during the 1960s, North Korea was reported to be spending close to 20 percent of its annual GNP on defense-related items.[36]

In addition to the tremendous resource drain into military endeavors, there has been a significant manpower drain on the North Korean economy in maintaining a large defense establishment. According to Western intelligence, some 700,000 North Koreans— one out of every twenty-five, or about 13 percent of North Korean males of military age (17 to 49)—are in the regular armed services, with many more committed to some form of militia or home-guard duties.[37] The manpower shortage remains particularly acute in agriculture, which has lost large numbers of workers to the military as well as to the growing industrial establishment. The North Korean army participates in harvesting crops and in constructing many civilian projects; nonetheless, the large military manpower requirements partly explain the chronic labor shortages in North Korea. Consequently, mechanization has been stressed by the Pyongyang regime in order to counter the labor shortage.

Another major resource drain on North Korea during the latter half of the 1960s and the early 1970s was its long-term program to build underground facilities to house important industrial and military facilities. This effort was part of Kim Il-song's widely publicized program in the early 1960s "to arm the entire people and to convert the whole country into a military fortress."[38] This expensive underground-construction program, designed to protect important industrial and military installations in the event of new, large-scale war on the Korean peninsula, undoubtedly diverted considerable manpower and capital equipment from other more productive sectors of the economy. (In general, underground construction is three to four times more expensive than similar aboveground construction and is much more time-consuming.)

A decline in the efficiency of central planning and planning errors can be listed as additional reasons for the north's industrial slow-down since the mid-1960s.

During the early 1970s, North Korea, probably noting the major, rapid economic development of South Korea, decided to make hasty and large-scale economic-growth efforts by importing advanced equipment and technology from Western Europe and Japan. In so doing, the DPRK set aside the *chuch'e* philosophy that was supposed to keep North Korea's external economic dependence at a bare minimum. In his speech to an important gathering of industrial managers in Pyongyang in early March 1975,[39] Kim Il-song made public a slight shift in the DPRK's economic policy by stating that North Korea could not satisfactorily meet all the requirements of rapid economic development if the country counted only on Communist countries and that Pyongyang must, in addition, actively seek out capitalist markets to procure necessary materials and machinery.

By the end of 1976, the North Koreans found themselves in economic trouble, culminating in their default on international debt payments. Figures on external debts varied, but according to reliable sources, North Korea owed a total of US$2 billion to the Communist bloc, Western Europe, and Japan at the end of 1976.[40] Of this, US$400 million was already overdue for repayment to non-Communist creditors alone. In the mid-1970s, Western and other creditors were angered by the DPRK's inability to honor contracts and to finance its growing deficits, and there was much talk of "bad faith." Imports of advanced machinery and technology from Western countries and Japan dropped sharply because of payment difficulties and, to a lesser extent, so did exports to those countries, thereby forcing North Korea to slow down its ambitious growth plan. Trade with the Communist nations was also reported to have shrunk severely. Renegotiations during 1977 apparently resulted in a five-year moratorium on the repayment of Pyongyang's long-overdue debts to Western European and Japanese creditors in exchange for an increase in the interest rates.

North Korea's balance of payments, coupled with its inability to pay its external debts, was in a difficult position for several reasons. First, in a frantic effort to push ahead of South Korea's rapidly growing economy, Pyongyang made its ambitious decision in late 1970, before the start of the six-year economic plan from 1971 to 1976, to push economic development too quickly by importing industrial plants and other heavy machinery in greater quantities than the nation could afford to pay for them. Second, North Korea's expected expansion of exports to the West and to Japan to pay for increased imports was dealt a severe blow by the worldwide energy (oil) crisis, inflation, and recession. These factors also substantially raised the cost of its imports. Third, Pyongyang suffered from a decrease in the price of its main exports— minerals and ores—because of the softening of world commodity markets in the post-energy-crisis period or because it could not sell its main export commodities overseas.

Foreign-trade debt problems continued to plague North Korea for the balance of the 1970s. According to a Japanese survey compiled in the mid-1970s by the semiofficial Japan External Trade Organization (JETRO), it would take at least ten years for North Korea to resolve its debt problems, even with strenuous efforts to expand exports.[41] DPRK officials said in 1977 that by the end of the ongoing seven-year economic plan (1978–1984), their exports of cement, ferrous and nonferrous metals, fertilizers, and other products would allow them to pay off all their external debts, asserting that North Korea's total export value would be much higher than US$4 billion by 1984.[42]

Largely because of the debt problem, but also because of a prolonged drought, North Korea's economy stumbled badly in 1976. Cutbacks in imported machinery and equipment, a shortage of hydroelectric power, and resource-allocation problems slowed industrial growth. (Fragmentary Western intelligence reports indicated that Pyongyang's economic problems were also intensified by a decrease in aid from the Soviet Union and from China.) Pyongyang fell short of many of its six-year plan (1971-1976) industrial targets. According to an American Central Intelligence Agency (CIA) study, electric-power production, for example, only reached 22 billion kwh (kilowatt hours), 6 billion kwh below the minimum target.[43]

These difficulties continued in 1977—which Kim Il-song had declared a "year of readjustment" before launching the new seven-year economic plan scheduled to begin on January 1, 1978. The economic hardships in the mid-1970s, however, were not necessarily serious enough to affect North Korea's ongoing military production programs over the next several years since the major investment was already in place. Nor did they appear to have deprived the population of the essentials of life or to have caused internal political crises.

In 1977, the DPRK announced the principal targets of the new seven-year economic plan from 1978 to 1984.[44] The plan called for a 220-percent increase in gross industrial output value, with an average annual growth rate of 12.1 percent. By 1984, electricity output would be 50 to 60 billion kwh, up from the 1977 level of 28 billion kwh; coal output, 70 to 80 million tons, from 53 million tons in 1977; steel, 7.4 to 8 million tons, from 4 million tons in 1977; machine tools, 50,000 units, from 25,000 units in 1976; chemical fertilizers, 5 million tons, from 3 million tons in 1975; cement, 12 to 13 million tons, from 8 million tons in 1977; and fishery products, 3.5 million tons, from 1.8 million tons in 1977.

North Korea would put more emphasis on the mining and transport sectors of the economy, which were growing in importance with the looming international energy crisis and with Pyongyang's need to modernize transport to meet a hoped-for expansion in trade. Agriculture, too, would be enormously developed, with grain production reaching 10 million tons by 1984, from approximately 8.5 million tons in 1977.

Except for electricity, all the announced targets were either equal to or considerably below the goals previously enunciated by the

Pyongyang hierarchy in 1974. This fact clearly suggested that, in light of the current economic difficulties, North Korea had established more realistic economic policies by readjusting (that is, lowering) its projections of economic growth for the next seven years. Even so, some Western experts said that the seven-year economic plan was too ambitious and that Pyongyang would have a hard time achieving the lowered targets unless assistance from the outside world—especially the Soviet Union and China—was forthcoming. But Japanese experts asserted that the ambitious targets of the seven-year plan were likely to be achieved with the possible exception of grain output set at 10 million tons.

At the Sixth Congress of the KWP in mid-October 1980, Kim Il-song made an overall evaluation of the economic performance of North Korea during the 1970s and presented a projection of economic tasks for the 1980s.[45]

He reported that during the 1970s, North Korea's industrial production had seen an average annual growth of 15.9 percent and its total industrial output had increased 2.8 times. In the same period, output of means of production had increased 3.9 times and consumer goods 3.7 times, he said. (As a result of the improvements in the North Korean economy, according to Kim, the average life span of citizens was now seventy-three years, thirty-five years longer than in 1945.)

To support his claims, Kim Il-song mentioned the following rates of increase in production: 120 percent for cement and 100 percent for thermal-power generation. (He said that thermal-power generation accounted for half of the total power generation.) He also cited the electrification of 1,600 kilometers of railways in 1970–1979, which boosted the ratio of electric traction to 87.5 percent, and the production of 9 million tons of grain in 1979.

Kim Il-song's report on the North Korean economy covered other topics as well: (1) 481 specialized schools for the training of technicians and scientists had been established during the 1970s; (2) North Korean scientists had invented a new metallurgical process using North Korean fuel and a new casting method, as well as new methods of producing seeds and cultivating crops; (3) the north's light industry was now capable of satisfying its own people's growing demand for consumer goods; and (4) the existing machine-building factories had been reinforced and many new ones were built, with special emphasis on the production of machine tools.

The North Korean chieftain presented ten economic goals to be attained by the end of the 1980s: the production of 100 billion kwh electricity, 120 million tons of coal, 15 million tons of steel, 1.5 million tons of nonferrous metals, 20 million tons of cement, 7 million tons of chemical fertilizers, 1.5 billion meters of textile, 5 million tons of marine products, 15 million tons of grain, and reclamation of 300,000 *jongbo* of land. (One *jongbo* is equivalent to 9917.3 square meters, or 2.45 acres.) He also called for an increase in exports of 320 percent during the nine years ahead. The average industrial growth rate was set at 12 percent a year, which is equal to the industrial growth set for the current seven-year economic plan. This figure is less ambitious than those for the 1960s and the 1970s and reflects a fairly conservative approach by the drafters.

According to South Korean observers, the DPRK's lowered targets for economic growth for the 1980s are still too ambitious and are impossible to attain. According to Japanese estimates based on current North Korean output levels, however, some of the targets—for instance, those for fertilizers, cement, and coal—are attainable if Pyongyang is provided with sufficient investment capital.

AGRICULTURE

Today, the basic farm production units are state farms and collective (cooperative) farms, with the latter predominating in share of output and in land under cultivation. The one negligible exception to state and collective ownership in agriculture is that individual farming households are permitted to cultivate small "garden plots" (50 *pyong*, or 0.04 acre) and fruit trees, as well as to raise poultry, pigs, and bees, both for home consumption and for sale at the "peasant markets."[46]

Traditionally, the north was the industrial center of the Korean peninsula while the south was the breadbasket. For this reason, the North Korean achievement in agriculture since 1945 is impressive. North Korean agriculture is highly mechanized, fertilizer application is probably among the highest in the world, and irrigation projects are extensive. (Pyongyang's irrigation system is believed to be one of the most elaborate and successful in the world.) During the past three and a half decades, for example, North Korea has been able to double its rice yields, and the country is now self-sufficient in rice, with a little to spare for export. Self-sufficiency has been claimed in grain products since the early 1960s.

Approximately 41 percent of the population lives on the land, but agriculture, forestry, and fishing constitute only 24 percent of the DPRK's total GNP. Of the three major types of agricultural activities (crops, livestock, and sericulture), grain crops, mainly rice and corn, are the principal farming activity in North Korea, as in most Asian economies. Corn accounts for 55 percent of the total harvest and rice for about 40 percent. Rice is the preferred grain in the north and is strictly rationed, which may account for the persistent reports of food shortages in North Korea. Stockpiling of grain may also be a factor in limiting the availability of food for current consumption.

Agriculture continues to be a lagging sector of the North Korean economy, in spite of substantial technological improvements and expansion in fertilizer production, mechanization, irrigation, land reclamation, and rural electric power. Various factors are responsible: the limited amount of arable land, the low priority assigned to agriculture by economic planners in terms of the state investment-allocation policy, the coercive nature of the collectivized farm operation, and the emphasis on a nonmaterialistic incentive system.

The DPRK regime claimed that the average annual growth rate of total grain production for the three-year plan (1954-1956), the five-year plan (1957-1961), and the seven-year plan (1961-1967) were 11.6 percent, 8.4 percent, and 6.7 percent, respectively.[47] According to the CIA study cited earlier, grain production increased an average of 5.4 percent annually between 1965 and 1976, and this performance was well above the 3 percent average growth in population, making North Korea nearly self-sufficient in grain supplies.[48]

According to Kim Il-song's report at the Fourth KWP Congress held in September 1961,[49] North Korea harvested 3,803,000 tons of grain from 2 million *jongbo* of fields in 1960. He added that 1,284,000 *jongbo* were used to grow rice and Indian corn.

In the 1970s, Pyongyang's agricultural policy focused on increasing farm acreage, with the goal of reclaiming 100,000 *jongbo*, as projected in the seven-year plan. The Pyongyang regime announced that 20.5 percent of its total investment went into agriculture in the 1970s. It is believed that most of the money was used for developing farm land and for building irrigation systems.

Efforts were also devoted to developing new varieties of rice plants. Since the cold, dry climate frequently damages crops, it is vital to develop new species of rice that have greater yield and that are resistant to severe weather conditions. The fact that Paek Sol-hui, who was credited with developing and breeding plant species, was chosen a candidate member of the Sixth KWP Central Committee suggests the great emphasis the government placed on this project.

The announcement that grain production in 1974 was 7 million tons indicated that North Korea's average annual increase in grain production during 1971–1974 was 228,000 tons. The post-1975 reports said that grain production jumped to 8 million tons in 1976, to 8.5 million tons in 1977, and still further to 9 million tons in 1979. By these accounts, the average annual increase in grain production during 1975–1979 amounted to 400,000 tons.

South Korean agroeconomists believe that the mountainous northern half of the Korean peninsula, with a limited acreage of arable lands and unfavorable weather condition, could not have produced 9 million tons of grain in 1979. They estimate the 1979 net grain production in North Korea at 6.12 million tons or even at 4.7 million tons, because Pyongyang's grain tonnage is based on unhulled grain, in the cases of rice, barley, and corn.

Kim Il-song's ten economic goals to be attained by North Korea by the end of the 1980s, which he presented at the Sixth KWP Congress of October 1980, included production of 15 million tons of grain and reclamation of 300,000 *jongbo* of land.[50]

FOREIGN TRADE

Foreign trade represents an important link in establishing what the DPRK hierarchy terms as "independent socialist economy." Foreign trade is completely controlled and conducted by the government and is geared to national economic planning. The regime clearly regards trade as an important part of its economic-development strategy. It needs to import machinery and such necessary raw materials as coking coal, oil, wool, sugar, and cotton to build a self-reliant national economy and other goods to meet short-term contingencies. It must also export some of its domestic products to earn foreign exchange to pay for those imports.

North Korea publishes no statistics on its trade performance. Information concerning the country's balance of payments is inferred mainly from trade data released by its trading partners and is, at best, incomplete.

Since its birth in 1948, the DPRK has transformed itself from an exporter of raw materials to a modern industrial state, exporting mostly semifinished and finished products.[51] In the early 1950s, North Korea was primarily an exporter of raw materials, chiefly mineral ores. As the level of industrialization increased, domestic manufacture became increasingly capable of absorbing many of the raw materials offered for export and converting them into semifinished products such as pig iron and rolled steel. Beginning in the early 1960s, manufactured goods such as machine tools, electric motors, and transformers were also made available for export.[52] Intensive efforts were also made to expand and diversify the number of semifinished and finished commodities available for export.

As North Korea's industrial base expanded, the composition of the imports shifted from machines, factory installations, and consumer goods to raw materials, fuels (notably petroleum and coking coal), and heavy, highly sophisticated machinery that was too advanced for domestic manufacturing capabilities. By the end of the 1960s, North Korea's imports were mostly capital goods, machinery, oil, and other products for expanding the industrial base, whereas imports of consumer items—mostly foodstuffs and luxuries—were being held at a minimum level.

For the past several decades, North Korea's trade volume has expanded steadily. During the 1960s, the volume of foreign trade increased rapidly, and the Pyongyang regime claimed that the volume of exports in the mid-1960s was three times the 1956 level. The total value of North Korea's trade in 1967 was estimated at about US$500 million, of which about 87 percent, or US$432.2

million, was derived from trade with Communist countries, especially the Soviet Union and China.[53] Pyongyang claimed that by 1968, trade relations had been established with over seventy countries. (The bulk of its trade was conducted with a limited number of countries, however.)

During the 1970s, the volume of North Korea's foreign trade grew 3.2 times, or at an average annual rate of 15.8 percent—from US$889,496,000 in 1971 to US$2,889,764,000 in 1979.[54] (In 1980, according to U.S. Government sources, North Korea's exports rose to US$2 billion while imports climbed to US$1.9 billion.)[55] In spite of a sharp drop of 22 percent from 1975 to 1976, exports increased 4.9 times in a six-year period, or an annual growth of 22 percent.[56] The rate was 6.2 percent higher than the average growth rate of overall trade. Imports rose only 2.3 times during the period from 1971 to 1979 due to reverses from 1975 to 1977.[57] Their average growth of 11.1 percent a year is nearly one-half that of the rate of export growth. In terms of balance of payments, however, available data indicate that imports outweighed exports, except in 1978 and 1979.[58]

The volume of North Korea's trade with Communist-bloc countries doubled during 1971–1979, registering an annual growth rate of 8.8 percent.[59] Trade with capitalist countries increased 10.6 times during the same period. The annual growth rate of 34.2 percent with capitalist countries was 25.4 percent higher than that with Communist nations.[60]

In the early years of the DPRK, prime importance was attached to trade with "fraternal" Communist countries, and more than 80 percent of North Korean trade was carried on with the Soviet Union and China. Although Pyongyang continued to stress trade with Communist countries, it also attempted to establish trade with non-Communist countries in order to achieve a measure of independence from the two major Communist powers and to obtain freely convertible foreign exchange.

In 1971, trade with Communist-bloc nations accounted for 85.1 percent of the total, compared to 14.9 percent with capitalist countries.[61] In 1979, the former dropped to 51.5 percent and the latter rose to 48.4 percent.[62] But the Soviet Union, China, and other Communist countries are still North Korea's main trading partners. In trade with non-Communist countries, the rate of growth with developing nations was more than twice as fast as with advanced countries.[63] The high rate of growth in trade with developing nations was due largely to expanded trade with Middle Eastern nations.

Beginning in the early 1960s, trade opportunities were actively sought with non-Communist countries, Japan in particular.[64] In 1957, the United Nations-imposed trade embargo against North Korea that had been in effect since the outbreak of the Korean War was lifted. Japan also lifted its embargo in 1961, and Pyongyang and Tokyo have conducted trade on an unofficial basis since then because the two countries have no diplomatic relations. Trade with non-Communist nations increased by more than 500 percent during the 1960s. In 1967, Japan accounted for about 55 percent (about US$36 million) of North Korea's commerce with non-Communist nations.[65] Trade with all other non-Communist countries reached almost US$30 million; the newly developing nations accounting for US$2 million.

Several factors make the two countries natural trade partners: geographical proximity, Japan's need for North Korea's marine and mineral resources, and Pyongyang's need for advanced Japanese technology and machinery. North Korea's most extensive trade contacts outside the Communist world are currently with Japan.[66] The Tokyo-Pyongyang trade, once deteriorated because of North Korea's failure to repay its trade debts, began to recover and grow rapidly in 1979. The two-way trade reached US$570 million during 1980, an increase of nearly 31 percent over a year earlier. The developing political and economic intercourse between Tokyo and Pyongyang suggests that pending full diplomatic normalization, their bilateral commerce will continue to grow in the form of memorandum-based private trade.

The Sixth KWP Congress of October 1980 set the export target at the end of the 1980s at more than quadruple (4.2 times) the 1979 volume of exports.[67] Measures to attain the proposed export goal included: (1) aggressive exploration of world markets for North Korean exports and preferential production of export goods; (2) qualitative improvement of merchandise; (3) strict observance of delivery schedules; (4) facilitation in transporting export goods; and (5) diversification of market and production lines.

The DPRK drive for trade expansion is expected to continue more actively in the 1980s, though the country is still handicapped by unpaid trade debts from the mid-1970s.

EVALUATION

For the past three and a half decades, the DPRK leadership has succeeded in restructuring and developing the economy rapidly without prolonged or excessive reliance on foreign aid. Thus, the North Korean economy seems well on the way toward an economic structure characteristic of a small industrialized country, on the model of, say, Austria or East Germany. The CIA estimated the 1976 per capita GNP of North Korea to be US$590, while the World Bank estimated it to be US$1,000 in 1978.[68] According to a State Department report, "The Planetary Product in 1980," North Korea's GNP amounted to US$15,908 million in 1980, which placed it fifty-seventh among 143 countries.

The DPRK is today self-sufficient in grain production and supplies with a small surplus of rice for export. In this connection, it is very significant that the reorientation of the North Korean economic structure from agriculture to industry has not created, as happened in many developing countries, a reliance on external sources of food, thus diverting foreign currency from the import of capital goods necessary for continued industrialization.

The DPRK enjoys a high degree of self-sufficiency in the following areas: (1) raw materials (by expanding the available supplies of domestic natural resources through exploration, by developing import-substitute industries, by increasing the production of synthetic raw materials, and by giving strong support to scientific research);[69] (2) consumer goods (although North Korean consumer products still have the problems of low quality, little variety, and high prices, and living standards in the DPRK are low because of strict consumption control); and (3) industrial machines and equipment of small, medium, and large sizes for domestic use (self-sufficiency in tractors and trucks in 1963[70] and 98 percent autarkic in machine tools in 1972[71]). In these areas, the *chuch'e* policy of self-reliance, or autarky to the fullest possible extent, has been remarkably successful.

But how self-reliant is the North Korean economy today in other areas? In the category of raw materials, North Korea is still dependent on the Soviet Union and China for coking coal and oil. But one bright spot on the economic horizon is that, when most nations are worrying about stability of oil prices and its availability,

Pyongyang relies on its abundant supplies of domestic coal and hydroelectric power for 95 percent of its energy needs. The DPRK is almost self-sufficient in its energy supply, of which only five percent is oil. North Korea generates about 45 percent of its electricity from domestic coal production and about 50 percent from its hydroelectric facilities. The heavy use of these resources has minimized the need to develop petroleum-related industries. Moreover, while North Korea imports oil from Iran and the Soviet Union, its main supplier is China, which agreed in 1978 to supply oil to Pyongyang at "friendship" prices: US$4 to 5 a barrel, which is half the US$11 per-barrel price tag for oil from the Soviet Union.[72] Recently, an oil refinery was built with Soviet support in Unggi, a port town near the Soviet border.[73] Approximately during the same period, the Chinese also built a pipeline connecting the oil fields in northeastern China (Manchuria) to a North Korean town along the border.[74]

The level of science and technology is still low, despite the DPRK government's strenuous efforts to improve the overall level of technical education and proficiency among the North Koreans in conjunction with the ongoing technical revolution. Accordingly, North Korea is, and will continue to be, heavily dependent on the Soviet Union and on the advanced industrial capitalist world for imports of highly sophisticated technology, machinery, and equipment. In this connection, it is important to note that the *chuch'e* policy of self-reliance has implicitly accepted this particular type of dependence on outside powers as a necessary, or even inevitable, exception to the policy of autarky. Furthermore, the DPRK regime believes that the limited dependence will not necessarily pose a threat to North Korea's *chuch'e* policy in general.

North Korea's foreign trade as a percentage of the national income is still relatively modest. Exports are low and there is a shortage of foreign exchange. In accordance with the *chuch'e* policy, the DPRK has mounted an intense effort to increase its degree of economic autarky by diversifying economic ties between China and the Soviet Union, on the one hand, and between Communist and non-Communist trade partners, on the other. Since the early 1970s, moreover, the Pyongyang regime has taken steps to expand its volume of export to establish a favorable balance of payments.

In conjunction with its desire to diversify trade in the world market, North Korea is faced with the need to improve the quality of its manufactured goods for export,[75] especially to the advanced capitalist world. The Communist-bloc countries may be willing to take North Korea's low-quality export items for political reasons, but such "soft goods" are difficult to sell on the non-Communist international market because of poor quality, strong competition, or lack of demand. Accordingly, a large and rapid increase in North Korea's export of manufactured goods to the advanced capitalist world must await further advancements in the North Korean economy and the further introduction of sophisticated technology from abroad.

Although North Korea pursues the *chuch'e* principle in its economy, it is not completely immune from the global impact of inflation and recession. In fact, foreign trade adversely affected North Korea's domestic economy in the mid-1970s.

The DPRK's future economic-expansion program faces several major problems if it is to have a fair chance of returning in the 1980s to the rapid growth it achieved up to the mid-1960s. Large amounts of investment capital are clearly needed. According to one non-North Korean outside estimate, Pyongyang's future expansion plans would require investment capital of about US$21–24 billion for the 1980s, with only about US$10–11 billion available from domestic savings. Unless the DPRK modifies its basic strategy of *chuch'e*-oriented, autarkic economic development and approaches the world capital market in the same fashion that China has done in pursuit of the "Four Modernization Program" after Mao's death in 1976, it will not find the credit abroad. Foreign (mostly Western and Japanese) credit of that magnitude, given North Korea's poor repayment record in the past, is not available.

Consequently, if the country is to insure the inflow of outside investment capital, it must push exports very hard to earn sufficient foreign exchange to meet all its debt obligations as promptly as possible. Recent directives from the leadership and signs of changes in the foreign-trade structure of the Pyongyang regime indicate a growing concern about balance-of-payments problems and possibly an awareness of the disadvantages of economic self-help.[76]

Since 1979, in fact, North Korea has been partially recovering from the economic slump of the mid-1970s and showing some signs of improving its international financial reputation by repaying its old debts.[77] At the same time, both its exports to and imports from Japan and other Asian nations have been increasing steadily in recent months.[78] Exports to these Asian nations grew more than 30 percent from 1978 to 1979 and were said to have increased a similar amount during 1980.[79] Rising world prices for nonferrous metals—an important North Korean export item—have been one of the major reasons for Pyongyang's improving trade record.

In addition to investment capital, North Korea is also in dire need of technical innovations and advancement at its present stage of economic development. Without the infusion of advanced Western technology and plants, it would be very difficult to maintain strong economic growth and achieve the high degree of industrialization desired for the 1980s. In the last analysis, whether the proposed goals for economic expansion for the 1980s can be attained will depend largely on investment capital and the level of production technology.

Another major problem related to North Korea's future economic expansion is the ever increasing ratio of military spending. As long as tension in the Korean peninsula remains high, the prospect is indeed slim that North Korea can and will cut its inordinately large military expenditures for maintaining *chuch'e* in the military field in order to reallocate domestic resources and funds for productive purposes. Moreover, the DPRK's dependence on Moscow and Beijing for the latest military weapons will continue for some time to come.

The North Korean-style autarkic, command economy has proven effective in transforming an excolonial, backward, agrarian society into an industrial state during the past several decades. As a small nation like North Korea becomes more advanced and complex, however, it becomes more dependent on external sources of raw materials and components because of the expanded needs created by increased economic sophistication. And equally important, can the North Korean political system based on the *chuch'e* ideology adjust satisfactorily now or in the near future to the more complex organizational and technical demands of an increasingly intricate economic system?

The DPRK leadership seems to have become aware of these problems and, keeping basic domestic economic strategy more or less intact, has so far responded in two ways. Kim Il-song recently made some changes in the structure of the DPRK cabinet in order to raise economic output by improving the efficiency of economic control from the top.[80] At the same time, the DPRK government implemented sweeping reforms in economic management by establishing economic-guidance committees at local and provincial levels to supervise compliance with central planning.[81]

Finally, an important question remains: to what extent will the political system of North Korea as embodied in the *chuch'e* ideology of Kim Il-song prove capable of solving the stark economic reality now prevailing in the DPRK? Pyongyang's current economic difficulties in the early 1980s—technological backwardness, shortage of capital, heavy military expenditures, and low industrial productivity—require it to expand economic cooperation with advanced capitalist countries more actively than the *chuch'e* policy of self-reliance or autarky allows.

It now appears that North Korea is slowly modifying its do-it-yourself style of economic modernization somewhat and is preparing to seek more assistance and trade opportunities with the outside, especially capitalist, world. The Pyongyang regime would perhaps like to minimize economic ties with the Soviet Union because of the political conditions that accompany them and turn more and more to non-Communist countries.

North Korea's current inclination to approach the capitalist world more actively to tap its technology and resources for the sake of its economic growth would not signal, however, that Pyongyang is going through more rational, liberal, and creative reforms in the economic system itself. Clear indications are that the DPRK wants to pursue a more flexible economic-development strategy by cautiously expanding economic exchanges with capitalist countries on a selective basis, as long as the expansion does not have an adverse effect on the existing ideological, political, and power structure of North Korea.

NOTES

1. The term "political culture" used in this context encompasses political beliefs, attitudes, feelings, and the general orientation of the population toward the political system. See Gabriel A. Almond and G. Bingham Powell, Jr., eds., *Comparative Politics Today: A World View* (Boston: Little, Brown and Co., 1974), pp. 42–51; Heinz Eulau et al., *Political Behavior* (Glencoe, Ill.: The Free Press, 1956), p. 36; and

Gabriel Almond and Sidney Verba, *The Civic Culture* (Boston: Little, Brown and Co., 1963), pp. 1–44.

2. "At the Central Committee Meeting of the KWP," *Nodong Sinmun*, December 15, 1956; and "For an Effective Fulfillment of the Economic Plan for 1957," *Nodong Sinmun*, December 16, 1956.

3. For an analysis of the Maoist concept of mass line, see Chalmers Johnson, "Building a Communist Nation in China," in Robert A. Scalapino, ed., *The Communist Revolution in Asia* (Englewood Cliffs, N.J.: Prentice-Hall, 1969), pp. 52–81.

4. Kim Il-song, "On Immediate Political and Economic Policies of the DPRK and Some International Problems," answers given by Kim Il-song to questions raised by newsmen of Japanese daily *Yomiuri Shimbun* on January 10, 1972, in Kim Il-song, *For the Independent Peaceful Reunification of Korea* (New York: International Publishers, 1975), pp. 151-56.

5. "For a Correct Understanding of *Chuch'e*," *Nodong Sinmun*, July 21, 1956.

6. Ilpyong J. Kim, "The Mobilization System in North Korean Politics," *Journal of Korean Affairs*, April 1972, pp. 3–15.

7. For a discussion of the theory of the North Korean-style mass mobilization, see Bruce G. Cumings, "Kim's Korean Communism," *Problems of Communism*, March–April 1974, pp. 24–41.

8. Kim Gyo-hwan, "The Ideology of Three Revolutions," *Vantage Point* (Seoul), June 1981, pp. 1–11.

9. Kim Il-song, *For the Correct Management of the Socialist Rural Economy* (Pyongyang: Foreign Languages Publishing House, 1969), p. 43.

10. *Kim Il-song Chojakchip* [Collected Works of Kim Il-song] (Tokyo: Miraisha, 1970), 1:297.

11. Ibid., pp. 313–20.

12. Kim Il-song, *Revolution and Socialist Construction* (New York: International Publishers, 1971), pp. 93–98; Kim Il-song, "On Communist Education and Cultivation," *Kim Il-song Sonjip* [Selected Works of Kim Il-song] (Pyongyang: Choson Nodong-dang Ch'ulpansa, 1960), IV:116–46; Kim Il-song, "On the Improvement of the Leadership Cadres' Attitudes Toward the Party, the Class and the People and of the Management Activities of the People's Economy," speech delivered December 19, 1964, in *Kim Il-song Chojakchip*, III:323; and Kim Yong-chu, "The Respected Leader Kim Il-song Is the Great Man of Thought and the Great Theorist in Our Times," *Nodong Sinmun*, April 13, 1972. For a discussion of North Korea's mass line policy, see B. C. Koh, "Ideology of Political Control in North Korea," *Journal of Politics*, August 1970, pp. 655–74.

13. Ha Ang-ch'on, "The Chollima Movement Is the General Line of the Korean Workers' Party in the Socialist Construction," *Kyo-no Chosen* [Korea Today], Japanese version, May 1961, pp. 1–21.

14. Kim Il-song, "On the Further Strengthening and Developing of the County Management Committee of the Cooperative Farms," in *Kim Il-song Chojakchip*, III:124. See also Ilpyong J. Kim, *Communist Politics in North Korea* (New York: Praeger, 1975), p. 83.

15. Kim Il-song, "On Further Developing the Taean Work System," speech delivered November 9, 1962, in *Kim Il-song Chojakchip*, III:108.

16. Kim Il-song, *Selected Works* (Pyongyang: Foreign Languages Publishing House, 1972), V:417–18.

17. For a detailed discussion of the DPRK's chuch'e policy in economic affairs, see Joseph S. H. Chung, "North Korea's Economic System and the New Constitution," *Journal of Korean Affairs*, April 1973, pp. 28–34; Adrian Foster-Carter, "North Korea: Development and Self-Reliance: A Critical Reappraisal," in Gavin McCormack and Mark Sheldon, eds., *Korea and South, The Deepening Crisis* (New York: Monthly Review Press, 1978), pp. 115–40; and B. C. Koh, "Chuch'esong in Korean Politics," *Studies in Comparative Communism*, Spring-Summer 1974, pp. 83–106.

18. Editorial Department, *Nodong Sinmun, Self-Reliance and Independent National Economic Construction*, June 12, 1963 (Peking: Foreign Languages Press, 1963), p. 8.

19. For a discussion of the COMECON, see Richard F. Staar, *Communist Regimes in East Europe*, 3rd ed. (Stanford, Calif.: Hoover Institution Press, 1977), pp. 239–60; and Heinz Köhler, *Economic Integration in the Soviet Bloc* (New York: Praeger, 1965), pp. 79–157.

20. For North Korea's opposition to the COMECON principles, see Kim Il-song, *Revolution and Socialist Construction*, pp. 91–93; *Nodong Sinmun*, October 28, 1963; *New York Times*, April 8, 1963; R. O. Freedman, *Economic Warfare in the Communist Bloc* (New York: Praeger, 1970), pp. 141–49; and Editorial Department, *Nodong Sinmun, Self-Reliance and Independent National Economic Construction*, pp. 7–8.

21. See references in note 20 of this chapter.

22. Kim Il-song said in 1962: "If we allow people to become mercenary, it will be impossible to realize the transition to communism." Kim Il-song, "On Further Developing the Taean Work System," November 9, 1962, in *Selected Works*, II:377.

23. Kim Il-song, *On Some Theoretical Problems of the Socialist Economy*, March 1, 1969 (Pyongyang: Foreign Languages Publishing House, 1969), p. 11.

24. For information on North Korea's natural resources, see U.S., Department of Army, *Area Handbook for North Korea* (Washington, D.C.: Government Printing Office, 1969), pp. 11–28.

25. Ibid., pp. 286–89, 295, 368.

26. Kim Il-song, "How to Develop State Industry and How to Manage the Enterprises," January 25, 1948, in *Selected Works*, I:188–89; and Chong Kwan-yong, "The Glorious Victory of the Party's Economic Line," *Nodong Sinmun*, August 5, 1967.

27. See note 35 of Chapter 3 for a breakdown of the foreign aid and loans given to North Korea by the Communist-bloc nations. Radio Moscow, in a March 17, 1981, program to celebrate the thirty-second anniversary of the signing of the Moscow-Pyongyang economic and cultural cooperation agreements of 1949, said that about sixty major factories in North Korea had been reconstructed or newly built with the assistance of the Soviet Union. Among them, according to the broadcast, were a Pyongyang thermal-power plant, Chongjin and Songjin iron and steel manufacturing plants, a Kimchaek steel company, Hungnam fertilizer plant, and textile factories in Pyongyang, Hyesan, and Hamhung. The broadcast further said that the production of those plants accounted for a greater proportion of North Korea's total industrial output: 60 percent of electricity, 42 percent of mining, and 30 percent of textile products.

28. Joseph S. H. Chung, *The North Korean Economy: Structure and Development* (Stanford, Calif.: Hoover Institution Press, 1973), pp. 92–93, 118–24.

29. Kim Il-song, "Everything for the Postwar Rehabilitation and Development of the National Economy," August 5, 1953, in *Selected Works*, I:421.

30. Gordon White, "North Korean *Chuch'e*: The Political Economy of Independence," *Bulletin of Concerned Asian Scholars*, April–June 1975, p. 50. See also note 27 of this chapter.

31. Richer in mineral resources than South Korea, North Korea has deposits of anthracite and lignite coal. Pyongyang still imports coking coal. Iron ore deposits from the Musan mine are mainly exported, but ores with 50 percent iron content are used for domestic consumption. Copper, zinc, mica, and tungsten are among the nonferrous ores.

32. The discussion of North Korea's economic development in industry, agriculture, and trade during the period from 1945 to 1981 in this chapter is taken from the following sources, unless indicated otherwise. In Suk Cho, "North Korean Economy," *Korean Journal of International Studies* 7, no. 1 (1975–1976): 23–40; Chung, *North Korean Economy*, pp. 1–212; Joseph S. H. Chung, "Economic Performance and Economic System: The North Korean Case," *Korea and World Affairs*, Spring 1977, pp. 67–86; Samuel K. Moak, "North Korea's Agricultural Policies in Collectivization," *Journal of Korean Affairs*, January 1974, pp. 25–36; Pong S. Lee, "North Korean Economy in the Seventies: A Survey," *Journal of Korean Affairs*, October 1974, pp. 3–17; Young C. Kim, "North Korea 1979: National Unification and Economic Development," *Asian Survey*, January 1980, pp. 53–62; Hong Young Lee, "Structure and Prospect of North Korean Trade," *Vantage Point*, September 1981, pp. 1–12; Joseph S. H. Chung, "The Six-Year Plan (1971–1976) of North Korea: Targets, Problems and Prospect," *Journal of Korean Affairs*, July 1971, pp. 15–26; *Area Handbook for North Korea*, pp. 286–88, 308, 323, 368; and White, "North Korean *Chuch'e*," pp. 46–54.

33. For a North Korean discussion of the importance of the machine industry, see Sin Tong-sop, "Further Development of the Machine Industry Is Urgent," *Kulloja*, March 15, 1969.

34. Kim Il-song, *Selected Works*, IV:441.

35. Ibid.

36. See note 48 of Chapter 2.

37. See Chapter 5.

38. See note 47 of Chapter 2.

39. *Kim Il-song Chojak Sonjip* [Selected Writings of Kim Il-song] (Pyongyang: Choson Nodong-dang Ch'ulpansa, 1978), VII:149–87; and *Korea Today*, no. 5 (1975), pp. 2–23.

40. *New York Times*, August 11, 1980; *Far Eastern Economic Review* (Hong Kong), April 9, 1976; and *Korea Herald*, May 4, 1976, and September 7, 1976.

41. Tai Sung An, "Korea: Democratic People's Republic of Korea," in Richard F. Staar, ed., *1981 Yearbook on International Communist Affairs* (Stanford, Calif.: Hoover Institution Press, 1981), p. 170.

42. Tai Sung An, "Korea: Democratic People's Republic of Korea," in Richard F. Staar, ed., *1980 Yearbook on International Communist Affairs* (Stanford, Calif.: Hoover Institution Press, 1980), p. 268.

43. National Foreign Assessment Center, CIA, *Korea: The Economic Race*

Between the North and the South (Washington, D.C.: January 1978), p. 8.

44. Tai Sung An, "Korea: Democratic People's Republic of Korea," in Richard F. Staar, ed., *1979 Yearbook on International Communist Affairs* (Stanford, Calif.: Hoover Institution Press, 1979), p. 258; and *Korea Today*, no. 1 (1978), pp. 18–28.

45. See *Foreign Broadcast Information Service*, Asia and Pacific, October 14, 1980, pp. D2–D28.

46. See Article 22 of the present DPRK Constitution adopted in 1972; and Joan Robinson, "Korean Miracle," *Monthly Review*, January 1965, p. 546.

47. See note 32 of this chapter.

48. *Korea: The Economic Race Between the North and the South*, p. 4.

49. Kim Il-song, *On the Building of the People's Government* (Pyongyang: Foreign Languages Publishing House, 1978), pp. 543–97; and Kim Il-song, *Selected Works*, III:57–204.

50. See note 45 of this chapter.

51. For the commodity composition of North Korean trade during the 1960s and 1970s, see *Korea: The Economic Race Between the North and the South*, p. 13; and Cae-One Kim, "Economic Interchanges Between South and North Korea," *Korea and World Affairs*, Spring 1981, pp. 88–94.

52. Chung, *North Korean Economy*, p. 106.

53. See note 32 of this chapter.

54. Lee Hong-yong, "Structure and Prospect of North Korean Trade," *Vantage Point*, September 1981, pp. 2–3.

55. *Far Eastern Economic Review*, May 14, 1982, p. 52.

56. See note 54 of this chapter.

57. Ibid.

58. Ibid.

59. Ibid.

60. Ibid.

61. *Korea: The Economic Race Between the North and South*, p. 12.

62. Lee Hong-youn, "Structure and Prospect," p. 2; and Cae-One Kim, "Economic Interchange," pp. 88–94.

63. Lee Hong-youn, "Structure and Prospect," p. 5.

64. *Far Eastern Economic Review Yearbook, 1970*, p. 216; *Far Eastern Economic Review Yearbook, 1973*, pp. 206–207; and *Area Handbook for North Korea*, pp. 373–374.

65. See references in note 64 of this chapter.

66. *Korea: The Economic Race Between the North and the South*, p. 12.

67. See note 45 of this chapter.

68. *Korea: The Economic Race Between the North and the South*, p. 2; and *1980 World Bank Atlas* (Washington, D.C.: 1980), p. 14.

69. For the DPRK's emphasis on these efforts, see, for example, O Tong-uk, "The Concept of Self-Identity and Our Scientific and Technological Development," *Kulloja*, July 30, 1968, pp. 21–24; Song Pok-ki, "The Central Problem in Chemicalizing the National Economy," *Kulloja*, November 30, 1967, pp. 51–59; and *Documents of the Fourth Congress of the Workers' Party of Korea* (Pyongyang: Foreign Languages Publishing House, 1961), pp. 60–64, 73.

70. R. O. Freedman, *Economic Warfare in the Communist Bloc* (New York: Praeger, 1970), p. 149.

71. Harrison Salisbury, *To Peking and Beyond: A Report on New Asia* (New York: Quadrangle Books, 1973), pp. 198–200. Mr. Salisbury visited North Korea in 1972.

72. Tai Sung An, "Korea: Democratic People's Republic of Korea," in Richard F. Staar, ed., *1979 Yearbook on International Communist Affairs* (Stanford, Calif.: Hoover Institution Press, 1979), pp. 259–60.

73. Young Whan Kihl, "North Korea: A Reevaluation," *Current History*, April 1982, p. 159.

74. Ibid.

75. The problem of production quality has been recognized by the DPRK leadership since the late 1960s. See, for example, An Yong, "Better Quality Control in Production Needed," *Minchu Choson*, July 19, 1968.

76. *Far Eastern Economic Review*, May 14, 1982, p. 52.

77. For example, the Japanese debt was renegotiated in 1978 and spread out over a ten-year period. So far, Japanese sources say, those debts are being paid. As a result, both exports to and imports from Japan are increasing. Japanese trade firms are reportedly paid promptly these days, either in British pounds or in West German marks that North Korea is believed to have obtained by selling gold.

78. Lee Hong-youn, "Structure and Prospect," pp. 10–12.

79. Ibid.

80. See note 76.

81. Ibid.

5

The Policy Aspects of the *Chuch'e* Ideology: Foreign Relations and Military Affairs

PYONGYANG-SEOUL RELATIONS: THE ISSUE OF REUNIFICATION

Korea is one of the oldest and most populous countries in the world. For 2,000 years, it was a homogeneous, unified nation, and today it has a combined population of 57 million inhabitants.

Absorbed in 1910 into the Japanese Empire, it remained subjugated until the end of World War II in 1945, when it was liberated. Korea was subsequently partitioned along the 38th parallel under terms of a secret wartime agreement, and it became enmeshed in the emerging cold war between the United States and the Soviet Union.[1] The division was further hardened by the establishment of the two antagonistic regimes in 1948, and the Korean peninsula has remained divided into two opposing political camps—the pro-Western Republic of Korea and the Communist-controlled Democratic People's Republic of Korea. Since 1948, each regime has been claiming to be the only "legitimate" government of the peninsula.

Both South Koreans and North Koreans believe that the division is unnatural, arbitrary, intolerable, and unjustifiable. They do not wish to see the unfortunate partition continued, regardless of their governments' ideological differences. The eventual reunification of the fatherland is the ultimate goal of the people of Korea, although many of them realize at present that a unified Korea under a single government is a remote possibility.

In the Korean peninsula, reunification has been a highly emotional issue as well as a sensitive political symbol for the political leaders of both South Korea and North Korea. They have repeatedly affirmed their desire for reunification of the divided peninsula by taking various policy positions on the subject.

Politicians on both sides have also found reunification a useful issue to be exploited for their political causes at home and abroad. In North Korea, for example, the Pyongyang regime under Kim Il-song has rationalized its programs for austerity, discipline, hard work, intensive political indoctrination, Stalinist-type economic development, and massive military build-up as the means of constructing a firm base for the eventual reunification of the fatherland. The DPRK regime has been quick to exploit any internal turmoil in South Korea, partly to reaffirm its own unification scheme and partly to divert the attention of its people from domestic problems.

As far as South Korea is concerned, successive regimes in Seoul since 1948 have often used North Korea's aggressive drive for unification as the rationale for cracking down on political opponents and other dissidents and for bolstering their political control. Furthermore, the Seoul regimes in recent years have wanted to deal with North Korea from a position of strength during both confrontation and dialogue, constantly stressing the need for rapid economic progress, internal cohesion, and full-scale military preparedness as a prelude to reunification. Externally, the two rival regimes have been carrying on intensive diplomatic campaigns, each portraying itself as the only legitimate government of the entire Korean peninsula.

Since the partition of the Korean peninsula in the aftermath of World War II, the Pyongyang regime has been remarkably consistent and persistent in its pursuit of the goal to unify Korea under Communist domination.[2] North Korea came close to achieving this goal in the summer of 1950, when it nearly defeated the combined South Korean-American forces. But it was soon overrun itself until the Chinese Communists intervened in the late fall of 1950. The armistice of July 1953 reestablished the division of Korea near the original partition line of 1945.

The DPRK's unification strategy under the *chuch'e* slogan has been that the Korean peninsula should be reunified by the Koreans themselves without any interference or intervention by foreign powers.[3] By taking this position, the DPRK leadership has made the most effective appeal to the nationalistic sentiment of the Korean people. The Pyongyang Government has blamed the United States for the continued division of the Korean peninsula, viewing the presence of American troops in South Korea as the greatest obstacle to a peaceful unification of Korea. North Korea has insisted on the complete and unconditional withdrawal of U.S. forces from the south so that both North and South Koreans can achieve their goal of an independent, peaceful reunification.[4]

Branded the aggressor in the Korean War by the United Nations in 1950, North Korea has condemned all United Nations actions in Korea during the conflict as illegal, and since then, it has continually attacked the United Nations as an "external force" that obstructs the independent, peaceful reunification of Korea by interfering without jurisdiction in Korean internal affairs.[5] The DPRK asserts that the problem of Korean reunification should be left to the Koreans themselves for solution. North Korea has long charged that the Korean question was imposed on the United Nations by the United States and that the world organization has been reduced to a belligerent in the Korean War and has therefore lost all competence and moral authority to deal impartially with the Korean question. The Pyongyang regime has insisted on the dissolution of the United Nations Command in Korea and the immediate and complete withdrawal of all foreign troops, charging that "the United States army is occupying South Korea under the camouflage of the United Nations flag" and arguing that the withdrawal of U.S. forces is "the prerequisite to a durable peace in Korea and to the solution of the Korean problem."[6]

In 1972, Kim Il-song changed his traditional hostility toward the United Nations somewhat and suggested that, if invited, the DPRK would participate in a debate on the Korean question at the United Nations General Assembly. The DPRK established its observer mission at the United Nations in New York in July 1972 and participated for the first time in the discussion of the Korean question at the 28th (1973) Session of the United Nations General Assembly. At the same time, representatives from Pyongyang were actively trying to line up votes from among the Communist countries and militant Third World countries.

The United Nations experience with the issue of Korean unification during the 1970s was an exercise in frustration.[7] The Korean question—a cold war issue that has plagued that body for more than two decades—disappeared from the agenda of the 1976 fall session of the General Assembly and has not been discussed by the world organization since then.

In 1972, when the mood of international détente began, the two Koreas agreed to end their twenty-seven years of bitterly hostile relations by opening a "dialogue of reconciliation" in two forums: one seeking arrangements to reunite families separated by the division of Korea, and the other aimed at eventual political reunification.[8] Each side spent considerable time probing the other's negotiating posture, and talks at both levels hardly advanced beyond the discussion of procedural matters. The suspicion between the two governments remained a formidable obstacle. More importantly, it was evident from the beginning that each had the ultimate objective of reunifying the Korean peninsula under its own political system and domination. The reunification strategies of Pyongyang and Seoul were the same as before; only the tactics had changed. As one astute South Korean observer said cogently, the two Koreas in 1972 moved "from confrontation without dialogue to a new era of confrontation with dialogue."

In both forums, South Korea took a gradualist approach by favoring step-by-step progress on nonpolitical or humanitarian issues in order to build mutual confidence before the central political issues were raised. Ever wary of the north's intention, Seoul demanded that Pyongyang in the first stage of negotiations prove its sincerity or good faith by taking a constructive attitude toward nonpolitical or humanitarian issues that were practical and feasible. From there, Seoul suggested, discussions could move into the more fundamental, comprehensive political realm. A close observer of the talks commented, perhaps correctly, that implicit in this strategy was an effort to break the North Korean political will.

The north argued that the south actually sought a perpetuation of the division of the Korean peninsula on the pretext of an evolutionary approach to unification. It offered a counter proposal for a quick, revolutionary jump to unification: a speedy political agreement must come first because humanitarian, economic, and cultural agreements must ultimately rest on a political solution. Pyongyang was apparently confident that, in this radical approach, its tightly controlled Communist system would eventually give it an edge over a "decadent" south.

The North Korean formula was rejected as an unfeasible attempt to solve the problem of reunification at one stroke—in other words, to put the cart before the horse. Détente talks between the two Koreas broke down in 1973, with fundamental disagreement over approaches to reunification and in the midst of mutual recriminations.[9]

After 1973, although it was willing, at any time, to pursue dialogue with North Korea on steps leading to a mutually acceptable reunification of the two Koreas, South Korea, in the interim, has favored a two-Korea solution (the application of the German formula to the Korean situation). More specifically, the south is willing to live with the status quo and contribute to its stabilization by reducing tensions on the Korean peninsula through such programs as (1) the conclusion of a peace treaty and nonaggression pact between North and South Korea, (2) the bilateral cross-recognition between each of the four powers (the United States, the Soviet Union, China, and Japan) and the two Koreas,[10] and (3) the admission of the two Koreas into the United Nations.[11]

South Korea believes that slowly, unevenly, and without official acknowledgment, a trend appears to be under way toward an increasing international accommodation to the day-to-day necessity to deal with separate political and economic entities on the Korean peninsula.

Under the *chuch'e* slogan, North Korea is actively seeking to revise the status quo in Korea. Hence, it welcomes signs of confrontation with the United States such as the current tension between Moscow and Washington while viewing with a jaundiced eye any emerging signs of the American-Chinese-Japanese entente.[12] Pyongyang adamantly opposes a two-Korea accommodation, denouncing it as a plot by "splitists" and contrasting the very "different" situations of Germany and Korea.[13] North Korea sees any steps that might stabilize and solidify the status quo as a threat to its ambitions to destroy the Seoul regime and unify Korea on its own terms. For this reason, Pyongyang has rejected all South Korea's specific proposals: dual representation in the United Nations; the replacement of the 1953 Armistice Agreement by a peace treaty between the two Koreas, along with a nonaggression pact and guarantees of security by the great powers; Russian and Chinese recognition of South Korea in return for American and Japanese recognition of North Korea; resumption of the south-north dialogue at the government level; and tripartite talks among South Korea, North Korea, and the United States.[14]

The current unification proposals of North Korea are only slight modifications of ideas previously advanced by the Pyongyang regime. The central premise of these proposals is the establishment of a "confederation" of North and South Korea under the name Democratic Confederal Republic of Koryo. Independent governmental systems on both halves of the peninsula would remain intact pending the settlement of thorny political issues by a nongovernmental body composed of equal numbers of representatives of political parties and social organizations in both parts of Korea as well as those representing overseas Koreans but excluding delegates from the Seoul Government.[15]

The north is demanding talks between representatives of political parties and social organizations rather than between governments in an apparent effort to buttress its policy of reunification through a grass-roots structure—a policy that favors Pyongyang. This North Korean proposal would also have the effect of legitimizing Pyongyang-sponsored opposition within the south without any reciprocity or hope of a fair vote in the north. The Seoul Government suspects that North Korea proposes the confederal system as an excuse for demanding the withdrawal of the American troops in South Korea and for excluding American participation in unification-related issues.

Ever since the two rival governments were established in 1948, their relations have been characterized by mutual distrust, hatred, competition, confrontation, and conflict. As a result, remarkably little has changed in the nature and substance of inter-Korean relations. The problems of security and unification on the Korean peninsula represent a dilemma. Neither side is willing to risk unification at the sacrifice of its own sociopolitical or economic system; meanwhile, the gulf between the two systems suggests that it will be impossible to integrate them into a common framework. The two parties will thus pursue policies that each believes will best protect its own interests, even if such a course contributes little to the real dialogue of unification. The probable course of inter-Korean relations is that both sides will continue to pursue mutually incompatible goals: legitimacy at the expense of the other, and reunification on each side's own terms.

The issue of Korean unification has not proven amenable to mediation by an outside power whose loyalty is well known and whose one-sided support of either of the two Koreas has continued for more than a generation. None of the great powers with big interests in Korean affairs, such as Washington, Moscow, Beijing, and Tokyo, would be acceptable to either Seoul or Pyongyang as an "honest broker." Accordingly, the mediator's role is realistic only in the context of a multiparty forum, as was tried in Geneva in 1954. Even that type of international forum ended in deadlock because of the conflicting interests of the great powers in Korea. No international conference of the Geneva type has since been convened to solve the Korean problem.

The frustrations resulting from the international negotiating efforts and the bilateral north-south talks have virtually halted all negotiating efforts for the moment. Given the slim prospects for meaningful negotiations and the wide gap between the two Koreas, none of the great powers today accords a high priority to Korean negotiations, although both Koreas are apparently willing to revive and sustain bilateral exchanges, partly to avoid being accused of opposing negotiations and partly to score propaganda points.

DIPLOMACY

In its external relations, the DPRK jealously guards its international position in the name of *chuch'e*. Since 1971, North Korea has been gaining diplomatic recognition from more and more countries.[16] As of February 1982, North Korea maintained diplomatic relations with 102 countries, 60 of which had extended diplomatic recognition to both Koreas simultaneously. Argentina, Australia, Chile, Iraq, and Mauritania suspended diplomatic ties with Pyongyang in the 1970s.

North Korea continues to assert that it is the only legitimate government on the Korean peninsula, even though the United Nations awarded that recognition to South Korea in 1948. Although it has pragmatically acceded to the recognition of both Koreas by some Third World and other countries, the DPRK continues to urge these countries to break relations with Seoul. Pyongyang has successfully pressed all Communist states to avoid relations with South Korea and has been particularly sensitive to any Chinese or Soviet contacts with Seoul.

In support of its ultimate objective of achieving the unification of the entire Korean peninsula under Communist domination, the DPRK pursues four major objectives in its foreign-policy operations: (1) maintaining close "comradely" relations with the Communist-bloc countries, especially the Soviet Union and China, to secure and safeguard its Communist base in North Korea; (2) raising Pyongyang's international stature by promoting friendly relations with all countries of the world, irrespective of differences in political ideologies and social systems, in order to gain broad international recognition and support; (3) removing the U.S. military presence from South Korea to enhance its own security and to facilitate Korean reunification on its own terms; and (4) weakening and isolating its rival regime in Seoul and eventually eliminating it.

From 1948 to 1970, North Korea seemed to be among the most hostile and isolated nations anywhere on earth. Pyongyang's foreign relations during that period remained heavily oriented toward the Communist states. But following the détente between the United States and the two major Communist powers in 1971, the DPRK began gingerly opening windows and doors to make contact with the outside world, especially the Third World.

Since 1971, Pyongyang has supplemented its efforts on the unification issue by becoming extremely active on the foreign-policy front, partly to undermine the international position of its rival regime in South Korea and partly to develop world support for North Korean policies.[17] In particular, the DPRK foreign policy has sought (1) to prevent recognition of the two-Koreas concept by the world community; (2) to isolate South Korea from both the Third World and the Communist bloc; (3) to gain full membership for the DPRK in the nonaligned movement; (4) to enlist diplomatic support for the United Nations vote on the withdrawal of United Nations (actually American) forces from South Korea; (5) to isolate the United States by strengthening ties with the Communist bloc and the nonaligned Third World countries in their anticolonial and anti-American campaigns and even by dramatizing its self-proclaimed vanguard role in the anti-United States struggle; and (6) to capitalize on contradictions between the United States and secondary capitalist powers such as France and Japan.

North Korea today maintains a militantly independent stance in its foreign policy in accordance with its doctrine of chuch'e. Nowhere is this more evident than in Pyongyang's relations with its two powerful Communist neighbors, the Soviet Union and

China.[18] Since the mid-1960s, the DPRK has pursued a nationalistic, self-reliant foriegn policy in Communist-bloc affairs by playing off the Soviet Union against China with Machiavellian astuteness. This policy of equidistance toward Moscow and Beijing has succeeded in the DPRK's steering an independent course between them.

In dealing with the DPRK leadership, the Soviets and the Chinese have experienced the full degree of Pyongyang's ideological-political rigidity and independence, and, on occasion, they have privately deplored excessive North Korean stubbornness. The Soviets and the Chinese have given matter-of-fact support to the DPRK's positions both in its détente talks with South Korea and in the United Nations debate on the Korean question. Moscow and Beijing have also urged the prompt withdrawal of American troops from South Korea, coupled with the dissolution of the United Nations Command. They have supported Pyongyang's stand for a direct United States-North Korean contact for settling the problem of the divided Korean peninsula and its North Korean program for reunification.

But military assistance to North Korea from the two major Communist powers is reported to have declined substantially in recent years.[19] In the prevailing mood of the post-cold war era, none of the big powers appears inclined to support any military moves in Korea. In recent months, Pyongyang's relations with both Moscow and Beijing seem to have been somewhat strained, although North Korea is still basically on friendly terms with both powers.

During 1979, the DPRK denounced Vietnam for its invasion and occupation of Kampuchea (Cambodia), a course of action that the Soviet Union supported. North Korea shares China's view on Kampuchea; neither recognizes the pro-Hanoi Phnom Penh regime supported by the Soviet Union and Vietnam. In mid-May 1979, Kim Il-song expressed Pyongyang's support for the ousted Khmer Rouge Pol Pot regime of Kampuchea, saying that, although the Kampuchean people were experiencing a severe trial, they would surely see the bright future of liberation and independence.[20]

According to Kim Il-song's good friend Prince Norodom Sihanouk, the Soviet invasion and occupation of Afghanistan in 1979—a clear example of what the DPRK regime contemptuously calls Soviet "great-power chauvinism"—seriously disturbed the DPRK leader.[21]

In early February 1980, at a meeting of Communist parliamentarians in Sofia, Bulgaria,[22] North Korea refused to join ten other Communist and left-wing states in publicly expressing support for the Soviet invasion of Afghanistan. During 1980, the Soviet Union was criticized by North Korea through its continuing references to "dominationism," a code word that embraces certain aspects of Soviet foreign policy.[23]

It is apparent that the DPRK now looks askance at China's ongoing revisionist reform drive started by Deng Xiaoping and other moderate post-Mao leaders. The injection of pragmatism and materialism into Chinese economic programs, the rapid turning outward to the advanced capitalist world for assistance, the decline of ideology, and the continuous attack on the cult of personality of Mao Zedong all represent trends that contrast considerably with Kim Il-song's leadership style and policy line. Moreover, China's increasing identification with the United States and Japan on critical strategic issues must be worrisome, despite Beijing's reassurance that it will stand fast with respect to North Korean interests.

A smouldering border dispute continued between North Korea and China in 1979 because China had long urged Pyongyang to give up 250 square kilometers of land near Mt. Paiktu, located on the border of the two countries, in return for military aid given during the Korean War.[24] The Pyongyang regime, wary of Beijing's anti-Mao leaders and its invasion of Vietnam in February 1979, was said to have fortified its border with China.[25]

Since 1971, the DPRK has exchanged various good-will delegations with the Third World countries and signed many agreements with them on trade, technical cooperation, cultural exchange, and science. North Korea has also exchanged visits by the heads of state and high-ranking government officials from the Third World, whose bloc has increasingly dominated the attention of the United Nations. It has given strong propaganda support to the Arab countries against Israel and Zionism in addition to maintaining cordial relations with the Palestine Liberation Organization.

With a view to getting diplomatic support from the nonaligned nations for its position in the United Nations on the Korean question and on its call for the withdrawal of U.S. troops from South Korea, North Korea has concentrated its efforts at the nonaligned summit meetings on a campaign for a strong anti-American stand. It is apparent that the DPRK now aspires to a leadership role in the nonaligned movement.[26]

Indications are that North Korea's courtship of the Third World has not gone well because of its diplomatic rigidity and stubbornness.[27] Many nonaligned countries voiced disinterest in 1977 in North Korea's aggressive diplomatic maneuverings on the Korean question, and former strong supporters such as Algeria and Yugoslavia appeared to be removing themselves from direct involvement in North Korea's diplomatic operations. These nonaligned nations were already skeptical about the usefulness of the annual discussions of the Korean question at the United Nations because the resolutions adopted had failed to bring the two Koreas closer to a peaceful settlement. The attitude toward Pyongyang now seems to be "let it alone." Consequently, the Korean question has not been discussed by the United Nations General Assembly since 1976. The DPRK's present moderation on the United Nations diplomatic scene can be attributed to such attitudinal changes among the nonaligned nations.

North Korea's diplomatic activity is relatively inactive in Western Europe, where it maintains diplomatic relations with Austria, Denmark, Finland, Iceland, Spain, Sweden, and Switzerland. (The French Government under socialist President Mitterrand is reportedly inclined to establish diplomatic relations with North Korea.)[28]

The United States maintains no representation of any kind in North Korea and conducts no trade with the Pyongyang regime. Since 1945, the United States has been North Korea's principal villain, the major stumbling block in its ambition to unify the entire Korean peninsula under Communist domination. Accordingly, the DPRK continues to conduct a hostile policy toward Washington.

In 1972, Kim Il-song appeared to want a new relationship with the United States. By opening up limited contacts, he presumably hoped to weaken domestic support in the United States for its continued troop presence in South Korea.

North Korea has long indicated that the withdrawal of the 40,000 American troops stationed in South Korea and the conclusion of a peace treaty between Washington and Pyongyang, excluding Seoul, are prerequisites to any moves toward ultimate reunification.

Accordingly, the DPRK has been pushing its own proposal for bilateral United States-North Korean talks, which, it believes, would be a useful propaganda move according it greater prestige, placing the south at a disadvantage, and adding a significant, new divisive element to Seoul-Washington relations. Such talks would enhance North Korea's claims to sole legitimacy and arouse not-too-latent southern fears of an American sellout of its interests behind its back.

The U.S. State Department has reiterated Washington's position that it will not establish direct contacts with North Korea unless South Korea is a full and equal participant; it has urged Pyongyang, instead, to resume direct discussions with the Seoul Government. The United States has repeatedly stated that it would be prepared to improve relations with North Korea, particularly in trade and cultural areas, provided China and the Soviet Union took similar steps toward South Korea.

In recent years, the DPRK has attempted to establish unofficial contacts with the United States by inviting a number of Americans and Korean-Americans to North Korea. During 1981, for example, Professors Donald S. Zagoria and Gregory Henderson, a delegation of Harvard University professors led by Professor Terry MacDougal, and a number of Korean-Americans visited North Korea. U.S. State Department spokesmen were quick to deny any "political significance" in these visits by American individuals. They also said that the United States government would not intervene in informal civilian contacts between the United States and North Korea when the Carter administration lifted travel restrictions on North Korea in March 1977.

The Reagan administration ruled out the possibility of improving relations with North Korea unless Pyongyang changes its old-fashioned attitude toward the United States. When President Reagan decided to firmly support President Chun Doo Hwan's government in South Korea in early 1981,[29] the DPRK leadership attacked him for pursuing "a more vicious Korean policy."[30]

Relations between North Korea and Japan have never been cordial. Suspicion and hostility toward Japan are still profound in the DPRK and can be traced to the Japanese occupation of Korea from 1910 to 1945. Because of the Japanese Government's strong opposition to a drastic reduction of U.S. ground forces in South Korea, Pyongyang accuses Japan of being excessively partial to

Seoul, of pursuing a policy of two Koreas, and of hostility toward North Korea. The North Korean media denounce the growing Japanese "imperialistic" stakes in South Korea and the alleged collusion of Tokyo and Washington to preserve their mutual "colonial interests" in the Korean peninsula.

Since the fall of 1971, however, the DPRK has softened its approach to Japan.[31] For example, countless visits to North Korea have been made by Japanese editors, newspapermen, broadcasters, public figures, politicians, and many businessmen. North Korea's motives seem to be (1) to cause the conservative-controlled Japanese Government to change its present exclusive involvement with Seoul and to enter into active relations with Pyongyang; (2) to ease Japan's tight travel restrictions to and from North Korea imposed on Korean residents in Japan; (3) to promote expanded trade and gain access to Japanese industrial machinery and technology needed to develop the North Korean economy rapidly; (4) to seek commercial and cultural ties as a first step toward eventual political recognition of the DPRK and the ultimate diplomatic isolation of South Korea; and (5) to sow seeds of dissent between, as well as within, Japan and South Korea to prevent a Japanese return to the Korean peninsula.

During the early 1980s, contacts between North Korea and Japan have continued to increase at the nongovernmental level, although official exchanges between the two countries do not appear likely in the foreseeable future. In early 1981, at the invitation of the Association of Japanese Parliamentarians for Japan-North Korea Friendship, a DPRK parliamentary delegation visited Tokyo for two rounds of talks with Japanese politicians. This was the first visit ever made to Japan by any political group from North Korea.

MILITARY ESTABLISHMENT

Chuch'e in national defense refers to the maintenance of a self-reliant, strong, and credible military capability. Support from outside is important in a war, but it is only an auxiliary role. The most important factor is self-reliant preparedness in military strength.[32]

Kim Il-song recognizes that the country's armed forces, the largest single component of national-security personnel in North Korea, constitute the keystone of the DPRK's past and future power. Because of its importance, he has taken elaborate measures to assure the tightest possible party control over the military. Kim regards the proper staffing of the military establishment as a vitally important vehicle of this control. In fact, the North Korean military establishment is one of the most intensely politicized in the world. The DPRK chieftain is a firm believer in the Maoist principle that the ruling Communist party controls the gun, and not vice versa.[33]

On questions of military strategy and tactics, the DPRK always gives ideology and politics first priority and continues to keep a firm lid on creeping military professionalism in the armed forces. But it also puts great emphasis on military techniques, technology, and weapons.[34] Kim Il-song stressed the importance of devising a military policy geared to Korea's natural features. He told the ruling KWP hierarchy to combine "the political and ideological superiority" of its army with "modern military techniques" and to modernize army, military science, and techniques to take into account Korea's many mountains and long coastlines.[35] On the nature of a modern war, he said that manpower and material resources must be fully prepared for a protracted war and that the Pyongyang Government should build "zones of strategic importance, develop the munitions industry, and create the reserves of necessary materials."[36]

The DPRK regime is constantly building its military strength with a professed aim of helping to "liberate" the southern half of the Korean peninsula and bring it into the Communist fold. The north is willing to pay a heavy price to maintain a credible military threat to the south in order to pressure the United States and South Korea into considering an alternative to the status quo. Kim Il-song said in 1970: "Frankly speaking, our spendings on national defense have been too heavy a burden for us in the light of the small size of the country and its population." But he exhorted the North Koreans to accelerate further "war preparations."[37] He said that the ruling KWP should combat "indolence and slackness" and that the people should "never be captivated with a pacifistic mood" and should guard against "the revisionist ideological trend or warphobia." He stressed that the strategic and tactical concepts as well as the Pyongyang regime's efforts to modernize the armed forces should be tailored to suit Korea's own conditions. He warned:

If we try, instead, to mechanically copy and dogmatically bring in foreign art of war and foreign weapons and military technical equipment allegedly to modernize the People's Army, it may bring a serious loss to the national defense building. We must perfect the art of war in such a way to make up for the defects in the People's Army, reinforce its weak links, and foster its strong points.[38]

It is clear that the North Korean forces are currently superior to those of South Korea, as indicated in Table 3. There has been a serious military imbalance in Pyongyang's favor for the past three decades, which is likely to continue for quite a few years before South Korea catches up. Meanwhile, it is apparent that the DPRK has no intention of acquiring nuclear weapons if—or as long as—South Korea also refrains.[39]

Table 3:
The North-South Military Balance in Korea, 1981-1982

Republic of Korea (South Korea)	Democratic People's Republic of Korea (North Korea)
Population: 38,800,000	Population: 19,000,000
Military service: Army and Marines, 2½ years; Navy and Air Force, 3 years	Military service: Army, 5 years; Navy and Air Force, 3-4 years
Total armed forces: 610,000	Total armed forces: 680,000-700,000
Estimated GNP: US$60.3 billion (1980)	Estimated GNP: US$14.1 billion (1980)
Defense expenditure: 5.5. to 6 percent of GNP	Defense expenditure: 15 to 20 percent of GNP
Army: 560,000 active personnel	Army: 600,000 active personnel
20 infantry divisions	6 tank divisions
1 mechanized division	5 armored brigades
2 armored brigades	3 motorized infantry divisions
7 tank battalions	35 infantry divisions (8 corps)
36 artillery battalions	2 independent tank regiments
	8 light-infantry brigades

Table 3 (continued)
The North-South Military Balance in Korea, 1981–1982

7 specialized-forces brigades	26 special-forces brigades
2 air-defense brigades	4 independent infantry brigades
1 SSM battalion with Honest John	4 reconnaissance brigades
2 SAM brigades with Hawk and Nike-Hercules	3 antiaircraft artillery divisions
33 SAM sites	3 antiaircraft artillery regiments
1,000 tanks	5 airborne battalions
700 armored personnel carriers	4 SSM battalion with Frog
5,400 mortars	20 artillery regiments
2,100 field artillery weapons	38-40 SAM sites
12,000 infantry antitank weapons	2,600 tanks
	1,000 armored personnel carriers
	1,500-2,000 multiple-rocket launchers
	9,000 mortars
	3,500-4,000 field artillery pieces
	25,000 infantry antitank weapons

7 specialized-forces
  brigades
2 air-defense brigades
1 SSM battalion with
  Honest John
2 SAM brigades with Hawk
  and Nike-Hercules
33 SAM sites
1,000 tanks
700 armored personnel
  carriers
5,400 mortars
2,100 field artillery
  weapons
12,000 infantry antitank
  weapons

Reserves: 1,000,000

Navy: 47,000 active
  personnel (including
  Marines)
Bases: 9
Total combat ships: 110,
  about 80,000 tons
10 destroyers
9 destroyer escorts
  (corvettes)
7 frigates
8 fast-attack craft
  (with standard SSM)
10 large patrol craft
28 coastal-patrol craft
8 coastal minesweepers
24 landing ships
  (amphibious craft)

Reserves: 25,000

26 special-forces brigades
4 independent infantry brigades
4 reconnaissance brigades
3 antiaircraft artillery divisions
3 antiaircraft artillery regiments
5 airborne battalions
4 SSM battalion with Frog
20 artillery regiments
38-40 SAM sites
2,600 tanks
1,000 armored personnel carriers
1,500-2,000 multiple-rocket
  launchers
9,000 mortars
3,500-4,000 field artillery pieces
25,000 infantry antitank weapons

Reserves: 260,000

Navy: 31,000 active personnel
Bases: 18
Total combat ships: 450 ships,
  about 59,000 tons
19 submarines (diesel)
4 frigates
33 large patrol craft
18-20 fast-attack craft (with
  Styx XXM)
320 fast-attack craft
80 landing craft

Reserves: 40,000

Table 3 (continued)
The North-South Military Balance in Korea, 1981–1982

Marines: 24,000 active
    personnel
1 Marine division
2 Marine brigades

Air Force: 32,600	Air Force: 51,000
378 combat aircraft	700 combat aircraft
10 helicopters	40 helicopters
12 jet-capable airfields	20 jet-capable airfields
54 F-D/E	120 MIG-21
228 F-5A/B/E	350 MIG-15/17/19
40 F-36F	85 IL-28
	20 SU-7
Paramilitary forces:	Paramilitary forces: 39,000
2,800,000 Homeland	security and border guards;
Defense Reserve Forces	a civilian militia (Worker-
	Peasant Red Guards) of 2,500,000

SOURCES: International Institute for Strategic Studies, *The Military Balance, 1979–1980* (London), pp. 68–69; International Institute for Strategic Studies, *The Military Balance, 1981–1982* (London), pp. 82–84; Chang Yoon Choi, "Korea: Security and Strategic Issues," *Asian Survey,* November 1981, p. 1125; Young Ho Lee, "Military Balance and Peace in the Korean Peninsula," *Asian Survey,* August 1981, p. 856; "U.S. Believes North Korean Troops Outnumber the South," *Los Angeles Times,* July 16, 1979; Japanese Defense Agency, *Defense of Japan 1979* (Tokyo), p. 54; *New York Times,* January 4, 1979; *Washington Post,* January 14, 1979; and *Korea Herald,* February 13, 1979.

North Korea has been concentrating on the modernization and expansion of armaments, in accordance with the four major military guidelines adopted in the early 1960s. Among other things, these called for modernizing the armed forces, arming the entire population, fortifying the entire nation, and, above all, preserving a self-reliant and strong military capability.[40] Twelve percent of the North Korean working-age population are in the regular armed forces. The pattern of the North Korean military expansion in recent years indicates a continued strengthening of armored forces, increased artillery and other firepower, greater airborne strength, greater ammunition reserves, and a continued build-up of naval strength, particularly submarines.

According to reliable Western intelligence reports, North Korea has been spending a much larger portion of its GNP on military activities than has South Korea. During the 1960s, for example, Pyongyang's military expenditures reached 15 to 20 percent of its GNP compared with 5.5 percent by South Korea, and the percentage was even higher during the 1970s.[41] North Korea's military spending as a percentage of GNP is second only to that of the Soviet Union.[42] Although the north has given absolute priority to its military build-up, it has so far been able to deprive its civilian economy without serious internal problems.

Initially, North Korean forces were supplied mainly with Soviet weaponry. As a result of the nation's advance in industrial technology, however, its domestic weapons-production capability has increased, and it is increasingly less dependent on military assistance from its Russian and Chinese allies.[43] North Korea's defense industry is capable of producing Pyongyang's own military hardware except for combat aircraft and other highly sophisticated equipment.[44] Currently, the DPRK produces small arms, recoilless rifles, mortars, rocket launchers, mobile artillery, AAA weapons, APCs, tanks, gunboats, and submarines. It relies on China and the Soviet Union for aircraft, missiles, and other technically sophisticated weapons.[45]

North Korea's military potential centers around a ground force of some 600,000 troops in forty divisions, with about 2,600 tanks. The airpower consists of some 700 combat aircraft, mostly MIG-19 and MIG-21 fighters, while naval forces include guided-missile patrol boats, torpedo boats, amphibious assault craft, and submarines. North Korean ground forces are characterized by armored units emphasizing concentrated strike power (five armored brigades and twenty artillery regiments). Guerrilla warfare is the strategic emphasis of the DPRK leadership, and the country appears to be training special forces for this purpose. North Korea also possesses powerful reserve forces centered around the 2.5-million-member militia (Worker-Peasant Red

Guards), which is better trained and equipped for rear-area security than is the south's militia (Home Defense Reserve Force).

Indications are that North Korea has concentrated its superior manpower and firepower near the DMZ by maximizing its geographical advantages and improving its prospects for achieving surprise. Heavy weapons, suitable for both offense and defense, have been concentrated in hardened forward positions closer to the DMZ. Approximately fourteen or fifteen crack army divisions with powerful artillery and air supports are also deployed near the DMZ, and some artillery and surface-to-surface missiles are thought to be deployed within striking range of Seoul. These forces are in a position to launch, at a moment's notice from the DPRK's supreme military council and without prior approval from either Moscow or Beijing, an all-out, three-dimensional, surprise attack against the south.

It is important to note that the North Korean forces are configured largely for blitzkrieg-type offensive operations, with both mobility and firepower, and therefore must be assumed to require a distinct superiority. North Korea has developed highly mobile armed forces, supported by airborne elements, for a surprise attack on the south that would aim, first, at capturing Seoul promptly and, second, at making rapid advances into other areas of South Korea. (A scenario often advanced by U.S. and South Korean military strategists is that the North Korean forces, taking advantage of the element of surprise, will rush to Seoul, seize the capital, control a high percentage of the population and industrial capacity of the south, and then seek negotiations from their new position of strength.) As happened during the initial stage of the Korean War in June 1950, the element of surprise and the strategic benefits of geography and terrain would give the north a distinct advantage. The north's recent emphasis on tunnel-digging was apparently designed to strengthen its blitzkrieg capabilities for a surprise attack that would neutralize South Korea's forward defenses along the DMZ.

Defensively, North Korea has invested heavily in dispersing industrial targets and in putting underground military as well as industrial facilities. Moreover, most of its military and industrial facilities are heavily protected by surface-to-air missiles (SAMs) and by antiaircraft artillery. With a substantial indigenous arms production and major stockpiling of ammunitions and other war materials, the north could extend an offensive for weeks or several months without relying on any external assistance or resupply.[46] According to a Hong Kong source, North Korea is believed to have stockpiled food and ammunition for a thirty-day war or perhaps for a conflict lasting several months, and has placed much of this in underground facilities in forward areas.[47]

Facing North Korea below the DMZ is a well-armed South Korean military establishment. But the North Korean forces outnumber those of the south in almost every significant aspect by enjoying, as Chang Yoon Choi describes accurately, "definitive advantages in air power and offensive strategic posture, and superiority in mobile assault weapons, shelling capability, naval capabilities, and unconventional warfare forces."[48] Specifically, the northern ground forces of 600,000 now outnumber the southern ground forces of 560,000, and Pyongyang's quantitative lead in weaponry is 2 to 1 in total mobile assault weapons (tanks, armored personnel carriers, assault guns), shelling capability (artillery, rocket launchers, and mortars), combat jet aircraft (although this is somewhat offset by qualitative inferiority), and more than 4 to 1 in antiaircraft guns and small, fast, heavily armed coastal-patrol vessels.

North Korea has a strong unconventional, or special, warfare capability in its four independent infantry brigades, which are organized specifically for commando-type infiltration and guerrilla-warfare activity in South Korea. The North Korean army, the fourth largest in the world, includes the world's largest commando force totaling 100,000 men. In the event of war, these forces would be able to infiltrate the south by land, air, and sea to mount diversionary attacks in the rear.

Concerning logistical support, South Korea is 6,000 miles away from its major ally, the United States, although it can receive immediate assistance from American forces stationed in South Korea and Japan. By comparison, North Korea has the advantage of a contiguous border with the Soviet Union and China, which would make it easy for them to furnish Pyongyang with supplies and weapons.

One major geographical disadvantage of the south is the location of its capital city, Seoul,[49] which is about twenty-five miles from the DMZ and thus falls within the range of North Korean surface-to-surface missiles (Soviet Frog-5/7).[50] Pyongyang, however, is about ninety-five miles north of the DMZ and is located well north of any direct firepower threat from the south's armed forces. Because of Seoul's proximity to the DMZ, the south cannot trade space for time in the event of an attack. Needless to say, North Korea has deployed its superior military forces to maximize the advantage derived from that proximity.

By and large, the North Korean military threat to South Korea is real, ever-present, and certainly growing. It should be emphasized, however, that the northern forces have a number of potential vulnerabilities that could become more pronounced in the 1980s. First, their air force is equipped with aging combat jet aircraft, the most modern being MIG-21s and SU-7s. Second, North Korea has a distinct disadvantage in its manpower and mobilization base, which are particularly crucial in a protracted war, and the drafting of 16-year-olds is apparently affecting its industrial manpower pool. Third, Pyongyang's economic base for continuing military build-up, modernization, and expansion in the future is inferior to that of the south. Fourth, the north may not have enough well-trained scientists and technicians, which puts Pyongyang at a disadvantage in the utilization of more sophisticated military technology. Finally, the north has no firm assurance from the Soviet Union and China that they would be eager to back another 1950-type war launched by Pyongyang. Although the North Korean forces are capable of capturing Seoul and a sizeable portion of the southern territory in an initial surprise attack, they would not be able to withstand a United States-South Korean counterattack without active and continuing support of its two major Communist allies. In the eventuality of failing to obtain such support, Pyongyang would once again be faced with widespread destruction and devastation.

NOTES

1. For a study of the origin of the partition of Korea, see Hak Joon Kim, "The Origin and Evolution of the South-North Korean Division," *Problems of Korean Unification* (Seoul: Research Center for Peace and Unification of Korea, 1976), pp. 9-66.

2. See, for example, *Nodong Sinmun*, August 15, 1955, February 20, 1958, November 6, 1962, December 17, 1962, September 8, 1966, and April 13, 1975; Kim Il-song, *For the Independent Peaceful Reunification of Korea* (New York: International Publishers, 1975), pp. 1-230; *Documents on the Eighth Session of the Second*

Supreme People's Assembly of the DPRK (Pyongyang: Foreign Languages Publishing House, 1960), pp. 8–62; *Documents of the Fourth Congress of the Workers' Party of Korea* (Pyongyang: Foreign Languages Publishing Hosue, 1961), pp. 384–88; and *Kim Il-song Chojak Sonjip* [Selected Writings of Kim Il-song] (Pyongyang: Choson Nodong-dang Ch'ulpansa, 1968), IV:53–54. See also Yong Soon Yim, *Two Koreas' Unification Policy and Strategy*, Occasional Papers/Reprints Series in Contemporary Asian Studies, no. 9 (School of Law, University of Maryland, 1978), pp. 5–42; and Sun Sung Cho, "Politics of North Korea's Unification Policies: 1950–1965," *World Politics*, January 1967, pp. 218–41.

3. See references in note 2 of this chapter.

4. See references in note 2 of this chapter.

5. Chong Han Kim, "The Korean Unification Issue in the United Nations," in Se-Jin Kim and Chang-Hyun Cho, eds., *Government and Politics of Korea* (Silver Spring, Md.: Research Institute on Korean Affairs, 1972), pp. 285–89. See also note 2 of this chapter.

6. See references in note 5 of this chapter.

7. For the United Nations experience with the issue of Korean unification during the 1970s, see this author's profiles on North Korea in Richard F. Staar, ed., *1973–1981 Yearbooks on International Communist Affairs* (Stanford, Calif.: Hoover Institution Press, 1973–1981); Jae Seung Woo, "Korea and the United Nations," *Korean Journal of International Studies* 5, no. 4 (Autumn 1974):19–32; and B. C. Koh, "The Battle Without Victors: The Korean Question in the U.N. General Assembly," *Journal of Korean Affairs*, January 1976, pp. 43–63.

8. For detailed accounts of the north-south negotiations in the 1970s, see Se-Jin Kim and Chong-Shik Chung, eds., *Korean Unification: Source Materials with an Introduction* (Seoul, Korea: Research Center for Peace and Unification of Korea, 1976–1979), 1:1–166, and II:1–250; Hak Joo Kim, "An Analysis of the Central Issues in the North-South Dialogue: The South Korean Perspective," *Korean Journal of International Studies* VI, no. 2 (1975):17–38; "Chronicle of South-North Korean Relations, 1945–1975," *Korean Journal of International Studies* 1, no. 4 (1975): 93–112; Sang Woo Rhee, "Overriding Strategy Versus Subversion Tactics: A Marco-Comparative Study on South and North Korean Unification Strategies," *Unification Policy Quarterly* II, no. 4 (1976):40–65; Hak Joon Kim, *The Unification Policy of South and North: A Comparative Study* (Seoul: Seoul National University Press, 1977), pp. 1–341; Yong Soon Yim, "The Unification Strategy of North Korea: Adroit Diplomacy or Fishing in Troubled Waters," *Korea and World Affairs*, Winter 1977, pp. 440–65; Jae Dok Kim, "Strategic Transition in North Korea's Unification Policy (1)," *Vantage Point*, Seoul, March 1981, pp. 1–13; and Jae Dok Kim, "Strategic Transition in North Korea's Unification Policy (2)," *Vantage Point*, April 1981, pp. 1–11.

9. See, for example, *New York Times*, January 22, 1982, and January 27, 1982; *Dong-A Ilbo* (Seoul), January 23, 1982; *Korea Herald*, January 23, 1982; and *Vantage Point*, September 1980, pp. 11–12.

10. In this formula, the United States and Japan would establish diplomatic relations with North Korea at the same time that the Soviet Union and China established diplomatic relations with South Korea. An exchange of North and South Korean ambassadors would appear to be a step in that direction.

11. Yong Chul Han, "South Korea's Unification Policy," *Unification Policy Quarterly* II, no. 2 (1976):16–21; *Korea Herald*, July 22, 1981; Hak Joon Kim, "Present and Future of the South-North Talks: As Viewed from Korea," *Korea and World Affairs*, Summer 1979, pp. 209–22; Shik-kwang Kang, "Unification Policy in the 1980s: Adapting to Changing Conditions," *Korea and World Affairs*, Spring 1981, pp. 120–38; Dong-Bok Lee, "Present and Future of Inter-Korean Relations: The January 12 Proposal and the Sixth Congress of the KWP," *Korea and World Affairs*, Spring 1981, pp. 36–52; Research Center for Peace and Unification, *The Republic of Korea's Basic Position on South-North Dialogue* (Seoul: March 1979), pp. 1–23; Lyeong Tae Yoon, "Rationality of South-North Nonaggression Pact," *Unification Policy Quarterly* II, no. 2 (1976):45–47; and Young Dae Song, "Prospect for Unification of Korea: In Connection with Three Basic Principles for Peaceful Unification of Korea," *Unification Policy Quarterly* II, no. 2 (1976):31–33.

12. See Yong Soon Yim, "North Korean Strategic Doctrine in the East Asian Regional System," *Korea and World Affairs*, Summer 1981, pp. 177–202.

13. North Korea firmly refuses to look to the German formula as a model for Korea. During a visit by East German Prime Minister Honecker to Pyongyang in early 1978, Kim Il-song forcefully rejected any parallelism between Germany and Korea, calling advocates of two Koreas "splitists." *Korea Today*, no. 1 (1978), pp. 29–32.

14. See *Korea Herald*, July 5, 1981, August 21, 1981, and November 26, 1981; Research Center for Peace and Unification of Korea, *South and North Korea: Differing Approaches to Dialogue* (Seoul: no date), pp. 1–53; The South-North Coordinating Committee (Seoul side), *A White Paper on the South-North Dialogue in Korea* (Seoul: July 1975), pp. 1–98; Chang Sun Kim, "North Korea's Unification Strategy," *Korean Signal* (Seoul), October–December 1975, pp. 29–33; Kwang Suk Choi, "Contrasting Unification Strategies of the Two Koreas," *Korean Signal*, October-December 1975, pp. 24–28; Hal Il Park, "A Diagnosis of the Proposal of the South-North Federation of Korea," *Unification Policy Quarterly* II, no. 2 (1976):69–71; Sung Chul Kil, "Strategic Background for the Proposed 'Grand National Congress,' " *Unification Policy Quarterly* II, no. 2 (1976):56–58; *Foreign Broadcast Information Service*, Asia and Pacific, October 15, 1980, pp. D1–D11; Dong-Bok Lee, "Present and Future," pp. 36–52; and Tuk-Chu Chon, "Is the 'Korean Confederation' Practicable? A Comparative Analysis of the East German Concept and the North Korean Concept of a Confederation," *Korea and World Affairs*, Summer 1980, pp. 349–62.

15. See references in note 14 of this chapter. At the Sixth KWP Congress of October 1980, for example, Kim Il-song presented a detailed ten-point program for reunification that was essentially a rehash of many old approaches. He proposed that a confederal government be established in the form of a "supreme confederal national conference" comprising an equal number of South and North Korean representatives plus an appropriate number of Korean residents from abroad. The conference would organize its standing committee to act as the de facto central government. The military section in his guidelines called for the reduction of each other's forces to 100,000–150,000 men, the removal of the military demarcation line (the 1953 cease-fire line) and military facilities there, and the disbanding of all other military units as well as the discontinuation of their military drills. Under a reunified

Korea, both sides would recognize each other's different social system and the north would not interfere with foreign investments in South Korea. He pledged that any reunified Korea would be neutral, nonaligned, and a "permanent peace and nuclear-free zone."

The presentation of the ten-point program was coupled with a stronger attack on the new Seoul Government under President Chun Doo Hwan. He repeated Pyongyang's branding of the South Korean Government as the "puppet of the United States imperialists" and called for the South Koreans to join North Korea's struggle against Washington and the Seoul Government. One passage of Kim Il-song's keynote speech seemed to hint that there would be no possibility of getting negotiations started again until the Chun government was swept out of power. He said that the overthrow of the "military fascist" regime in South Korea was a major condition for the unification of the divided peninsula. *Foreign Broadcast Information Service*, Asia and Pacific, October 15, 1980, pp. D1–D11.

16. In his keynote speech at the Sixth KWP Congress of October 1980, Kim Il-song said that during the period from 1970 to 1980, the DPRK had established diplomatic relations with sixty-six countries. *Foreign Broadcast Information Serivce*, Asia and Pacific, October 15, 1980, p. D12.

17. For the details, see Rinn-sup Shinn, "Changing Perspectives in North Korea: Foreign and Unification Policies," *Problems of Communism*, January–February 1973, pp. 55–71.

18. See note 17 of Chapter 1. See also Tai Sung An, "New Winds in Pyongyang?" *Problems of Communism*, July–August 1966, pp. 68–71; and Roy U. T. Kim, "Sino-North Korean Relations," *Asian Survey*, August 1968, pp. 708–22.

19. Gareth Porter, "Time to Talk with North Korea," *Foreign Policy*, Spring 1979, p. 59.

20. Pyongyang Radio, May 21, 1979.

21. *Far Eastern Economic Review*, November 14, 1980, p. 48.

22. *Washington Post*, February 9, 1980; and *Korea Herald*, February 9, 1980.

23. In his keynote speech at the Sixth KWP Congress of October 1980, Kim Il-song made repeated reference to North Korea's support for the "anti-imperialist independence forces" against the "imperialists and dominationists," and called for unity of the nonaligned countries to "counter the dominationist forces." *Foreign Broadcast Information Service*, Asia and Pacific, October 15, 1980, pp. D12–D18.

24. *Indian Express* (New Delhi), July 20, 1965; *Ming Pao Daily* (Hong Kong), March 30, 1979; *Ta Kung Pao* (Hong Kong), September 23, 1981; and *Korea Herald*, April 1 and 22, 1979.

25. See references in note 24 of this chapter.

26. See notes 49 and 50 of Chapter 1.

27. See, for example, Nayan Chanda, "The Ice Is Broken But the Chill Lingers On," *Far Eastern Economic Review*, March 5, 1982, pp. 32–34.

28. *Le Monde* (Paris), June 23, 1982.

29. See, for example, the Chun-Reagan joint communique of February 2, 1981, reprinted in *Korea Herald*, February 3, 1981.

30. *Nodong Sinmun*, February 4, 1981.

31. *Yomiuri Shimbun* (Tokyo), January 11, 1972, January 13, 1972; and *Asahi Shimbun* (Tokyo), September 27, 1971.

32. Kim Il-song, *Selected Works* (Pyongyang: Foreign Languages Publishing House, 1971), IV:539.

33. See, for example, Chong Pyong-gap, "The People's Army of Korea Is a Trustworthy Protector and Defender of the Revolution," *Kulloja*, February 25, 1967, pp. 35–41.

34. Ibid., p. 37.

35. *Kim Il-song Chojak Sonjip* IV:364–65; Choe Hyon, "Arming of the Entire People and Fortification of the Entire Country," *Kulloja*, no. 12 (1966), pp. 7–17; *Nodong Sinmun*, December 5, 1967; and Kim Il-song, *Report on Work of Central Committee to Fifth Congress Workers' Party of Korea* (London: Africa-Magazine Ltd., 1971), pp. 49–50.

36. See references in note 35 of this chapter.

37. Kim Il-song, *Report on Work of Central Committee to 5th Congress Workers' Party of Korea*, p. 49.

38. Ibid.

39. South Korea's nuclear-energy production capability is believed to be several years ahead of North Korea's, which has only one small-scale nuclear-research reactor. Young Sun Ha, "Nuclearization of Small States and World Order: The Case of Korea," *Asian Survey*, November 1978, p. 1141.

In his interview with the editor-in-chief of the Japanese magazine *Sekai* on March 26, 1976, Kim Il-song said: "We have no intention of arming ourselves with nuclear weapons. We have not enough money to produce nuclear weapons or adequate place to test them." And he added: "Even if war bursts forth in Korea, they would not be able to use nuclear weapons. How can they use nuclear weapons here in Korea when friend and foe will grapple with each other? Should the enemy use nuclear weapons, he will also get killed." Kim Il-song, "Talk with the Editor-in-Chief of the Japanese Politico-Theoretical Magazine *Sekai*," *Korea Today*, no. 238 (July 1976), pp. 11–12.

40. See Ki Won Lee, "North Korean Military Affairs," *Korean Journal of International Studies* VIII, no. 1 (1975–1976):65–78.

41. U.S. Central Intelligence Agency, National Foreign Assessment Center, *Korea: The Economic Race Between the North and the South* (Washington, D.C.: January 1978), p. 6; and U.S. Arms Control and Disarmament Agency, *World Military Expenditures and Arms Transfers, 1967–1976* (Washington, D.C.: July 1978), p. 50.

42. According to U.S. CIA reports, the Soviet Union is now devoting between 16 and 20 percent of its GNP to military purposes, with spending rising 4 to 5 percent a year, while China's military costs are only 5 to 10 percent of a much smaller GNP and are growing at 1 or 2 percent a year. By comparison, military spending in major Western European countries range from Great Britain's 5.8 percent to Italy's 2.4 percent, and India, the largest military power in South Asia, spends 3.5 percent.

43. For example, Moscow's military assistance to North Korea has reportedly declined in both quantity and quality in recent years. More specifically, total North Korean arms imports from Russia fell from US$249 million in 1973 to US$32 million in 1976. Gareth Porter, "Time to Talk," p. 59.

44. Paek Hwang-gi, "Armament Industry of North Korea," *Vantage Point*, March 1982, pp. 1–10; and April 1982, pp. 1–10.

45. For arms transfers to North Korea from the Soviet Union and China in the

1960s and 1970s, see note 35 of Chapter 2.

There is no indication that the Soviet Union has acceded to North Korean requests for more sophisticated military equipment, including MIG-23s, although the North Koreans have received ground weapons, including Frog 7 missiles, air-defense systems, and technology for submarines and high-speed attack boats. North Korea has reportedly complained bitterly of Moscow's refusal to provide MIG-23s.

46. U.S. Senate, Foreign Relations Committee, *U.S. Troop Withdrawal from the Republic of Korea, January 9, 1978* (Washington, D.C.: U.S. Government Printing Office, 1978), p. 31.

47. Dale Van Atta and Richard Nations, "Kim's Build-up to Blitzkrieg," *Far Eastern Economic Review,* March 5, 1982, p. 28.

48. Quoted from Chang Yoon Choi, "Korea: Security and Strategic Issues," p. 1138. See also Table 3.

49. Seoul, whose population now exceeds 8 million, constitutes the political, commercial, industrial, and cultural centers of South Korea.

50. The flying time between the DMZ and Seoul is only three minutes.

6

The Cult of Kim Il-Song
and His Family

One major characteristic of the DPRK's political system is the excessive personality cult of Kim Il-song, which has now elevated him to the status of a demigod. Since its beginning, idolatry of Kim Il-song, which is designed to create the desired image of the all-wise, omnipotent, and infallible leader, has become one of North Korea's major preoccupations. Through the intensive campaign of his personality cult, Kim has made it abundantly clear that he has no equals in the DPRK leadership.

The foundation of the cult has derived largely from his anti-Japanese revolutionary past in Manchuria in the 1930s, from his *chuch'e* ideology, and from the DPRK's achievements allegedly based on it. As Sung Chul Yang observes correctly, "the sources and substance of Kim's cult are not all outright and groundless fabrication."[1] Nevertheless, the aggrandizement of the DPRK chieftain has required the unscrupulous twisting of truth and the exaggeration or falsification of historical facts by the North Korean hagiographers involved in the cult-building enterprise.

The DPRK dictator is commonly called the *suryong* ("supreme leader") or the *widaehan chidoja* or the *yongdoja* ("great leader").[2] His speeches are referred to as "the teachings," and they have priority over decisions made by the ruling KWP and the government; no dissenting opinion is permitted. Indeed, the North Korean people have been indoctrinated to accept Kim's utterances as cardinal truth in all aspects of governance. The regime says that it is "immense glory, paramount happiness and holy duty to submit themselves totally and unconditionally to the Great Leader . . . by

Kim Il-song

carrying out his 'teachings' unconditionally and by accepting his authority absolutely."[3] For the people of North Korea, "glory is theirs, whether they are alive or dead, as long as they have dedicated themselves to the task of carrying out the 'teachings' of the Great Leader."[4]

Every citizen wears a small pin with Kim's likeness placed over the left breast pocket of a jacket or dress. His writings are read every day. Moreover, the face of Kim Il-song is everywhere: it adorns every home, school, public office, factory, street, bus, train, and park. In many homes, his image occupies the central place on the family altar, replacing the ancient tablets as the principal object of worship.

The DPRK regime apparently recognizes the basic utility of a secular political religion combined with the powerful unifying figure of Kim Il-song and the cult of his personality. While there may be some undercurrent of disaffection with the Kim cult in intellectual circles, the worship of Kim is apparently too intimately embedded in the entire fabric of the North Korean political system to be publicly ridiculed or scorned. It is not surprising that essays, speeches, and sermons by important DPRK leaders and propagandists, as well as the daily conversations of the North Korean people, are usually composed of fragments of Kim's past utterances, in the same way that a Christian cleric or zealot would produce a sermon from the attributed words of Jesus.

In the absence of confirmed data, it is difficult to estimate the extent of Kim Il-song's appeal to the North Korean people. One should not, however, discount the possibility that substantial numbers of the masses really adore the North Korean chieftain. Neither is it known how deeply Kim's militant ideas, particularly the idea of continual revolutionary rebirth and momentum, have penetrated the minds of the people.

The personality cult of Kim Il-song is neither an accidental nor a sudden phenomenon; it has grown gradually from 1945. In its formative years between 1945 and 1958, during which Kim gradually eliminated all his rivals for power, there was a considerable effort by the Pyongyang Government to reinforce his image as the savior of Korea—a figure around whom the toiling masses could rally and with whom they could identify their hopes and dreams. In the task of constructing a new Communist society in North Korea, he was depicted as prophet, agent of the birth, and possessor of revealed truth.

During the formative period of the DPRK, the Kim cult was also used as a political weapon to strengthen Kim Il-song's prestige and personal power by exalting his revolutionary credentials. Immediately after the end of World War II, there was little doubt that a major qualification for a leadership position in the newly emerging Communist state in North Korea was to have had a good record in the pre-1945 anti-Japanese independence movement. Kim was portrayed as the unsurpassed hero of Korea's preliberation anti-Japanese independence campaign. Kim's North Korean biographers rewrote history in accordance with his canons and in a manner calculated to accentuate his exclusive, indispensable role and merits in the cause of anti-Japanese national liberation while discrediting or even denying contributions made by his rivals.[5] (North Korea is a nation where the ruling power faction controls not only the present, but the past.)

At a certain stage of its development, the cult gained its own momentum. Since the consolidation of Kim Il-song's dictatorial power in the early 1960s, a serious campaign developed to establish his personality cult firmly and to create a myth about him and his family. As the Kim cult gradually assumed more of the functions of a religion, Kim himself, and later his likeness or image, has become increasingly cloaked with the quality of the sacred. The most important device for nurturing and strengthening the cult of the sacred being is ritual, in which both myth and symbol are combined.[6] The ritualized expression of loyalty to Kim has, in fact, become commonplace. Until now, the most familiar rituals in North Korea are associated with the DPRK's National Day on September 9, when hundreds of thousands of the faithful would participate in and witness those spectacles of reinforcement and regeneration of the faith that were highlighted by the appearance of the DPRK dictator.

In the early 1960s, the DPRK regime began to propagate the "Kim Il-song Thought" as a magic or supernatural weapon, the proper application of which would aid in the solution of most problems and a number of physical afflictions as well. In the mid-1960s, for example, the DPRK mass media widely circulated the story of a North Korean fishing boat named "Minchungho" that was beset by a storm in March 1963.[7] The entire crew, according to the story, gathered together in the captain's cabin and chanted Kim Il-song's biography, "Recalling the Period of the Anti-Japanese Armed Struggle,"[8] for more than twenty minutes, beseeching the help of the North Korean chieftain. Suddenly and miraculously the storm subsided, and the crew was saved.

Since the 1960s, all DPRK publications, including newspapers, magazines, textbooks, and academic works, have been used to promote the Kim cult. A 745-page *Political Dictionary* published in October 1970 included 2,604 references glorifying Kim Il-song—an average of 3.5 references per page, or 1.5 references per entry. Dictionaries of economics and philosophy, newspapers, yearbooks, and other mass-communication media in the early 1970s had a similar orientation. In 1970, 35 percent of the elementary-school textbooks dealt with class struggle and 65 percent, with the cult of Kim Il-song.

Kim Il-song's birthday has become the most important "national holiday" in North Korea. Academic seminars, debates, movie festivals, artistic performances, sports competitions, memorial tree plantings, awards, memorial editorials, and beautification campaigns have been undertaken on or around Kim's birthday.

At the Fifth KWP Congress of November 1970, the bards of the Kim Il-song cult surpassed themselves, reaching new heights in the public adulation of the chieftain. Not only was he credited with all North Korea's achievements, but his "creative thinking" was said to be a unique and original contribution to Marxism-Leninism and the only correct strategy for the world revolutionary movement in general.

Kim Il-song's 60th birthday (according to Oriental belief, the most auspicious moment in life), on April 15, 1972, became a milestone in the campaign idolizing the person of Kim Il-song and his family members going back five generations. Kim's closest associates from the Manchurian period and other loyal followers published a series of essays and articles in the KWP organ, *Nodong Sinmun*, in the most laudatory terms.[9] His birthday was celebrated throughout the country, and he was hailed in terms such as these in a five-hour speech by a KWP Secretariat member:

> The revolutionary thinking of the great Marxist-Leninist Kim Il-song is an encyclopedic idea which gives comprehensive scientific answers to all the theoretical and practi-

cal questions covering all fields of revolution and construction—politics, economics, ideology and culture—
which have been arising in different stages of the revolution, and shows the correct ways and means for their
implementation. It is an idea giving the most correct and
overall answers to all new theoretical and practical
problems and fundamental needs of our time.[10]

Since 1972, significantly, Kim Il-song's status has been elevated to
the "great leader of the international Communist movement and
world revolution" and the "savior of humanity" from previous
adulations of "one of the outstanding leaders of the international
Communist and labor movements" and the "national hero." The
idea of *chuch'e* has become synonymous with "Kimilsongism" in
the DPRK propaganda, and its publications are devoted to an
exposition of Kim's thoughts and theory.

Kim Il-song's 60th birthday was also celebrated with the dedication
of the Revolutionary Memorial Museum in his honor. At the same
time, a massive twenty-three-meter-high, seventy-ton bronze
statue of Kim Il-song was erected in front of the colossal building
that houses the museum. The statue faces south and symbolically
promises the return of North and South Korea under Communist
rule. To add cosmetic prestige, the statue was coated with more
than seventeen kilograms of gold. Because of this, Kim was called
"Golden Boy" by foreigners residing in Pyongyang. In September
1978, however, shortly before the festivals marking the thirtieth
anniversary of the founding of the DPRK, the gold layer was
removed. A Japanese journalist reported that the "degilding" was
the consequence of a Chinese wish.[11]

As early as January 1981, North Korea started making preparations
to celebrate the 70th birthday, April 15, 1982, of Kim Il-song with
gala events. For example, a prospectus for a literature and art
contest was announced as part of the program for the celebration.
Preparations for the birthday events also included a nationwide
refurbishing and polishing of some of the 30,000 statues and monu-
mental busts of Kim Il-song, including the twenty-three-meter-high
statue in Pyongyang.[12]

The birthday anniversary on April 15, 1982, was the most festive
national holiday in the long history of all Korea. North Korea

invited 209 delegations from 118 countries to join the celebration. (Among the foreign guests from Communist countries were neither governmental officials nor delegates of Communist parties, except in the case of Yugoslavia.) On April 10, 1982, North Korea completed the extension work on Moranbong Stadium in Pyongyang, and on April 14, the Pyongyang Government renamed it Kim Il-song Stadium. On April 15, the DPRK dedicated a sixty-meter-high arch of triumph, constructed at the entrance of Kim Il-song Stadium, as a symbol of his "march of triumph into Pyongyang to liberate the Korean people from Japanese colonial rule in 1945."[13] At the same time, a grand ceremony was held in Pyongyang to unveil the Tower of the *Chuch'e* Idea, which was erected to symbolize the firm will of the KWP and the North Korean people to bequeath Kim Il-song's "immortal revolutionary idea and achievements generation after generation and to complete the *chuch'e* revolutionary cause generation after generation."[14]

On the morning of April 15, Kim Il-song was decorated with the title "Hero of the Democratic People's Republic of Korea, Gold Medal and the Order of National Flag, First Degree."[15] He received a congratulatory message that, written jointly by the KWP Central Committee, the Central People's Committee (North Korea's supercabinet) and the Administration Council (cabinet), praised him as "savior of the nation" and a world leader who "contributed greatly to the international Communist movement and world revolutionary movement." There were also elaborate eulogies for the DPRK chieftain in North Korea's mass media and at the commemorative mmeetings in Pyongyang and in other parts of the country.[16] A grand ceremony was held at Kim Il-song Stadium on April 16, 1982, to present letters of loyalty in the name of the entire North Korean people to Kim Il-song on his 70th birthday.[17]

Kim Il-song is today surrounded by perhaps the most extravagant personality cult in the world. The North Korean media almost invariably refer to him in such terms as the "respected and beloved fatherly leader of the Korean people," "peerless patriot," and "ever-victorious, iron-willed brilliant commander, the greatest military strategist the world has ever known," the "greatest philosopher-politician in the annals of human history," and so forth.[18] He is acclaimed as "the most profound revolutionary genius of all time," "without precedent in the West or East, in all ages, the sun of the nation," and adored by all "world revolutionary people." His birthplace at Mankyongdae, which is a national shrine, is said to be the "cradle of the world revolution," and a pilgrimage to his birthplace is a must for both citizens and foreign visitors. The country's leading university and several other important educational institutions are named after him. The word "communism" has been eliminated from all official publications in North Korea and replaced by the term "Kim Il-song ideology." Objects he touches at official functions—even ashtrays and pencils—are either covered with a white veil or put into vitrines labeled with the date.

Shortly after the Sixth KWP Congress of October 1980, where his son was made future political heir, *Nodong Sinmun* wrote that Kim Il-song was "the greatest leader of the working class who has extraordinary wisdom, outstanding leadership and a lofty, virtuous Communist character which no one has ever had before."[19] It continued: "People of the world, if you are looking for miracles, come to [North] Korea. Christians, do not go to Jerusalem. Instead, come to [North] Korea. Do not believe in god, believe in the great man [like Kim Il-song]."[20]

The cult of Kim Il-song has been carried to an extreme that is without parallel in recent history. Communist dictatorships have characteristically developed personality cults, as with Stalin and Mao Zedong. But the personality cult of Kim has thus far surpassed those of Stalin and Mao both in its intensity and its scope. The cults of Stalin in Russia and Mao in China were modest by comparison. Even though giant portraits of Stalin and Mao were often hung in Red Square and in Tien-an-men Square alongside those of Marx, Engels, and Lenin, only the picture of Kim Il-song is displayed in public places and private homes throughout North Korea. The cult of the DPRK chieftain is strictly a one-man show.

Similarly, the works of Marx, Engels, and Lenin, printed and distributed by the tens of millions in the Communist world, are rarely seen in the bookstores and libraries of North Korea. In the bookstores, one can only find books by or about the "Great Leader," DPRK President Kim Il-song. Kim's office bookshelf is said not to contain a single work by Karl Marx.[21] The multivolume works of Kim Il-song compensate for this absence of the Communist classics. Theoretically, at least, everyone in the country is supposed to devote at least two hours a day, and four hours on Saturday, to the study of Kim Il-song's political ideology.

The DPRK mass media constantly stress that loyalty to Kim and his ideology must continue from generation to generation;[22] and the people are supposed to renew a daily oath—in schools, at their jobs, or wherever else they may be—that they will follow his instructions forever.

In the mid-1970s, the DPRK entered the present, and apparently final, stage of the deification campaign of Kim Il-song. This final stage is distinguished by the extension of the Kim cult to cover simultaneously all his family members, dead and alive, and by the elevation of his son Kim Chong-il to the position of successor-designator.

Simultaneously with the intensified campaign of the Kim Il-song cult, even the genealogy of the North Korean chieftain has become an object of idolization. Those included in the family cult are Kim's paternal great-grandfather, grandparents, parents, uncle, and his younger brothers, eldest son, and deceased first wife, in addition to his grandfather and an uncle on his mother's side (see Table 4). All are constantly canonized for having been "ardent, brilliant, and foremost revolutionary fighters and patriots who devoted their lives unselfishly to the cause of Korea's liberation and national independence, generation after generation."[23] (It should be mentioned in this connection that evidence to support this claim is lacking.) North Korean propaganda maintains that "such a revolutionary family record would be hard to find anywhere in the world."[24] The canonization of Kim Il-song's family members seems intended to demonstrate that the Kim clan represents North Korea's best family of revolutionaries and also that it would be quite natural for the DPRK regime and the North Koreans to seek Kim Il-song's future political successor from such a prominent family.

As part of the glorification campaign of Kim Il-song's family, a great deal of propaganda is disseminated on their behalf. Kim's family roots are widely studied and discussed at every school, administrative organization, agricultural cooperative, and military organization, and various monuments, historical buildings, and sites have been dedicated to Kim's family members. Some public educational institutions have been named after the Kim clan, as exemplified by the Kang Ban-suk (Kim's mother) Revolutionary Academy in Nampo City and the Kim Hyong-jik (Kim's father) Teacher's College in Pyongyang. The burial mounds for deceased relatives are equal in size to those of Korea's ancient kings, and the

Table 4:
Kim Il-song's Family and Relatives, Including Those in the Idolization Campaign

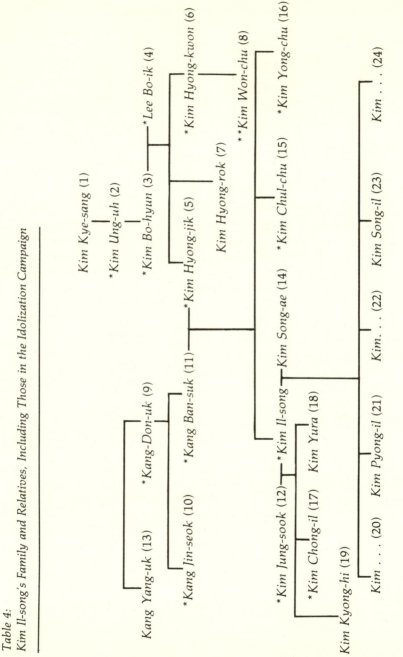

*Included in the family cult

Kim Kye-sang (1)
*Kim Ung-uh (2)
*Kim Bo-hyun (3)
*Lee Bo-ik (4)
*Kim Hyong-jik (5)
*Kim Hyong-kwon (6)
Kim Hyong-rok (7)
*Kim Won-chu (8)
**Kim Won-chu (8)
*Kang-Don-uk (9)
Kang Yang-uk (13)
*Kang Ban-suk (11)
*Kang Jin-seok (10)
*Kim Hyong-jik (5)
Kim Song-ae (14)
*Kim Chul-chu (15)
*Kim Yong-chu (16)
*Kim Il-song
Kim Yura (18)
*Kim Jung-sook (12)
*Kim Chong-il (17)
Kim Chong-il (17)
Kim Kyong-hi (19)
Kim . . . (20)
Kim Pyong-il (21)
Kim. . . (22)
Kim Song-il (23)
Kim . . . (24)

Table 4 (continued)

LEGEND

(1) Dead. Kim Il-song's paternal fifth-generation great-grandfather. Kim's ancestors used to live in Chunju, in southern Korea. Kye-sang emigrated to Pyongan Province in northern Korea and lived a vagabond life.

(2) Dead. Kim Il-song's fourth-generation great-grandfather, Kim Ung-uh settled down near Pyongyang as a grave keeper for the Lee Pyong-taek family. Enshrined as a "great patriot" who led the Pyongyang citizenry to the Taedong River and who sank "the U.S. imperialist pirate ship General Sherman" in 1886.

(3) Dead. Kim Il-song's grandfather. Depicted as a stout anti-Japanese patriot who "gallantly stood behind his offspring in their revolutionary struggles, preserving his loyalty to the fatherland and courageously fighting against the aggressors, despite persecutions by the Japanese imperialists."

(4) Dead. Kim Il-song's grandmother. Depicted as a gallant anti-Japanese fighter.

(5) Dead. Kim Il-song's father. Credited with having founded the Korean National Organization. The Japanese source does not mention the father's active participation in any anti-Japanese movement. Now canonized in North Korea as the foremost leader of the anti-Japanese resistance movement in Korea after 1919. At least one college is named after him.

(6) Dead. Kim Il-song's uncle. Praised as a member of Kim Il-song's anti-Japanese guerrilla band in Manchuria in the 1930s.

(7) Dead. Kim Il-song's uncle who died in his late 20s.

(8) Dead. Kim Il-song's cousin. Praised as an anti-Japanese revolutionary patriot.

(9) Dead. Kim Il-song's maternal grandfather. Depicted as a patriotic fighter against the Japanese.

(10) Dead. Kim Il-song's maternal uncle. Depicted as a patriotic anti-Japanese fighter.

(11) Dead. Kim Il-song's mother. Canonized as a brilliant and dedicated anti-Japanese revolutionary fighter, the "pioneer of world women's movement," and the founder of the Korean women's movement.

(12) Dead. Kim Il-song's deceased first wife. Praised as an unsurpassed Communist warrior. Tomb and museum are dedicated in her honor.

(13) Dead. Kim Il-song's maternal great-uncle. Former Presbyterian minister. Former vice-president of the DPRK. Kang Yang-uk died on January 9, 1983 at the age of 80.

(14) Alive. Kim Il-song's present wife. Chairman of the Korean Democratic Women's Union. Also a member of the Sixth KWP Central Committee.

(15) Dead. Kim Il-song's younger brother who died a natural death in Manchuria in 1935 at the age of 19. Depicted as an "indomitable and dedicated anti-Japanese revolutionary fighter."

Table 4 (continued)

(16) Possibly dead. Kim Il-song's younger brother. Former member of the Politburo of the ruling KWP, and former deputy premier. Once praised as a true Communist revolutionary fighter.

(17) Alive. Kim Il-song's eldest son. Chong-il is Kim's only surviving son by his first marriage. Emerged as the second most powerful person in the DPRK at the Sixth KWP Congress. Depicted as "a genius of ideology and leadership and a compassionate instructor of the people," "a brilliant instructor of our party and people," and "the rays of the sun."

(18) Dead. Kim Il-song's second son by his first marriage, who died shortly before the Korean War.

(19) Alive. Kim Il-song's first daughter by his first marriage.

(20) Alive. Kim Il-song's first daughter by his second marriage. Her full name is not available.

(21) Alive. Kim Il-song's first son by his second marriage.

(22) Alive. Kim Il-song's second daughter by his second marriage.

(23) Alive. Kim Il-song's second son by his second marriage.

(24) Alive. Kim Il-song's third daughter by his second marriage. Her full name is not available.

beautified tomb of Kim Il-song's deceased first wife, along with 100 other burial mounds of Kim's relatives, have been declared the tombs of heroic revolutionaries. The DPRK has launched the glorification campaign of Kim Il-song's family to such an extent that it seems as if the country is a dynastic kingdom under the Kim clan. In addition, the cult of the chieftain and his family is intended to pave the way for the creation of a family dynasty by demonstrating that the roots of the emerging Communist monarchy under the Kim clan are deep and legitimate.

Another important characteristic of DPRK politics is that the government of North Korea has become, in effect, a family affair because of extensive nepotism. Perhaps Kim Il-song's nepotism indicates that he would not trust the political reliability of even his most trusted colleagues from the Manchurian period and other loyal followers in a crisis. Nepotism is, of course, commonplace among Communist dictatorships, but Kim Il-song is a champion practitioner who has pushed innumerable relatives into strategically important positions in the North Korean power structure. For all

intents and purposes, North Korea today is run by the DPRK dictator, his family members, and his old Manchurian comrades, and
Kim Il-song appears to have laid a firm basis for the ultimate succession of his son Kim Chong-il, who has emerged as the second
most powerful man in North Korea, as will be discussed in Chapter
7.

The vast array of key committee memberships in the ruling KWP
apparatus and other top-level affiliations strengthen the power base
of the Kim clan. Kim Il-song's wife, Kim Song-ae, is chairman of
the Central Committee of the 2.7-million member Korean Democratic Women's Union, a regular member of the Sixth KWP Central
Committee, and a member of the Standing Committee of the
Supreme People's Assembly (legislative branch). (His younger
brother, Kim Yong-chu, was a member of the Fifth KWP Politburo
and Secretariat and also a vice-premier of the State Administration
Council before he faded away from the scene in 1975.) His daughter
Kim Kyong-hi is deputy head of the international affairs section of
the KWP apparatus. His maternal great-uncle, Kang Yang-uk, who
was a Presbyterian minister, was the country's vice-president and a
member of the Central People's Committee until his death in mid-
January 1983.

Prestige and authority are shared at all levels of Kim Il-song's
family tree, including cousins, nieces, nephews, and their spouses.
A cousin, Kim Chung-suk, is deputy chairman of the Korean
League of All Vocations. Her husband, Ho Tam, is an alternate
member of the Sixth KWP Politburo and also serves concurrently
as deputy premier and foreign minister. Her sister, Kim Sin-suk, is
vice-president of the ideologically important Academy of Social
Sciences. This woman's husband, Yang Hyong-sup, is a regular
member of the Sixth KWP Central Committee and also president of
the Academy of Social Sciences. Kim Pyong-ha, the husband of
one of Kim Il-song's nieces, is head of the powerful National Security and Political Affairs Bureau, North Korea's intelligence and
secret police organization. A nephew, Hwang Chang-yop, is chairman of the Standing Committee of the Supreme People's Assembly
and one of the Sixth KWP Central Committee secretaries, while a
cousin on his mother's side, Kang Hui-won, is an alternate member
of the Politburo of the Sixth KWP Central Committee and a member of the Central People's Committee. Another cousin on his
mother's side, Kang Hyong-su, is a regular member of the Sixth

KWP Central Committee, chairman of the South Pyongan Provincial People's Committee and first vice-chairman of the Control Committee of the Sixth KWP Central Committee. Kang Song-san, a nephew of Kim Il-song's mother, is a regular member of the Politburo of the Sixth KWP Central Committee and first deputy premier. There are unconfirmed intelligence reports indicating that Pak Song-chol, North Korea's former premier and current vice-president, is also related to Kim Il-song by marriage.

The extravagant, religion-like personality cult of Kim Il-song probably leads observers to ask: What accounts for this extraordinary phenomenon in North Korea? Although there are numerous explanations for and speculations about the Kim cult, no single theory can explain it fully. Accordingly, a combination of many factors seems to be responsible for the rise and the never-ending phenomenon of the Kim cult.

There are indications that Kim Il-song craves personal power, fame, glory, and public acclaim, so the cult has developed partly to caress his limitless ego. Boundlessly ambitious, yet perhaps inwardly insecure, he has an impressive need for hero worship. In this way, the cult of personality has played a significant role in meeting his psychic needs.

Kim Il-song is intensely obsessed with his own revolutionary biography and his place in history. Nothing is more important to the DPRK chieftain, who is driven to view himself as North Korea's most unique, outstanding, and revolutionary leader in the past, the present, as well as the future. As a result, he himself initiated certain steps to create his personality cult during the formative years of the DPRK in the late 1940s, and he has since taken care to see the cult gain its own momentum and develop intensely without interruption. He has shown that obsession by his own actions, by those of functionaries representing him, and by his acceptance of the officially inspired adultation as it intensified during the 1950s. Since the establishment of the DPRK in 1948, he has made no single, genuine gesture (as Lenin did),[25] or shown the mask of modesty (as Mao did),[26] to discourage his growing personality cult. Besides, his *chuch'e* ideology, especially with respect to the individual superman-like leadership, by itself serves as a ready-made rationalization for encouraging and sustaining the Kim cult. Seen in this context, it is not farfetched to say that Kim Il-song has been the master builder of his own cult.

Kim Il-song has always wanted obedience more than consultation from his colleagues. Further, he has found it convenient to let himself be turned into the symbol of the socialist revolution and construction in North Korea, which enabled him to mobilize and direct the masses to do his bidding more easily.

Moreover, Kim Il-song's closest associates from the Manchurian period and other loyal followers have undoubtedly fanned the flame of his personal ego trip. It is important to note that the flattery of rulers, coupled with the idolatry toward them, is a centuries-old art for career advancement in the Orient in general and particularly in Asian countries (China, Japan, and Korea), whose traditional political cultures were based on Confucian ethics. (The classical Chinese writings referred to the emperor as the "Son of Heaven" exercising the "Mandate of Heaven.") It is difficult for people of these countries to overcome such deep-rooted ruler-worshipping traditions overnight.[27]

The "palace cheerleaders"—members of Kim Il-song's Manchurian inner power circle—have genuinely devoted themselves to the DPRK dictator or truly perceived him to be the uniquely qualified, supreme, and charismatic leader of their country who deserves to be adored. Other loyal followers at the second level of the DPRK power structure—many of whom are perhaps sycophantic careerists—who may have lacked strong qualifications to be included in Kim's inner power sanctum, have been shrewd enough to grasp the opportunities for self-advancement inherent in the cult enterprise.

Within each group, everyone has tried to outperform others in the Kim cult-building process in order to remain in his good graces or to curry favor with him, even by twisting the truth and falsifying or exaggerating historical facts. At the same time, competition has developed between the two groups to see which one has done a better job of massaging Kim's bottomless ego. Historically, egomaniacal or megalomanic rulers have usually encouraged such competitive biddings among their loyal followers for their maximum idolization. (Even Kim Il-song's wife, younger brother, and son have had to participate actively in his worship.)[28] In the process, these glorifiers have ignored their scruples and stilled their consciences by pushing the cult enterprise even to the height of absurdity.

Indeed, it is ironic that some sort of "religious" function (with corresponding religious roles and structures) is found even in atheistic Communist countries, where, as Karl Marx said,[29] religion is considered the "opium" of the people and where those institutions usually regarded as religious are destroyed. It is obvious that religion serves certain vital societal and individual needs and thus is, in the words of Elizabeth K. Nottingham, "a universal function of human societies wherever they are found."[30]

Kim Il-song has been in power for thirty-four years. As the long political history of mankind demonstrates, political power tends, by nature, to be centripetal rather than centrifugal. The longer one rules, the more power one is tempted to accumulate; and the more power one amasses, the greater the possibility of succumbing to the enchantment and thrill of mass acclaim and adulation of one's rulership. Accordingly, a parallel may be drawn between the ever intensifying personality cult of Kim Il-song in North Korea and Lord Acton's dictum that "all power tends to corrupt and absolute power corrupts absolutely."[31]

Kim Il-song has been shrewd enough to realize that mass worship would help dislodge his critics and opponents within the ruling elite and thus make his political supremacy in the future more unassailable. He has also used his cult as a myth-making device to claim both temporal and spiritual "infallibility" in the past, the present, and the future.

Historically, Marxism-Leninism has demanded a strong personal leadership capable of rallying the masses behind his revolutionary banner, given the inability of the working class spontaneously to organize themselves for a revolutionary cause.[32] Most Communist regimes have manifested varying types of personality cults, ranging from the godlike Kim Il-song in North Korea to the grandfatherly Tito in Yugoslavia. Such cults also seem to be natural otugrowths of a personal rule that has no checks and balances to restrain it.

A well-established rule of modern mass-oriented politics suggests that, regardless of ideology and/or system, any society undergoing a radical revolution requires a great man, a political "genius," a charismatic leader. Such a leader serves as a unifying element in mobilizing the masses during the radical, extremely difficult, and complex transformation of the society.[33] And the quest for such coherent unity contains within it an affinity for a highly personalized symbol in the form of a personality cult. As far as the DPRK is concerned, Kim Il-song personifies this type of a leader.

Moreover, the unity of purpose and action under a highly

personalized leadership can eliminate internal factionalism, anarchism, and external interference. Given Korean communism's history of chronic, notorious, and pathological factionalism,[34] the emergence and the maintenance of Kim Il-song's one-man dictatorial rule in North Korea seem to have been a sheer necessity for the nation's survival and development as a modernizing Communist state.[35]

The DPRK leadership has demonstrated a keen understanding of the integrative, symbolic function of Kim Il-song and of the cult that has grown up around him. In a nation not far removed in time from the Confucian-based ethical tradition of ancestor and emperor worship, they understand as well the individual needs of people for a personalized symbol of authority to whom allegiance can be transferred.

The regime also appears to have perceived the immensely important role of the Kim cult as an inculcator of social values and as a medium or instrument for forming a consensus about the nature and content of these values. In other words, the Kim-cult enterprise justifies and legitimizes the DPRK chieftain's dictatorial regime and policies by stimulating unconditional and unswerving loyalty to him. To the DPRK, the psychological element of loyalty (ch'ungsong) is the most important political and social value that sustains North Korean society.

The progress of Kim Il-song's personality cult may also derive from the fact that it may be more difficult for the North Korean masses, who were, as Joan Robinson writes, "hurled suddenly from a blank of [Japanese] colonial past, without a clue, into socialism,"[36] to identify with new, impersonal processes and institutions than with a personal leader. In other words, it is vastly easier to relate their loyalties to an individual leader than to a set of new abstract values and ethics that may take a considerable length of time for most of them to grasp.[37] The ultimate objective of the personality cult campaign is that loyalty to the North Korean chieftain can and will eventually be extended concurrently to the DPRK institutions.

NOTES

1. Quoted from Sung Chol Yang, "The Kim Il-song Cult in North Korea," *Korea and World Affairs*, Spring 1980, p. 161.

2. In the Korean Language, both *widaehan chidoja* and *yongdoja* are synonyms; they are used interchangeably.

3. "The Immense Glory and Happiness of Our People Led by the Great Leader," *Kulloja*, April 1974.

4. Ibid. For the expression of similar exhortations, see, for example "It Is the Unshakable Revolutionary Will and Faith of Our People to Remain Loyal to the Great Leader Forever," *Nodong Sinmun*, February 18, 1976; "Loyalty to the Party and the Leader Is the Basic Trait of *Chuch'e*-type Communist Revolutionaries," *Nodong Sinmun*, October 5 and 6, 1980; "Let Us Firmly Establish Revolutionary World Outlook Like Unheralded Heroes," *Nodong Sinmun*, Feburary 19, 1980; Yi Chong-ok, "The KWP Is the Great Guide Leading the Republic Along the Road of Prosperity and Grandeur," *Nodong Sinmun*, September 15, 1980; and O Paek-yong, "Respected and Beloved Comrade Kim Il-song Is the Leader Who Laid a Solid Foundation for the Founding of Our Party," *Nodong Sinmun*, September 2, 1980.

5. From 1945 to 1962, Han Sol-ya was Kim Il-song's official biographer in North Korea. See his article "General Kim Il-song as Seen by a Writer," *Minsong* (Seoul), January–February 1947, pp. 30–31; and his book *Hero General Kim Il-song* (Tokyo: Chosen Shinbo-sha, 1962). Han was purged in 1972; Baik Bong has since served as the DPRK's senior official biographer of Kim Il-song.

6. "The essential truth of the myth," writes S. H. Hooke, "lies in the fact that it embodies a situation of profound emotional significance—a situation, moreover, which is in its nature recurrent, and which calls for the repetition of the ritual which deals with the situation and satisfies the need evoked by it . . . " Samuel H. Hooke, ed., *The Labyrinth* (New York: Macmillan, 1935), p. ix.

Myth thus provides a powerful symbolic force for bridging the gap between leaders and the masses, and provides those symbols of sentiment and identification that assist in arousing and strengthening faiths and loyalties. Harold D. Lasswell and Abraham Kaplan, *Power and Society: A Framework for Political Analysis* (New Haven, Conn.: Yale University Press, 1952), p. 119.

7. This story is cited in *North Korean Political System in Present Perspective* (Seoul: Research Center for Peace and Unification, 1976), p. 26.

8. Yim Chun-chu, *Hangil Muchang T'uchaeng Shiki rul Hoesang hayo* [Recalling the Period of the Anti-Japanese Armed Struggle] (Pyongyang: Choson Nodong-dang Ch'ulpansa, 1960), pp. 1–313.

9. See *Nodong Sinmun*, April 1–23, 1972.

10. *Pyongyang Times*, April 15, 1972.

11. In response to a North Korean request for more economic aid, Chinese Deputy Premier Deng Xiaoping allegedly said, when he visited Pyongyang in 1978, that things could not be too bad in North Korea's economy if the country could afford the luxury of a gold monument. Kikuchi Masato, "Golden Statue of President Kim Changed to Bronze on Deng Xiaoping's Advice," *Yomiuri Shimbun*, April 30, 1979. See also *Frankfurter Allgemeine Zeitung*, July 18, 1979.

12. *New York Times*, March 17, 1982.

13. *Foreign Broadcast Information Service*, Asia and Pacific, April 21, 1982, pp. D11–D12.

14. *Nodong Sinmun*, May 9, 1982; and *Foreign Broadcast Information Service*, Asia and Pacific, April 20, 1982, p. D7.

15. *Foreign Broadcast Information Service*, Asia and Pacific, pp. D2–D3.

16. See, for example, Yim Chun-chu, "The Respected and Beloved Comrade Kim Il-song Is the Great Leader Who Has Glorified Our People as a Prestigious and

Independent Nation," *Nodong Sinmun*, March 16, 1982; O Chin-u, "The Future Path of Our Revolution Under the Leadership of the Great Comrade Kim Il-song Is Endlessly Bright," *Nodong Sinmun*, February 26, 1982; and "The Respected and Beloved Leader Comrade Kim Il-song Is a Great Ideological Theoretician and Man of Action," *Nodong Sinmun*, April 11, 1982.

17. *Foreign Broadcast Information Service*, Asia and Pacific, April 19, 1982, p. D1.

18. According to a British newspaper reporter who visited North Korea in the spring of 1979, a North Korean guide chanted the phrase "our Great Leader Kim Il-song" certainly not fewer than 500 times in a ninety-minute tour around the Revolutionary Memorial Museum in Pyongyang. *Daily Mail* (London), April 25, 1979.

19. "The People Praise Their Leader," *Nodong Sinmun*, December 22, 1980.

20. Ibid.

21. *Economist* (London), October 18, 1975.

22. See, for example, "It Is the Unshakable Revolutionary Will and Faith of Our People to Remain Loyal to the Great Leader Forever," *Nodong Sinmun*, February 18 and 19, 1976.

23. Choson Nodong-dang, Chungang Wiwonhoe Chiksok Tang Yoksa Yonguso [Party History Study Center, Central Committee, KWP], *Pulgul ui Panil Hyokmyong T'usa Kim Hyong-jik Sonsaeng* [Mister Kim Hyong-jik, the Indomitable Anti-Japanese Revolutionary Fighter] (Pyongyang: Choson Nodong-dang Ch'ulpansa, 1969), pp. 1–142; Pyongyang KCNA in English, April 21, 22, 23, and 24, 1975, March 23, April 21, June 13, and June 14, 1976, July 10, 1980; *Nodong Sinmun*, January 12, March 23, March 24, June 12, July 9, and July 31, 1976, July 9, 1980, June 28, July 12, and August 19, 1981; *Kulloja*, April 1975; *Kita Chosen Kenkyu* (Tokyo), March and June 1975; *Political Dictionary, 1972*, published on December 31, 1973, by the Social Sciences House Publishing House, Pyongyang, pp. 1–3; and *Foreign Broadcast Information Service*, Asia and Pacific, June 30, 1980, pp. D10–D11, July 11, 1980, pp. D7–D8, and June 30, 1980, pp. D10–D11.

24. Baik Pong, *Minjogui Taeyang, Kim Il-song Janggun* [General Kim Il-song, the Sun of the Nation] (Pyongyang: Inmin Ch'ulpansa, 1969), 1:9.

25. See Robert C. Tucker, ed., *The Lenin Anthology* (New York: W. W. Norton, 1975), pp. lx–lxiv.

26. See Edgar Snow, "Snow and Mao," *Kansas City Star*, September 28, 1969, pp. F7–F8; and Edgar Snow, "A Conversation with Mao Tse-tung," *Life* (Magazine), April 30, 1971, p. 46.

27. Such scholars as Robert A. Scalapino, Chong-sik Lee, and Bruce C. Cumings extrapolate that the Kim cult in North Korea is related to traditional reverence toward the emperor. Robert A. Scalapino and Chog-sik Lee, *Communism in Korea* (Berkeley and Los Angeles: University of California Press, 1972), II:1314–15; and Bruce C. Cumings, "Kim's Korean Communism," *Problems of Communism*, March–April 1974, p. 34.

28. See, for example, Kim Yong-chu, "The Respected Leader Kim Il-song Is the Great Man of Thought and the Great Theorist in Our Times," *Nodong Sinmun*, April 13, 1972. See also Chapter 7.

29. Karl Marx, "Contribution to the Critique of Hegel's Philosophy of Right," *Marx and Engels in Religion* (New York: Schocken Books, 1964), p. 42.

30. Quoted from Elizabeth K. Nottingham, *Religion and Society* (New York: Random House, 1954), p. 1.

After discussing the cult of personality with Mao Zedong in 1965, Edgar Snow observed: "Mao liked to make fun of gods and idol worship, but he was well aware that the supernatural holds great attraction for many indigenous people. Among them, the cult was a powerful weapon." Edgar Snow, "Snow and Mao," *Kansas City Star*, September 28, 1969, p. F8.

31. Lord Acton (John Emerich Edmund Dalberg-Acton), *Essays on Freedom and Power* (Boston: Beacon Press, 1948), p. 364.

32. For this view, see Ellen Brun and Jacques Hersh, *Socialist Korea* (New York and London: Monthly Review Press, 1976), pp. 406–407.

33. For this theoretical exposition, see Edwin R. A. Seligman, *The Economic Interpretation of History*, 2d ed. rev. (New York: Gordian Press, 1966), pp. 97–98; Joan Robinson, "Korean Miracle," *Monthly Reivew*, January 1965, pp. 548–49; and Brun and Hersh, *Socialist Korea*, pp. 407, 410, 413–14.

34. See Chapter 1, especially note 14.

35. Koon Woo Nam, *The North Korean Communist Leadership 1945-1965* (University, Alabama: University of Alabama Press, 1974), pp. 141–42; and Brun and Hersh, *Socialist Korea*, pp. 415–16.

36. Quoted from Joan Robinson, "Korean Miracle," pp. 548–49.

37. Brun and Hersh, *Socialist Korea*, p. 414.

7

Dynastic Succession: Kim Chong-il's Ascendancy as Heir Apparent

The decision to elevate Kim Il-song's son Kim Chong-il to the position of future political successor has been carefully planned and executed by the Pyongyang regime. It was not a premeditated plan concocted after the establishment of the DPRK in 1948. Instead, the task of grooming Kim Chong-il as the political heir was initiated and put in high gear during the 1970s, well in advance of its official pronouncement at the Sixth KWP Party Congress of October 1980, in response to particular domestic conditions and the external environment, particularly Communist-bloc affairs.

For a while, Kim Yong-chu, Kim Il-song's younger brother, was believed to be slated to succeed his elder brother. In 1966, Kim Yong-chu entered the political limelight, having been appointed director of the important Organization and Guidance Department of the Fourth KWP Central Committee, which was in charge of all party personnel matters. He also became a member of the Fourth KWP Politburo and Secretariat concurrently. In 1970, he was the sixth-ranking member in the DPRK power structure, after his continuing membership in the Fifth KWP Politburo and Secretariat.

Coinciding with the appearance of Kim Chong-il on the political scene in the spring of 1973, however, Kim Yong-chu was demoted from sixth to thirteenth place in the Pyongyang hierarchy. In February 1974, he was dismissed as director of the Organization and Guidance Department of the Fifth KWP Central Committee and demoted to one of several insignificant deputy premiers, foreshadowing demotions and disappearances of the KWP figures personally associated with him.

Kim Yong-chu was reputed to be extremely loyal to his brother, but he was stubborn and somewhat violent in temper. He had been in bad health for a long time, and in late 1973, he was reported to be suffering from an incurable disease.[1] He has been less and less in the forefront since 1973 and has not been seen in public since April 1975. He was not reappointed to the new fifteen-member Central People's Committee when the DPRK reshuffle took place in December 1977. Nor was he retained as the DPRK's deputy premier. He is perhaps dead by now.

In early 1974, Kim Chong-il began to receive increasing attention as the likely heir apparent. Officials of the pro-Pyongyang General Association of Korean Residents in Japan (Chochongnyon) reported, after a visit to North Korea in 1975, that Kim Chong-il already held several important positions in the DPRK regime—possibly as a candidate member of the Fifth KWP Politburo, as a secretary of the Fifth KWP Secretariat, and as a member of the KWP's propaganda division.[2] (When a Korean-born professor of political science at George Washington University visited North Korea in August 1975, he, too, was told by a key KWP official that Kim Chong-il was serving in an important—possibly senior—party position.)[3] The Chochongnyon officials reported that they had seen pictures of Kim Chong-il side by side with his father in all the homes they visited in North Korea, and that they had been informed that the "party center" *(tang chungang)*, often mentioned euphemistically in KWP directives, referred to Comrade Kim Chong-il. North Korean foreign ministry officials told the Chochongnyon representatives that Kim Chong-il's official appointment as his father's "sole" successor would probably be announced at the Sixth KWP Congress.[4]

Even before the reports from the Chochongnyon representatives, the Pyongyang regime obliquely revealed its scheme to undertake hereditary rule in North Korea. The 1970 edition of *Dictionary of Political Terminologies*, published by the DPRK's Academy of Social Sciences, defined the term "hereditary succession" as follows:

Hereditary succession is a reactionary custom of exploitative societies whereby certain positions or riches may be legally inherited. Originally a product of slave societies, it was later adopted by feudal lords as a means to perpetuate dictatorial rule. . . . The custom is still followed in capitalist societies, where landowners and capitalists rely on it to dominate the working class, just as feudal aristocrats did earlier. (p. 414.)

Significantly, this item, entitled "Hereditary Succession," was simply deleted in the 1972 edition of *Political Dictionary*, published on December 31, 1973, by the same institution under the name Social Sciences Publishing House.

In the mid-1970s, in short, everyone in North Korea knew that Kim Chong-il occupied the second most powerful position in the country, and the DPRK regime never bothered to deny or squash persistent rumors about his forthcoming dynastic succession. Indeed, the DPRK launched a mass-media build-up for Kim Chong-il by using a subtle system of code words, slogans, and symbols— tending to counter any doubt about the junior Kim's intended future.[5]

The mass-media campaign proceeded on the premise that "the revolutionary cause pioneered and guided by the Great Leader" could not be completed in a generation, so it would be completed only through the efforts of succeeding generations. As was amply demonstrated in the past under the sole leadership of Kim Il-song, the single successor to the DPRK chieftain, who must emerge from the younger generation, was bound to play a decisive role in this historic task to "correctly inherit, defend and complete the Great Leader's revolutionary cause."[6]

The North Korean mass-media build-up for Kim Chong-il with the title "party center" in the 1970s was designed to bestow on the junior Kim a measure of authority and legitimacy as the truly worthy "sole" successor to the North Korean dictator. Since Kim Chong-il lacked the anti-Japanese revolutionary credentials that constituted the hallmark for top leadership in the Pyongyang regime, it was necessary to create an aura about him that would "prove" to the North Korean people that he possessed the extraordinary qualities necessary to be his father's single heir and the DPRK's future supreme leader. Thus, the mass media portrayed the junior Kim as a man "who is boundlessly loyal to the Great Leader, perfectly embodying his ideas, outstanding leadership, and noble traits, and brilliantly upholding his grand plan and intention at the highest level."[7] It was also said that Kim Chong-il had "bright wisdom, deep insight, strong sense of revolutionary principles and strong will."[8] In the 1970s, the DPRK mass media, as Morgan E. Clippinger says cogently, "attempted not only to transfer to the son the charisma of the father, but also to depict a father-son unity."[9]

Beginning in late 1973, KWP members and the populace referred to Kim Chong-il by the title "Comrade Leader" *(chidoja tongji)*.[10] Seminars or study sessions on Kim Chong-il's succession to the DPRK chieftain were held throughout the country. The junior Kim's pictures were hung on the walls of KWP headquarters and offices, other public buildings, schools, and private homes, along with the portraits of Kim Il-song and his family. Kim Chong-il's pictures, which were sold in department stores and bookstores, even became collectors' items for the North Korean people. His birthday was celebrated with athletic events, youth rallies, loyalty-oath sessions, and other observances.

There is a lack of solid information about Kim Chong-il, 43, and only the barest biographical details are available.[11] He is married and reported to have one daughter. He was born on February 16, 1940, in the Soviet Union, and is the North Korean chieftain's only surviving son by his first marriage. (Chong-il's Russian nickname was "Zhura," and he was raised by a Russian kitchen maid. His younger brother was born in 1943, also in the Soviet Union, and called by the Russian nickname "Yura." He was drowned in the Taedong River shortly before the Korean War.) Chong-il moved to Pyongyang with his family in 1945. He was in Manchuria during the Korean War.

He attended Nam-San School in Pyongyang, the predecessor of the present Red Flag Mankyongdae Revolution School, which is the DPRK's special elite school reserved exclusively for the children of high-ranking party officials. He later majored in politics and philosophy at the nation's best university, Kim Il-song University, which is also located in the capital. Shortly before or after graduating from the university in 1963, he may also have spent some years at the East German Air Force Academy.

While in his 20s, Chong-il acted as his father's personal secretary and worked for the KWP's Organization and Guidance Department under his uncle Kim Yong-chu. In the 1970s, he appears to have been promoted to progressively more influential posts in the Pyongyang regime. In 1972, he was named party secretary in charge of organization, propaganda, agitation, the three most important and powerful functions of the KWP apparatus. A year or two later, he is said to have been appointed a member of the all-powerful Politburo of the KWP. Since February 1974, the junior Kim has reportedly been in charge of North Korea's operations toward South Korea and Japan. In the mid-1970s, Kim Chong-il was apparently second to his father in supervising and overseeing the affairs of both the nation and the ruling KWP.

Since 1973, Kim Chong-il has been in the forefront of the DPRK's Three-Revolution Campaign,[12] which was personally sanctioned by Kim Il-song to raise the North Korean people's education, increase their technical know-how, and intensify their knowledge of the DPRK chieftain's ideology. The campaign comprises between 40,000 to 50,000 youths, both party and nonparty members, who are dispatched in groups of twenty to fifty members (the Three-Revolution Teams—TRT) to various administrative, educational, cultural, and other institutions to arm them with revolutionary thought and to teach them modern techniques of promoting production. The Three-Revolution Teams, which have been described as the North Korean counterpart of the Chinese Red Guards, operate separately from the party's existing organizational chain of command and report directly to the "party center"—that is, personally to Kim Chong-il.[13] Unmistakably, the Three-Revolution movement, of which the junior Kim is in charge, is an important step toward putting him at the top of the North Korean power hierarchy.

Kim Chong-il is said to have played an important role in the August 18, 1976, incident at Panmunjom in which two American officers were killed by axe-wielding North Korean soldiers. The incident resulted in a strong show of U.S. force. Strategic B-52 and F-111 bombers were dispatched to South Korea as a large force of American troops entered Panmunjom to cut down the tree that had been the center of the dispute resulting in the axe-death. After the incident, the North Korean chieftain expressed "regret" in language that was far more moderate and conciliatory than his usually belligerent anti-American pronouncements. To many foreign observers, the senior Kim's term of "regret" represented an apology.

Shortly after the Panmunjom incident, Kim Chong-il dropped from sight for two and a half years, leading to rumors in Japan that he had become a human vegetable following an assassination attempt on his life.[14] It appears that the junior Kim, who was blamed for endangering his country by exposing it to a potential U.S. countermove, was summoned back by his father to receive more political schooling and to serve more apprenticeship.

Beginning in the early spring of 1979, the expression of the "party center," which had not been used for the preceding two and a half years, began to reappear increasingly in the North Korean mass media.[15] As the renewed use of this designation began to escalate in 1979, reports of his visits to industrial plants and farms increased sharply. At the same time, some high-ranking DPRK officials and the League of Socialist Working Youth called for loyalty to the "glorious party center" in their speeches and meetings.[16] *Nodong Sinmun* has also been editorializing that the party, the army, and the public should rally behind the "party center." The DPRK mass media, as well as many political, social, and professional organizations, have attributed the country's achievements in every field during the past ten years to Kim Chong-il.[17] He was particularly credited with launching a successful drive to infuse the whole North Korean society with the *chuch'e* idea.[18]

According to U.S. Congressman Stephen Solarz (Dem.-New York) who visited the DPRK in July 1980, his North Korean guide openly acknowledged Kim Chong-il as the second man in the Pyongyang regime, saying that he would be the head of the country as a result of "our own choice."[19]

A North Korean propaganda broadcast beamed to South Korea in early 1980, which was monitored in the south and in Japan, said that it was the "glory and duty of the masses to uphold the successor to the Great Leader in high esteem," even though the North Korean dictator is still alive.[20] It also said that Kim Chong-il was a perfect extension of the DPRK chieftain himself.[21]

North Korean sources in Tokyo said in 1982 that Kim Chong-il was already running things in the DPRK on a day-to-day basis.[22] In mid-April 1980, meanwhile, North Korean reporters in Panmunjom said that the junior Kim was being referred to as "dear comrade leader" (*chinnaehanun tongji chidoja*) instead of the previous term "heart of the party."[23] Asked when Kim Il-song would retire and the DPRK would hold a formal ceremony installing Kim Chong-il as the country's top leader, they replied that that would be unthinkable before the senior Kim's *chingap* (70th birthday).[24] (This point was confirmed by the DPRK chieftain in mid-September 1980, when he, in his meeting with the visiting Dietmen of Japan's ruling Liberal-Democratic party, ruled out a major party reshuffle at the then forthcoming Sixth KWP Congress.)[25] The resumption of the elaborate campaign for Kim Chong-il's hereditary succession in the spring of 1979 was followed with the DPRK regime's announcement that the long-awaited Sixth KWP Congress would be convened in October 1980.[26]

Until his name and party positions were officially announced for the first time at the Sixth KWP Congress, Kim Chong-il's name had rarely appeared in the DPRK mass media, except as the "party center." This reticence was presumably to prevent South Korea and other enemies of the DPRK from gaining propaganda advantage by accusing the DPRK chieftain of dynastic ambitions.[27] Pyongyang also seemed to be sensitive to, or fearful of, adverse reactions from elsewhere in the Communist world, which views hereditary succession as ideologically repugnant, as well as from Third World countries whose friendship has been assiduously courted by the North Korean diplomacy. Probably for these reasons, Kim Chong-il's activities remained unpublicized. He seldom made public appearances, and he apparently had not received prominent foreign visitors.

Along with Kim Chong-il's rapid advance within the North Korean power structure, a posthumous deification of his deceased mother, Kim Jung-sook, has also taken place. (Until then, she had hardly been mentioned by the North Korean regime.) On the commemoration of International Women's Day in March 1975, Kim Song-ae (the present Madame Kim Il-song and Kim Chong-il's stepmother) eulogized her predecessor as an "indomitable Communist revolutionary fighter and outstanding woman activist" who "fought for the sake of the Great Leader, sacrificing her youth and life" through many years of anti-Japanese resistance.[28] Six months

later, she again praised the virtues and accomplishments of Kim
Chong-il's deceased mother as a revolutionary as well as for her
"total allegiance to the Great Leader."[29]

The twenty-sixth anniversary of Kim Jung-sook's death in 1975
was marked by special ceremonies, including the unveiling of a
bronze statue of her erected in the Tomb of Revolutionary Patriots
on Mt. Taesong in Pyongyang. On that occasion, North Korea's
vice-president Kim Tong-kyu (who was purged two years later)
paid homage to her as a devoted revolutionary fighter, among
whose services to the revolution were "screening the Great Leader
with her body and shooting down the enemy (that is, the Japanese."[30] "Sometimes she washed the Great Leader's wet socks and
dried them in her bosom, and sometimes she cut her hair to spread
it in the Great Leader's shoes." But she did not serve the Great
Leader alone. "She also held a comrade-in-arms who was suffering
from a fever to her bosom to protect him from the storm and rain.
There are simply too many stories to relate of the warm love
extended by Comrade Kim Jung-sook to the revolutionary comrades-in-arms."[31]

A song has also been composed in her honor, entitled "Mother
Kim Jung-sook, A Star of Loyalty."[32] And in recent years, portraits,
busts, and statues have been set up in many places (including her
birthplace, Haeryong, South Hamgyong Province), labeled with
such honorific titles as "unparalleled Communist revolutionary
fighter," "an independence (chuch'e)-oriented woman revolutionary
who devoted her life to the goal of Communist construction," and
so forth.[33] A revolutionary museum in her honor was built in
Haeryong recently.[34]

Undoubtedly, these campaigns to build up a posthumous
personality cult of Kim Jung-sook are designed to strengthen the
status and image of Kim Chong-il, subtly suggesting that his
revolutionary spirit and total loyalty to his father have been inherited
from his mother. In the same way, Kim Song-ae's praise for her
husband's deceased first wife subtly signaled that, as the country's
First Lady, she was fully prepared to accept the principle of
primogeniture and thus certify the legitimacy of the forthcoming
hereditary ascendancy of her stepson after the aging dictator's
retirement or death. Incidentally, she perhaps did this more
grudgingly than wholeheartedly, for the personal relationship

between Kim Chong-il and his stepmother reportedly has never been cordial and smooth. (In this connection, it is significant to note that Kim Song-ae was demoted in party ranking from 67th at the Fifth KWP Congress in 1970 to 105th at the Sixth KWP Congress in October 1980, where the junior Kim rose to the status of Crown Prince.)

The current campaign to build up Kim Chong-il as his father's political heir coincides with reports of the elder Kim's failing health in his old age and of the generational shift in the top echelons of the political power structure. Numerous photographs reveal a large lump on the back of Kim Il-song's neck, and he is said to have made a secret visit to Romania in late 1974 for treatment of this lump.[35] Some reports suggested that the lump was cancerous. However, the consensus of intelligence analysts, diplomats, and other government officials in Seoul and Tokyo is that the lump is benign and that Kim is in no immediate danger.[36] No hard evidence has so far surfaced to indicate any extraordinary physical problems.

Nevertheless, the senior Kim is 70, and there is reason to believe that he is not in the best of health. (He is a chain smoker.) He was reported to have prerecorded his 1976 New Year's message, which he had never done before; and the speech lasted only twenty minutes, one-third the length of his previous message. Ten days later, the DPRK media declared that it was the "most sacred duty" of the North Korean people "to ensure the longevity of the Great Leader," and urged a maximum effort to "lessen, even a little, his concerns for the country."[37]

In addition to his failing health, the DPRK chieftain is surrounded by a team of aging loyalists who have helped him run the country ever since their return from Russia in 1945. The average age of North Korea's top leaders in 1982 (excluding Kim Chong-il) was seventy years. As the old guard of first-generation leaders fade away, North Korea must undergo a critical period of transition in the top leadership of the party and the government. Indeed, illness and death have forced a major reshuffling of the DPRK's top political lineup in recent years. So far, Kim Il-song has been able to replace losses among the old guard with other long-time supporters, but replacements will soon have to be found among the ranks of the younger generation. The North Korean dictator must arrange a timely, orderly transfer of power to younger men or time will intrude to preempt a decision. The Fifth KWP Congress, which met in 1970, merely reconfirmed the existing leadership pattern. But the Sixth KWP Congress was highlighted, among other things, by a gradual generational shift in leadership.

Presumably, Kim Il-song is well aware that the succession of leadership following the demise of a dictatorial Communist ruler has been the most troublesome question for all Communist regimes. Therefore, while he is alive and still powerful enough to impose his will, he wants to prepare a smooth transfer of power.

The DPRK chieftain knows that the leadership will soon pass to the younger generation—men who have no active revolutionary background or who reached adulthood after his regime was installed in Pyongyang in 1948. His overriding concern in this context is to ensure that the younger generation, including the technocrats with a rational (nonideological) approach to economic and social affairs, will remain faithful to the revolution he has led for the past several decades, which is based on his nationalistic, militant *chuch'e* ideology. Kim emphasized the problem several times during his five-and-a-half-hour speech delivered on October 14, 1980, to the Sixth KWP Congress:

> The generation is changing in our revolution and this reality makes it all the more urgent to inherit and develop our revolutionary traditions. By steadfastly carrying on the struggle to inherit and develop the revolutionary traditions as an important task of party works, we should push ahead briskly with the revolution and construction and admirably carry forward the revolutionary cause of *chuch'e* to completion.[38]

With the upsurge of "postliberation" technocrats and younger cadres in the various state apparatus, Kim seems to fear that after his death, the younger generation may drift away from the norms of his "glorious revolutionary tradition," particularly his lifelong goal to reunify the divided Korean peninsula under Communist rule, and backslide into the seductive and "poisonous" bourgeois way of life. The Khrushchev-Brezhnev period in the Soviet Union and the Deng Xiaoping rule in post-Mao China are stark examples of such degeneration, and Kim Il-song seems determined to prevent a repetition of the Soviet and Chinese "tragedies" in his own country. The article "To Protect and Complete the Revolutionary Task Launched by the Great Leader Is the Firm Resolve and the Revolutionary Creed of Our Party," which appeared in the February 1977 issue of *Kulloja*, said in part:

> The traitors of the revolution are always maneuvering to sterilize and eradicate the revolutionary tradition. The history of the international Communist movement clearly demonstrates that if revisionist tendencies are allowed to surface, they will prevent the revolution from making any further progress.

In other words, Kim Il-song has been haunted by the need to place the most trustworthy successor in the power center to perpetuate his militant, fiercely nationalistic revolutionary cause as the governing ideology of North Korea after his death, without meeting the same fate as Stalin and Mao suffered after their disappearance from the scene.[39] Kim Il-song is aware that Mao Zedong did not fare well with both Liu Shaoqi (Liu Shao-ch'i), his heir apparent before the Cultural Revolution, and Lin Biao (Lin Piao), his constitutionally designated heir after the Cultural Revolution. Liu was purged as "China's Khrushchev" in the mid-1960s,[40] and Lin Biao allegedly died in Outer Mongolia in the aftermath of his failure to assassinate Chairman Mao in 1972.[41] Shortly after Mao's death in 1976, his wife, Jiang Qing, who wanted to carry forward the banner of Maoism, was purged by his hand-picked premier, Hua Guofeng, thus signaling a reversion to moderation in China's domestic affairs.

Meanwhile, Kim Il-song is perhaps impressed by the impeccable filial and political piety demonstrated by President Chiang Ching-kuo of Taiwan toward his father, Chiang Kai-shek. The only significant recent case of hereditary political succession outside of traditional monarchies occurred in Taiwan when Chiang Ching-kuo succeeded his deceased father some years ago. In dealing with his own problem of political succession, in short, Kim Il-song has apparently placed his faith in the old adage that blood is thicker than water. His own son's ascendancy as political successor signifies a firm guarantee that succeeding generations will inherit, defend, and complete his revolutionary cause of *chuch'e*. The DPRK regime asserts that the junior Kim's hereditary succession is a cornerstone of the *chuch'e* idea.[42] North Korean spokesmen are quick to add that Kim Chong-il has been chosen, not because of his bloodline, but because of his "embodiment" of the DPRK chieftain's revolutionary spirits.[43]

Kim Chong-il's designation, by and large, seems to be his father's own decision, probably made in consultation with his old Manchurian partisan colleagues, who have weathered all the political turns and twists by solidly supporting him and who now dominate the Pyongyang regime. His close comrades-in-arms, choosing their lifelong loyalty to their master and self-interests in power and security against Communist principles, have decided to support Kim Chong-il's succession actively.

The Sixth KWP Congress began on October 10, 1980, and ended on October 14.[44] It was attended by 3,062 voting delegates and 158 nonvoting delegates, along with foreign delegations from 118 countries (and 100 foreign media representatives). Among the foreign delegates were a member of the Soviet Communist party's Politburo, V. V. Grishin, and a vice-chairman of the Central Committee of the Chinese Communist party, Li Xiannian.

This was the first congress in ten years, although the KWP Charter provides for one to be held every four years to elect central party organs and to discuss and make decisions on major problems facing the ruling party and the nation. There was no plausible explanation why the ruling KWP had not held the congress for such a long time.

The Sixth KWP Congress was held to evaluate party achievements in the ten years since the Fifth Congress in October 1970, to adopt new programs, and to elect officials of the central party organs. But the main purpose of convening the Sixth KWP Congress for the Communist hierarchy in Pyongyang was to confirm officially Kim Chong-il as his father's future political successor. (Shortly after the meeting, *Nodong Sinmun* exhorted that loyalty to Kim Chong-il was a "fundamental requirement for flourishing the revolutionary tradition forever to firmly guarantee the [continuing correct] leadership of our Party," stressing that the Sixth KWP Congress "splendidly resolved the fundamental issue relating to the fate of our Party and the future course for our revolution.")[45]

For the DPRK regime, in short, the Sixth KWP Congress was an international showcase to display North Korea as a modern, economically strong country ready to be ruled by a new generation of younger leaders. As part of its important business, the congress elected the members of the Sixth Central Committee of the KWP (145 regulars and 103 alternates) and 14 members of the Central Auditing Committee.[46] The first plenary session of the new Central Committee elected the party's General Secretary (Kim Il-song was reelected) and the following members of the Presidium of the Politburo, the Politburo, the Secretariat, the Military Commission, and the Control Commission.

> *Presidium of the Politburo* (5)
> (in order of rank)
>
> Members: Kim Il-song, Kim Il, O Chin-u, Kim Chong-il, Yi Chong-ok
>
> *Politburo* (34)[a]
> (in order of rank)
>
> > Regular members: Kim Il-song, Kim Il, O Chin-u, Kim Chong-il, Yi Chong-ok, Pak Song-chol, Choe Hyon,[b] Yim Chun-chu, So Chol, O Paek-yong, Kim Chung-nin, Kim Yong-nam, Chon Mun-sop, Kim Hwan, Yon Hyong-muk, O Kuk-yol, Kye Ung-tae,[c] Kang Song-san, Paek Hak-im
> >
> > Alternate members: Ho Tam, Yun Ki-pok, Choe Kwang, Cho Se-ung, Choe Chae-u, Kong Chin-tae, Chong Chun-ki, Kim Chol-man,[d] Chong Kyong-hui, Choe Yong-nim, So Yun-sok, Yi Kun-mo, Hyon Mu-kwang, Kim Kang-hwan, Yi Son-sil
>
> *Secretariat* (10)[e]
> (in order of rank)
>
> General Secretary: Kim Il-song
>
> Secretaries: Kim Chong-il, Kim Chung-nin, Kim

Yong-nam, Kim Hwan, Yon Hyong-muk, Yun Ki-pok, Hong Si-hak,[f] Hwang Chang-yop, Pak Su-tong[g]

Military Commission (19)
(in order of rank)

Chairman: Kim Il-song

Members: O Chin-u, Kim Chong-il, Choe Hyon,[b] O Paek-yong, Chon Mun-sop, O Kuk-yol, Paek Hak-im, Kim Chol-man,[d] Kim Kang-hwan, Tae Pyong-yol, Yi Ul-sol, Chu To-il, Yi Tu-il, Cho Myong-nok, Kim Il-chol, Choe Sang-uk, Yi Pyong-won, O Yong-pang

Control Commission (7)
(in order of rank)

Chairman: So Chol

Vice-chairmen: Kim Chwa-hyok, Chu Chang-pok

Members: Kim Chang-hwan, Chong Kwan-yul, Yi Yong-mo, Han Sok-kwan

[a] Of the 34 Politburo members elected at the 6th KWP Central Committee, Choe Hyon died, Kye Ung-tae was demoted to candidate member, Kim Chol-man was purged, and Choe Yong-nim and So Yun-sok were promoted to regular members. Those who were newly elected to the Politburo's candidate members after the 6th KWP Congress are Kang Hui-won, Hong Song-nam, Chon Pyong-ho and Kim Tu-man.

[b] Died on April 9, 1982.

[c] Demoted to candidate membership in the Politburo in 1981.

[d] Purged in 1981.

[e] Hyon Mu-kwang, So Kwang-hui and Ho Chong-suk were elected to the Secretariat after the Sixth KWP Congress.

[f] Dismissed in 1981.

[g] Dismissed in 1982.

After the Sixth KWP Congress, only thirteen of the top party functionaries who were elected to run the party (and the government) in the 1980s had the same Manchurian guerrilla background as Kim Il-song. Several are old and sick and so theirs are largely honorary positions. The DPRK at the time of the Sixth KWP Congress was gradually undergoing an alteration in its political generations, grooming Kim Chong-il as its top leader. Another important sign of a generational change in the ruling hierarchy at the Sixth KWP Congress was the emergence of a group of technocrats in their mid-50s, which does not necessarily mean the entry of technocracy but which may merely substitute the younger breed of fanatics for aged ones.

Kim Il-song named five members, including himself and his son, to the Presidium of the Politburo, the supreme ruling machinery of the KWP. The three non-family members of this all-powerful party organ represent the three influential groups in the DPRK regime, respectively: Vice-President Kim Il, the top-ranking party cadre; Premier Yi Chong-ok, the technocrat; and People's Armed Forces Minister O Chin-u, the military man. But these three top leaders are old and will soon retire or die. (Moreover, they are not on the Secretariat, the KWP's nerve center.)

In terms of real power, the Presidium of the Politburo has only a two-man membership: Kim Il-song and Kim Chong-il. Kim Il, for four decades a colleague of Kim Il-song, has had little influence since ill health forced him to resign his premiership in 1976. Yi Chong-ok holds his position as the leading technocrat of the government, but he is believed to exercise little political influence. O Chinu, who is also a long-time associate of the North Korean chieftain, has his own power base by virtue of his long career in the army. But the 73-year-old defense minister is on the verge of retirement, due partly to his advanced age and partly to his ill health.

It appears that General O Kuk-yol, chief of staff of the North Korean army, who is about 50 and relatively young, has been gradually taking over the top army command post, since the middle of 1979, from General O Chin-u, to whom he is believed related. General O Kuk-yol is believed to be a close associate of Kim Chong-il, and he can ease the military's displeasure over the junior Kim's position.

Of the thirty-two new members of the Sixth KWP Politburo, besides Kim Il-song and Kim Chong-il, 31 percent, or ten persons, are connected with the military. If Kim Chung-nin and Chung Kyong-hui, both reportedly top anti-South Korean strategists, are included, the figure would rise to 37 percent, far above the 25 percent recorded during the Fifth KWP Congress in November

1970. With the backing of such top military figures, plus the support of other powerful generals close to Kim Il-song such as General Chon Mun-sop, head of the presidential security force, Kim Chong-il's claim to the succession is solidly based.

This military support is considered vital because the 700,000-man army has a strong voice in North Korean affairs. No one could hope to remain leader in North Korea without the support of the military. Now it seems that the junior Kim has become the military's candidate for the succession, though it is impossible to know whether this relationship is based on loyalty to his father or to the son.

The Sixth KWP Congress installed Kim Chong-il as the second most powerful man in North Korea. Specifically, he is second in the party Secretariat, fourth in the newly created five-man Presidium of the Politburo, and third in the party's Military Commission. The only persons ranked ahead of him were his father and two other aging or slowly fading party leaders. More importantly, only he and his father hold concurrent posts in all three strong arms of the ruling KWP apparatus. The formalization of the junior Kim's ascent was an explicit action installing him as heir apparent—just short of writing it into the party constitution, as happened in China to Lin Biao in 1969. The only other leadership positions that Kim Chong-il must fill to complete his one-man control of the DPRK in his father's fashion are in the Supreme People's Assembly, the country's rubber-stamp legislature, and on the Central People's Committee, the highest government organ.

It was clear at the Sixth KWP Congress that, as long as he remained healthy, Kim Il-song was reluctant to recede into the background by yielding power. At 70, he is still apparently in good health and not particularly old for leadership in Asia. The Confucian-based ethics of East Asia tend to respect the wisdom of older men over the vigor of the young. China's Senior Deputy Premier Deng Xiaoping is 77, Zenko Suzuki became prime minister of Japan at 70, while Taiwan's ailing President Chiang Ching-kuo is 71.

The Sixth KWP Congress revealed an intangible resistance of North Koreans to Kim Chong-il's heirship, indicating that the junior Kim's position as successor to his father was not yet firm. In his speech to the congress, Public Security Minister Yi Chin-su publicly acknowledged that there had been dissidence in the course of establishing Kim Chong-il's leadership and that there was still potential opposition to the junior Kim's hereditary succession.[47] Yi said, "Antagonistic and anti-revolutionary elements whose number was very small still remained." "We will protect our socialist state and system by preventing maneuverings of espionage agents, destructive and harmful elements, impure elements, and ferreting out all of them," he added.[48] He urged the workers of his public-security ministry to remain absolutely loyal to Kim Il-song and his son.

Warnings against "traitors of the revolution" who were disloyal to the DPRK chieftain and who opposed Kim Chong-il's leadership, coupled with the clarion calls for loyalty to the two Kims, continued after the Sixth KWP Congress. On the eve of Kim Il-song's 69th birthday in April 1981, *Nodong Sinmun* warned against "turncoats who discarded their revolutionary conviction"—their loyalty to the elder and young Kims.[49] "A man with conviction can be forgiven though he makes a mistake, but a man can be neither reformed nor forgiven when he sways and betrays his colleagues who stick to the revolutionary conviction," it said.[50]

An editorial in *Nodong Sinmun* on February 22, 1982, implied that some troubles were developing in cementing Kim Chong-il's leadership. The editorial "All Party Cadres and Members Should Become Real Revolutionaries Armed with an Unyielding Revolutionary Spirit" indicated that the youth of the junior Kim posed somewhat of a problem, when it said: "During the anti-Japanese struggle period there were the persons who were older than young General Kim Il-song, but who safeguarded and assisted him in earnest." The editorial twice repeated the following passage: "All party cadres and members should not forget their pledge of loyalty to the Party and the revolution throughout their lifetime, which they made when they were admitted to the Party."

Since the Sixth KWP Congress, there have been recurrent editorials in *Nodong Sinmun* stressing that loyalty to Kim Il-song also involves being loyal to his son. The most explicit appeal came on November 11, 1980, when *Nodong Sinmun* argued that "the revolution should be carried out just in the way the Great Leader wants and seeks to have it done." Other editorials in the party newspaper insisted that only "traitors of the revolution" or "phony comrades" were critical of their leader while they called for discipline and loyalty to the "party center" as he was carrying out the ideas of the "Great Leader."[51] An editorial in *Nodong Sinmun* on December 22, 1980, "Faithfulness Hotter Than Fire," exhorted the North Koreans to remain totally and absolutely loyal to Kim Il-song and Kim Chong-il by emulating and following the "noble example" of Kim Jung-sook.

North Korea, on April 25, 1981, urged all members of the Korean People's Army to uphold the party leadership, saying that "the army belongs to the KWP led by the party center." The call came through an editorial in *Nodong Sinmun*, "The Korean People's Army Is Invincible Revolutionary Force Which Preserves Our Revolutionary Ideas Under the Party Leadership," that appeared on the forty-ninth anniversary of the founding of the army. "All soldiers and officers should protect the party center politically and ideologically at the risk of their lives and guarantee the leadership authority of the party by all means," the editorial said.

As soon as the Sixth KWP Congress ended, the DPRK launched a campaign to create an image abroad of Kim Chong-il's "outstanding leadership." While bent on revealing "the greatness and virtue" of the junior Kim, North Korean broadcasting stations have been focusing their reports on world repercussions toward his leadership quality. For example, they have repeated reports of "congratulatory messges to Comrade Kim Chong-il from foreigners and their praise of his leadership."[52] Radio Pyongyang has reported lectures and meetings held outside North Korea to "praise the greatness and virtue of the cherished leader Comrade Kim Chong-il."[53] The apparent aim of this DPRK publicity campaign to promote the personality cult of the junior Kim is to implant the image of the young leader as one who is being "extolled" by foreign leaders, governments, and peoples, as well as to blunt possible domestic resistance to the plan for hereditary succession.

Since the Sixth KWP Congress, the DPRK regime has vitalized its drive to promote the personality cult of Kim Chong-il, crediting him with everything from having guided the overachievement of production targets to being the inspiration for new inventions and works of art.[54] An article in *Nodong Sinmun* on June 18, 1981, depicted Kim Chong-il as a "great luminary brightening the world with his brilliant wisdom." *Nodong Sinmun* declared on July 13, 1981, that "the road of revolution along which our People's Army and people should advance is the road our party center indicates." All North Koreans have been urged to study a thesis on the *chuch'e* ideology recently written by Kim Chong-il.[55] According to *Nodong Sinmun* on April 1, 1982, the junior Kim's thesis, which was read by Party Secretary Kim Yong-nam at the closing session of the national forum on the *chuch'e* idea on March 25–31, 1982, to mark the elder Kim's 70th birthday anniversary, is a guideline for party and state activities.

Since October 1980, Kim Chong-il has made numerous public appearances and embarked on a series of "on-the-spot guidance tours" similar to those undertaken by Kim Il-song for many years to inspire workers or to hand down new policy directives.

The cult of Kim Jung-sook, Kim Chong-il's deceased mother, has intensified since the Sixth KWP Congress. On August 17, 1981, two administrative units and two schools in Shinpa district, Yanggang Province, were renamed after her.

In mid-February 1982, North Korea awarded Kim Chong-il the title "Hero of the Democratic People's Republic of Korea," on the occasion of his 42nd birthday.[56] On February 28, 1982, the junior Kim, along with 614 other deputies, was elected to the Seventh Supreme People's Assembly. In the new DPRK government formed on April 15, 1982, however, his name was excluded from the new administrative leadership lineup. All the evidence shows that Kim Chong-il's delayed appointment as top government leader reflects discretion rather than denigration or uncertainty.

Probably to fend off the possible scorn of the Soviets, Chinese, or other Communists, the DPRK stresses the *chuch'e* ideology with regard to Kim Chong-il's political succession.[57] It asserts that the North Korean-style hereditary movement is justifiable in terms of the *chuch'e* ideology.

The Soviet Union and China, both of which had their own personality cults of infamy, must privately look on the extravagant personality cult of Kim Il-song and the dynastic political succession in North Korea with some distaste.[58] Mikhail Pak, a noted Korean-Soviet historian from Moscow who spent the first half of 1982 at the University of Hawaii as a visiting professor of history, told a South Korean poet, also a visiting professor, that the Soviet

Government was annoyed by Kim Il-song's rule based on political shamanism.)[59] But Moscow and Beijing have been very reluctant to reproach North Korea for fear of unnecessarily antagonizing Kim Il-song to their own disadvantage in the context of the continuing Soviet-Chinese rift. It was clear even before the convocation of the Sixth KWP Congress that the Soviet Union and China had no choice but to accept Kim Chong-il's ascendancy to power. After the congress, the two major Communist powers seem to have acquiesced to the junior Kim's new status, but without voicing their formal endorsement.[60]

NOTES

1. *Mainichi Shimbun* (Tokyo), October 12, 1976; and David Rees, *North Korea: Undermining the Truce,* Conflict Resolution Studies, no. 69 (London: Institute for the Study of Conflict, March 1976), p. 8.

In 1972, Kim Yong-chu became co-chairman (representing the DPRK) of the South-North Coordinating Committee, which discussed the political future of reunifying Korea, but he never attended any of the committee meetings in the mid-1970s. Throughout the inter-Korean contacts, he had been represented by Pak Song-chol, now Vice-President of the DPRK.

2. Tokyo Kyoto News Service in English, August 12, 1975.

3. Young C. Kim, "The Democratic People's Republic of Korea in 1975," *Asian Survey,* January 1976, p. 92.

4. See note 2 of this chapter.

5. For a detailed study of the DPRK mass media's build-up for Kim Chong-il through the use of semi-esoteric communication in the mid-1970s, see Morgan E. Clippinger, "Kim Chong-il in the North Korean Mass Media: A Study of Semi-Esoteric Communication," *Asian Survey,* March 1981, pp. 289–309.

6. See Chapter 3.

7. For this kind of mass-media praise of Kim Chong-il in the 1970s, see "Table 2: Treatment of the Same Theme in Official North Korean Documents and Mass Media," in Clippinger, "Semi-Esoteric Communication," pp. 299–300. For the repetition of this kind of praise by Pyongyang's mass media in the 1980s, see *Foreign Broadcast Information Service,* Asia and Pacific, October 14, 1980, pp. D33–D36, and January 7, 1981, pp. D5–D7.

8. See references in note 7 above.

9. Quoted from Clippinger, "Semi-Esoteric Communication," p. 304.

10. See excerpts from a DPRK educational booklet for use in KWP cadres training courses, written on October 10, 1975, the thirtieth anniversary of the founding of the KWP, reprinted in *Korea Herald,* September 7, 1976.

11. For the published biographical sketches of Kim Chong-il, see Kim Myong Chol, "Biography of an Infant Prodigy," *Far Eastern Economic Review,* March 5, 1982, pp. 30–32; and Shim Jae Hoon, "Watching the Son's Rise with Suspicion,"

ibid., pp. 30–31. Kim Myong Chol is editor of the Tokyo-based pro-North Korean publication *People's Korea*. Shim Jae Hoon is a South Korean.

12. The Three-Revolution Campaign covers the fields of ideology, technology, and culture. For the details, see Kim Gyo-hwan, "The Ideology of Three Revolutions," *Vantage Point*, June 1981, pp. 1–11.

13. On February 13, 1981, the DPRK regime disclosed that the Three-Revolution Teams were under the direct control of Kim Chong-il. *Nodong Sinmun*, February 13, 1981.

14. See *Tong-il Ilbo* (Tokyo), February 2, 1978; and *Japan Times* (Tokyo), February 4, 1978. See also this author's article in *Far Eastern Economic Review*, July 7, 1978, pp. 27–28; and John Sharkey, "The 1st Marxist Monarchy," *Washington Post*, October 15, 1978.

15. *Vantage Point*, March 1979; *Kita Chosen Kenkyu*, June 1979, pp. 9–10; and *Foreign Broadcast Information Service*, Asia and Pacific, January 10, 1980, p. D1.

16. See *Nodong Sinmun*, March 2, April 25, June 4, 1979; and *Foreign Broadcast Information Service*, Asia and Pacific, February 7, 1980, p. D3.

17. *Nodong Sinmun*, July 24, 1980, July 25, 1980, August 8, 1980, September 5, 1980, September 12, 1980, and December 29, 1980.

18. See references in note 17 above.

19. *Nodong Sinmun*, July 22, 1980.

20. *Foreign Broadcast Information Service*, Asia and Pacific, April 30, 1980, pp. D12–D14.

21. Ibid.

22. *New York Times*, March 4, 1982; and *Foreign Broadcast Information Service*, Asia and Pacific, April 19, 1982, p. D26.

23. *Korea Herald*, April 19, 1980.

24. Ibid.

25. *Foreign Broadcast Information Service*, Asia and Pacific, September 17, 1980, p. D7.

26. The nineteenth plenary session of the Fifth KWP Central Committee, held on December 12, 1979, adopted a decision to convene the Sixth KWP Congress in October 1980.

27. On October 14, 1980, the Japanese daily *Sankei Shimbun* criticized North Korea's nepotistic ruling system in connection with the imminent naming of Kim Chong-il as the successor to his father. "Could it be possible for North Korea, [which] calls itself a democratic people's republic, to hand over the reins of power to the ruler's son without resistance?" *Sankei Shimbun* also harshly accused the DPRK of fostering a personality cult, saying that North Korea was not qualified to criticize South Korea's internal situation, such as the suppression of human rights.

In a full-length essay published in the September 1979 issue of the Japan Communist party's monthly theoretical journal, *Zenei (Vanguard)*, Central Committee Secretary General Tetsuzo Fuwa of the JCP, in an unprecedented move, wrote a scathing criticism of the personality cult system created by Kim Il-song and of the political basis of his one-man despotism now reigning in North Korea.

28. *Kita Chosen Kenkyu*, March 1975.

29. Dong-Bok Lee, "North Korea and Its Succession Issue," *Korea and World*

Affairs, Spring 1977, p. 54.

30. Cited in *Economist* (London), October 18, 1975.

31. Ibid.

32. Seoul Hapdong, in English, March 16, 1976; and *Vantage Point,* September 1981, p. 16.

33. Pyongyang KCNA, in English, January 18, January 28, and April 26, 1976. See also *Nodong Sinmun,* February 20, 1976.

34. *Foreign Broadcast Information Service,* Asia and Pacific, December 30, 1980, p. D9; and *Vantage Point,* September 16, 1982, p. 16.

35. Eske Pirinen, "Son Takes Over After Kim," *Helsingin Sanomat,* April 16, 1976.

36. See, for example, *Washington Post,* March 1, 1982.

37. "It is the Unshakable Revolutionary Will and Faith of Our People to Remain Loyal to the Great Leader Forever," *Nodong Sinmun,* February 18, 1976.

38. *Foreign Broadcast Information Service,* Asia and Pacific, October 15, 1980, p. D25.

39. For the DPRK regime's expression of this need, see *Nodong Sinmun,* February 9, 1980, April 15, 1980, September 22, 1980, November 8, 1980, and December 7, 1980.

40. See Lowell Ditter, "Death and Transfiguration: Liu Shaoqi's Rehabilitation and Contemporary Chinese Politics," *Journal of Asian Studies,* May 1981, pp. 455-80.

41. For the Lin Biao affair, See Tai Sung An, *The Lin Piao Affair* (Philadelphia: Foreign Policy Research Institute, 1974), Monograph Series no. 17, pp. 1-67; and Michael Y. M. Kau, *The Lin Piao Affair: Power Politics and Military Coup* (White Plains, N.Y.: International Arts and Sciences Press, 1975), pp. 1-591.

42. See Chapter 3. See also "We Must Arm Our Society with the Idea of *Chuch'e* to Fulfill Our Historical Revolution," *Kulloja,* February 1977; and *Foreign Broadcast Information Service,* Asia and Pacific, July 17, 1980, pp. D1-D3, and August 4, 1980, pp. D11-D12.

43. *Foreign Broadcast Information Service,* Asia and Pacific, April 19, 1982, p. D26.

44. For the proceedings of the Sixth KWP Congress of October 1980, see Dong-Bok Lee, "North Korea After the Sixth KWP Congress," *Korea and World Affairs,* Fall 1981, pp. 415-40.

45. "Let Us Strongly Uphold, Splendidly Succeed to and Develop the Glorious Revolutionary Tradition of Our Party," *Nodong Sinmun,* December 8, 1980.

46. For the lists of these elected members, see *North Korea News* (Seoul), November 10, 1980, pp. 1-6.

47. For the full text of Yi Chin-su's speech on October 13, 1980, see *Foreign Broadcast Information Service,* Asia and Pacific, November 5, 1980, pp. D17-D20.

48. Ibid.

49. "The Revolutionary Conviction," *Nodong Sinmun,* April 13, 1981.

50. Ibid.

51. See, for example, "Loyalty All the Way Through the Anti-Japanese Revolution," *Nodong Sinmun,* January 25, 1981; and "Comradeship," *Nodong Sinmun,* January 26, 1981.

52. See, for example, *Foreign Broadcast Information Service,* Asia and Pacific, November 26, 1980, pp. D1–D2, December 1, 1980, pp. D5–D7, December 3, 1980, pp. D1–D3, December 5, 1980, pp. D5–D6, December 8, 1980, pp. D3–D6, December 10, 1980, pp. D7–D8, December 12, 1980, p. D6, December 18, 1980, p. D2, December 19, 1980, pp. D5–D7, December 29, 1980, p. D18, December 30, 1980, pp. D9–D10, and January 6, 1981, pp. D7–D10.

53. See references in note 52 above.

54. *Foreign Broadcast Information Service,* Asia and Pacific, February 18, 1982, pp. D5–D7, March 3, 1982, p. D3; and "Let Us Live Eternally as Kimilsongists," *Hyongmyong Choson,* February 16, 1982.

55. "The *Chuch'e* Idea Is the Great Guiding Ideology of Revolution Based on the Demands of a New Era and the Experience in the Revolutionary Struggle," *Nodong Sinmun,* May 31, 1982; "The *Chuch'e* Idea Is a Great Ideology Which Has Elucidated Afresh the Basic Principles of Social Movement and Revolutionary Movement," *Nodong Sinmun,* June 7, 1982; and "The Leading Principles of the *Chuch'e* Idea Are Powerful Revolutionary Weapons Leading the Cause of Independence to Victory," *Nodong Sinmun,* June 28, 1982.

56. *Foreign Broadcast Information Service,* Asia and Pacific, February 16, 1982, p. D10.

57. See Chapter 3. See also "Respected and Beloved Leader Comrade Kim Il-song Is the Great Leader Directing the Cause of *Chuch'e* to Shining Victory," *Nodong Sinmun,* November 19, 1980; "Modeling the Whole Society on the *Chuch'e* Idea Is the General Task of Our Revolution," *Nodong Sinmun,* November 24, 1980; and "Great Programmatic Work Indicating the Way to Brilliantly Accomplish Our Cause Under the Banner of *Chuch'e* Idea," *Nodong Sinmun,* October 20, 1980.

58. Textbooks of the Soviet Communist party conclude that personality cults run directly counter to Marxism-Leninism. It is the belief of Marxist-Leninists that history depends on the decisive role of the working class and the struggle of the masses. Such a historical viewpoint is incompatible with the cult of personality. "Personality cult is an ideology opposed to Marxism and it is derived from the world view of feudalism and bourgeois individualism," defines an official Soviet party publication. *Fundamentals of Marxism-Leninism* (Moscow: Foreign Languages Publishing House, 1963), p. 83.

In early October 1980, the Chinese Communist Party directly criticized Stalin for the first time in an attack on the personality cult, which also besmirched the late Chairman Mao Zedong. The party's theoretical journal, *Hongqui (Red Flag),* wrote in October 1980 that "although Stalin brought the personality cult to a peak, we went even further for Mao's personality cult during the Cultural Revolution." *Hongqui,* no. 17 (October 1980). For the post-Mao Chinese Communist regime's criticism of Mao's personality cult, see also "Power Should Not Be Concentrated in the Hands of Individuals," *Beijing Reivew,* November 3, 1980, pp. 15–17; and "On Personaltiy Cult and Other Questions," *Beijing Review,* December 29, 1980, pp. 13–15.

Chinese Deputy Premier Deng Xiaoping, in an interview with Italian journalist Oriana Fallaci in mid-1980, called such nepotism as the dynastic political succession in North Korea "feudal," hardly words of support for Kim Chong-il. Oriana Fallaci, "Deng: Cleaning Up Mao's 'Feudal Mistakes,'" *Washington Post,* August 31, 1980.

Stalin's portraits, along with those of Marx, Lenin, and Engels, were removed in August 1980 in connection with the removal of all portraits of Mao Zedong, except one that remains on top of the entrance to the Forbidden City in Tien-an-men Square, scene of mammoth support demonstrations during the Cultural Revolution.

59. Ku Sang, "After Meeting with a Korean-Soviet Professor," *Dong-A Ilbo*, June 30, 1982.

60. *Foreign Broadcast Information Service*, Asia and Pacific, March 8, 1982, p. D4; and *North Korea News*, December 21, 1981, p. 2.

Conclusion

As the 70-year-old Kim Il-song nears his twilight, he appears to be approaching the end of his long and remarkable career. And the DPRK is in transition from his long one-man dictatorship to the world's first Communist dynasty under his son Kim Chong-il. An important question arises, then, about what will happen in North Korea after the DPRK dictator passes away.

It must be emphasized that projecting the future of North Korea after Kim Il-song can be no more than an educated speculation at best. As of the present, no definite prognosis about the future of North Korea can be made since much will depend upon the pressures generated from its internal contradictions and its international crosscurrents.

Leaving aside those internal and external parameters of the unpredictable, ever changing world political configuration for the rest of the 1980s, there are some fixed political realities that will chart the future course of North Korean politics. They can be briefly stated. There will be a smooth transition of power from Kim Il-song to his son, as is planned now, so North Korea will remain for some years a doctrinaire society with a closed political system. In other words, the short-term trend of the post-Kim Il-song era would seem to favor the general thrust of the DPRK dictator's legacy. Whether Kim Chong-il's forthcoming ascendancy to the top leadership position would mean continued stability or potential instability in the politics of North Korea after the death of Kim Il-song remains to be seen.

Kim Il-song's closest associates and other loyal followers are confident, at least for the public record, that they resolved the succession problem at the Sixth KWP Congress. Privately, however, they seem to be fairly uncertain about whether the political succession scenario can survive long after the death of its originator. For one thing, North Korean pronouncements are frantically replete with the themes of loyalty, unity, and discipline, which seems to presuppose a tortuous path ahead for Kim Chong-il. If this analysis is correct, the political arrangement about the junior Kim may stand on more shaky ground than the DPRK regime is prone to admit, leaving the North Korean leadership succession an open and potentially thorny issue.

The tendencies and factors that have shaped the Kim Il-song era will influence but not predetermine the future course of North Korean politics, although the incumbency holds distinct advantages. Unpredictability can play havoc with North Korean politics as much as with any other politics. Kim Chong-il's capacity for outstanding leadership, or his lack of it, remains a critical question during this transitional stage. Will he match, or even surpass, his father in this regard? The answer will crucially affect the viability of the junior Kim's dynastic political rule in the future.

Kim Il-song believes that the maintenance of a highly nationalistic, militant, and rigid ideological regime is vital to the survival and preservation of his dictatorship in North Korean society. The concept of the ruling KWP apparatus as a disciplined missionary elite whose purposes transcend the daily affairs of the society it dominates has been essential, in his view. His thirty-four-year rule has provided a high degree of political stability and political consistency, but, concurrently, it has stifled individual creativity and initiative, thereby turning political stability into political stagnation and political consistency into policy dogma.

Under Kim Il-song (as in Russia under Stalin and in China under Mao) the mythology of the monolithic, continuous, and infallible supreme leader has been carried to its extreme. Flying in the face of the natural tendency of political men to divide over issues of power and policy, as the experiences of both post-Stalin Russia and post-Mao China clearly demonstrate, the insistence on political monolithism in the form of a dictatorship reinforces rather than reduces the potential for conflict within its ranks. Accordingly, conflicts within and among the broader groups in the North Korean system may begin to surface as soon as Kim Il-song disappears from the scene, althoug the very nature of Kim Chong-il's political succession is intended to prevent and even suppress these potential conflicts.

Change is the universal law of history, and no system—whether it be political, economic, religious, or some other complexion—can remain immune from this historical imperative. As the economy develops and the complexity and division of social functions become prevalent, the monopolistic position of an exclusive ideology may be gradually undermined. The present North Korean political system under Kim Il-song's unitary ideology is no exception to this rule, as such transitions in social phenomena are often experienced. In fact, there has already been tension between competence and ideology, as industrialization has advanced and the bureaucratic (technocratic) organization has expanded. The anguished attacks on "bureaucratism" by Kim Il-song and other top DPRK leaders relate directly to this and similar problems.

One illustration can be offered in support of the hypothesis of change. Kim Il-song's anti-Japanese armed revolutionary tradition in Manchuria in the 1930s has been invaluable to him in capturing and sustaining his power in North Korea. But almost a half century has passed since that tradition was established. To many North Koreans, therefore, his "glorious revolutionary tradition" may sound like a "splendid anachronism." In a rapidly changing world, they would consider it an irrational act to refer constantly to the fifty-year-old past for inspiration and guidance for the future. Therefore, the DPRK regime's endless references to Kim Il-song's anti-Japanese armed struggles as a model for all organizational and developmental works can be (as has already been shown) irrelevant and counterproductive in adapting to the new organizational and management requirements of a modernizing, increasingly pluralistic North Korean society.

Consequently, the need to bridge the gap between the ideological-political mission of the ruling KWP apparatus and the practical business of ruling and managing a modernizing industrial society would become all the more pressing after Kim's death. The crisis of "Red" versus "expert" would develop and deepen in this situation. In the highly politicized North Korean Communist system, where a union of both elements even in a single individual is stressed, there is no clear dichotomy between Red and expert. Nevertheless, the struggle between the two elements would be bound to be aggravated both within a single man and between all social groups of North Korean society. Seen in this context, the roots of the perceived cleavage in the post-Kim Il-song era can be located mainly in the tensions between the imperatives of a revolutionary ideology and the requirements of ruling and managing an increasingly complex industrial society.

Even now, some underground resistance appears to exist within the KWP and the government against the Kim Il-song orthodoxy and Kim Chong-il's political succession, as was revealed at the Sixth KWP Congress. There is no way yet to measure the extent of opposition, if any, among the carefully controlled North Korean populace. It is evident, however, that any possible opposition or dissident group constitutes a very small and silent, or muzzled, minority without any power base to challenge Kim Il-song's dictatorial rule.

There is a distinct possibility that a group of technocrats (middle- and upper-level bureaucrats in the party and government) may be secretly leaning more toward technocracy than toward Kim Il-song's militant revolutionary ideology and heritage. At the same time, they may be seeking to adapt the DPRK regime's theory and practice to the realities of a modernizing North Korea and a changing outside world, which would represent the type of revisionism that Deng Xiaoping encouraged in China after the death of Mao Zedong. Perhaps they blame the DPRK for the considerable economic problems or for mismanagement at the highest levels of the Pyongyang regime, as well as for an unbalanced sense of national priorities. This group may especially believe that the military expenditures—some observers put it as high as 20 percent of North Korea's GNP—limit the resources available for economic development and consumer production. According to these technocrats, the most pressing economic issues facing the DPRK are the need to improve its technical know-how and to acquire foreign capital in order to grow out of its persistent economic stagnation. They may believe that the Pyongyang regime must move increasingly in the direction of pragmatism or utilitarianism so as to obtain capital and modern technology from the advanced Western world and from Japan.

The role of technocrats is the central problem Kim Il-song faces in ensuring a stable leadership, dedicated to his doctrine, after his death. The development of the North Korean economy, especially during the 1970s, created a need for technocrats to run industry, the economy, and even some party functions. Their priorities of rational policy and access to modern technology may increasingly place them in conflict with the *chuch'e*-oriented policies of Kim Il-song. The DPRK chieftain frankly admitted this internal conflict during the Sixth KWP Congress. He warned:

> Party organizations must combat the self-centered tendency manifested among economic officials. Now this tendency is glaringly in evidence among them, hampering socialist economic construction to a considerable degree. Self-centeredness is a variety of egoism and expression of love of fame. Self-centered persons are fame-seekers who work for their personal honor and career. Party organizations must wage a major ideological battle against the self-centered tendency among economic officials, so that they work responsibly in the overall interests of the revolution from a firm party and state standpoint.[1]

Despite this criticism, North Korea's technocrats possess skills that are indispensable if the economic and social goals of the DPRK regime are to be reached, so their status and prestige are steadily rising. In other words, a new elite, armed with new power and influence, is emerging in North Korea, and this tendency is accelerating over time. As the ruling KWP apparatus seeks to replenish the DPRK regime by nurturing politically entrenched Kimilsongists, it is also placing great emphasis on training a huge army of technocrats in which each individual must acquire additional technical skills and experience.

U.S. Congressman Stephen Solarz observed during his visit to Pyongyang that English was one of the important foreign languages taught in North Korean schools,[2] an indication of the value placed on Western contacts. And the influence of post-Mao China's modernization campaign has begun to filter in, another sign of pragmatic inclinations.

The hypothetical resistance by North Korea's dissident technocrats in the post-Kim Il-song era must be balanced against the natural and powerful inclination of the Kim Chong-il regime to prevent any pluralistic tendencies from acquiring autonomous force within the DPRK political system. The new Pyongyang regime under the junior Kim will have its own logic and determination to survive and will thus strive to retard and contain pressures for change that threaten its political supremacy. Kim Chong-il is unlikely to seek to square the circle between revolutionary sweep and efficiency, between ideology and reality, by turning the focus of his regime from dogma to science or by making it less an ideological leadership and more a managerial apparatus.

The Kim Il-song legacy will live in the political foundation of the Kim Chong-il regime, and no mere exorcism could destroy it. But should the dissidence become more than hypothetical, Kim Chong-il would accuse North Korea's dissident technocrats of attempting to permit subversive ideas to gain a foothold in North Korean society, and he would assert—sooner rather than later—the necessity for imposing firmer ideological and political controls inside the country. Indeed, it would not be surprising if one of the junior Kim's reactions against dissident technocrats would be to move closer toward the extreme glorification of his father and the Kim Il-song legacy.

The tension or friction in the post-Kim Il-song era between Kim Chong-il and his die-hard political loyalists (the orthodox group) and the pragmatic technocrats (the reform group) can be generally defined in several areas. In domestic policy, the orthodox group will stress the ideological function of the KWP apparatus, doctrinal continuity, self-reliance, austerity, maintenance of highly centralized control of the economy, close supervision of the intelligentsia, and a heavily weighted industry-defense resource-allocations policy. The reform group, by contrast, will lean toward innovation and flexibility, pragmatic solutions of economic problems, greater reliance on material rewards than on ideological stimuli, more local initiative and less centralization, and concessions to the consumer.

In external affairs, the orthodox group will emphasize the necessity of continuing the "class struggle" abroad, especially against South Korea, the dangers from outside enemies, and the *chuch'e*-oriented policy of isolation. The reform group will stress the solution of internal problems, the prospects for a relatively stable international environment, the possibilities of developing less dangerous forms of struggle with the adversary abroad, the acceptance of "peaceful co-existence" with South Korea, and a turning outward to the advanced industrial societies so as to tap the most modern science and technology.

These, broadly speaking, are the poles around which the political struggle will likely evolve in the post-Kim Il-song period. Between the extremes, of course, the struggle over power and policy may produce a complex pattern of changing political combinations and shifting alignments. In this connection, it is important to note that the two groups in this struggle will continue to share one goal: they will remain fully committed to preserving the dominant role of the ruling KWP apparatus over society at large. Therefore, the reform group will not represent conscious champions of some form of democratization leading to the dismantling of the KWP dictatorship over society, though the orthodox group may accuse the reformers of this heresy if and when its future survival is at stake. The reform group will likely address itself to the problem of rule in the post-Kim Il-song North Korea: how can the ruling KWP apparatus, which was originally conceived as an instrument of revolution, be made into an effective agency of governance? Meanwhile, the orthodox group will devote itself to offering a relatively consistent, old-fashioned solution to the problem of justifying the role of the ruling Communist party establishment that is in danger of becoming an anachronism in an increasingly modernizing, complex society.

The possibility of resistance by dissident technocrats is an important indication that Kim Chong-il's future task in preserving doctrinal stability and continuity as his father's political successor will be arduous. An educated forecast is that Kim Chong-il will have to resolve several other major problems before he will be able to consolidate his power.

The ongoing de-Maoization in China may signal ominous signs for Kim Chong-il's dynastic political succession. Recent Soviet and Chinese history proves that disparate and contrary views are often hidden behind the facade of monolithic rule. And those who are secretly opposed to the junior Kim's succession would emerge once Kim Il-song were no longer on the scene to protect his son. (Korean history has numerous instances of treachery by high-ranking palace officials during critical transitions from elder king to younger one of the same dynastic family or from one dynasty to another.)

Another problem is related to Kim Chong-il's leadership position, which he did not earn through his own efforts but which was bestowed by his father: charisma cannot simply be passed on from his father to him. The North Korean people are not going to tolerate a bad performance, even though he happens to be Kim Il-song's son. The junior Kim will have to demonstrate his leadership qualities and competence and thus establish his legitimacy for hereditary succession when his father has gone. To do this while his father's awesome presence continues will not be easy, however.

An even more fundamental problem may be that political stability and economic development under Kim Il-song's long dictatorial rule have spawned a significant number of North Koreans who want more out of life than a self-sacrificing work ethic provides them. If the almost-fanatical devotion to the elder Kim's philosophy of *chuch'e* pulled a war-torn nation by its bootstrap, it also led North Korea to the stage where it perhaps epitomizes the best and worst of a fully nationalized "workers' paradise." The Democratic People's Republic of Korea is a misnomer—being neither a republic nor a democracy—and the economic gains made since 1953 have come at the expense of the individual.

Indeed, many North Koreans, particularly those of the postwar generation, may scorn the code of selflessness, hard work, austerity, and social conformity that the Kim Il-song regime has imposed. They may want more individual lives, less dominated by organizational and societal duties.

As North Korea has moved toward a modernizing socialist state, the various bureaucratic, professional, and intellectual groups within the system have become increasingly articulate. While none of these groups speaks with a single voice, each represents communities of interest and outlook. The DPRK leadership can less and less afford to ignore their weight and influence. The demand for reforms, popular pressures for greater welfare and material rewards, the desire for personal security and legality, and the stirrings for more freedom of expression will accumulate among these groups.

By and large, the silent majority of the North Korean population may secretly believe that their country has been gaining little from the *chuch'e*-oriented policy of inward exlcusivism under Kim Il-song's leadership. They may be weary of agonizing political pressures, austerity, and rigorous ideological drives. When the DPRK chieftain passes away, they may want to see the excesses of the Kim Il-song orthodoxy replaced by an orderly, moderate society with some scope for freedom and a good life.

Perhaps in recognition of these popular desires for reform and change, the DPRK's current seven-year economic plan puts more emphasis on the "improvement of the people's life" in the form of increased materialistic incentives to boost output. Whether this definition of improvement will satisfy the average North Korean remains to be seen. (After taking over his father's power, Kim Chong-il may assume that the domestic pressures on the ruling KWP apparatus could be contained if the long-neglected material wants of North Korean society could be satisfied to some extent. However, such a formula for bridging the gap between the DPRK regime and society will be inadequate on the face of it.)

It is also possible that there is still a group of dedicated ideologues within the KWP who are committed to orthodox Communist doctrine as it relates to the question of hereditary succession. This group may include some high-ranking DPRK officials who may harbor their own secret ambitions to rise to the top after Kim Il-song's death. These ideologues would be bent on restoring textbook doctrine, believing that Kim Chong-il's succession represents an outmoded, bourgeois, and reactionary practice.

There is also speculation that a group of professional North Korean military officers—particularly among the younger generation and in the technical branches—may not be enthusiastic about Kim Chong-il's succession. The recent appointment of O Kuk-yol as the armed forces chief of staff was probably intended partly to calm this group's discontent or opposition. These military officers may disagree with Kim Chong-il, who, like his father, will probably want to control and politically orient the military in accordance with the cardinal KWP principle of "putting politics in command of military affairs." So far, they appear to have positioned themselves to be patient and remain reticent. But as soon as Kim Il-song disappears from the scene, they will be likely to become vocal in demanding less stringent political control of the armed forces and more professional orientation of the military establishment based on expertise and specialization.

It is clear, however, that all the dissident or opposition groups, both real and potential, now constitute a very small, silent minority without any power base of their own to challenge directly or openly Kim Chong-il's forthcoming succession. They may be temporarily acquiescing to the junior Kim's ascendancy, hoping, meanwhile, that Kim Chong-il's power will last only as long as his father and/or the Manchurian partisan colleagues stay alive. But they are likely to become more vocal and assertive in the post-Kim Il-song era by jockeying for power behind the scene.

When Kim Chong-il succeeds to his father's leadership position, it is unlikely that he will immediately inherit Kim Il-song's power untrammelled and unencumbered. It is probable that the elder Kim's dictatorial authority will be shared by a collective leadership, as happened in Russia immediately after Stalin's death, with the junior Kim playing a dominant role within the collective leadership. For the time being, at least, Kim Chong-il will not be strong enough to rule North Korea single-handedly as his father has done. He will not have the personal appeal and stature of an authoritative national leader, and he will also lack his father's unrivaled prestige with which to enforce unity among the top leadership team.

Internationally, Kim Chong-il seriously lacks experience and skill in dealing with other Communist nations, including the Soviet Union and China. He will need support from his two powerful Communist neighbors if he is to succeed in establishing a firm power base in his country. Domestically, his relative inexperience in the art of governing will require him to seek the support, advice, and expertise of more-experienced party functionaries in discharging his responsibilities.

Kim Chong-il is really an unknown quantity. Only the members of North Korea's inner power circle have had opportunities to observe him and become acquainted with him. If he turns out to be weak and incompetent, the new Communist dynasty under the Kim clan would rest on very shaky foundations. Chong-il would gradually be relegated to the status of a paper tiger or even removed from office. In such circumstances, it is possible that his stepmother, Kim Song-ae, or her son Kim Pyong-il would try to fill the junior Kim's shoes, in collaboration with other personalities in the ruling group, in order to rescue the crumbling Kim dynasty. Madame Kim is an important political personality in her own right, and she has an unshakable faith in her husband's revolutionary orthodoxy and policy line. Her son Pyong-il is reputed to be bright, capable, and ambitious, and the sibling rivalry between him and his half-brother Chong-il has been reportedly tense and often stormy. Pyong-il is reported to have been sent to an East German university for a period, possibly to maintain family peace.[3]

On the other hand, if Kim Chong-il proves to be an able, intelligent man with the requisite traits of shrewdness, personal commitment, and drive, coupled with a necessary measure of ruthlessness to survive the endless intrigues of dictatorship, his dynastic rule would be likely to last a long time.

Educated speculation suggests that the junior Kim has the necessary qualities to survive. It is difficult to believe that Kim Il-song, who does not lack astuteness, would ever have contemplated the dynastic transmission of power to Kim Chong-il if his son has failed to live up to his expectations with respect to leadership quality and revolutionary devotion. As a seasoned revolutionary (and politician), the elder Kim must know that the survival-of-the-fittest doctrine operates with a vengeance in a Communist dictatorship, no matter who is involved in the scramble for power and leadership.

Kim Chong-il would surely try to consolidate and strengthen his position in order eventually to restore one-man rule in the fashion of his father. He would gradually eliminate the old guard and bring in younger men who were more dependent on him, and he would also infuse new blood into the top leadership. He would not be disposed to tamper with the highly centralized regime by which the country has been goverened for many years. As long as he controls the key centers of political power, there would be little relaxation either in North Korea's militant world outlook or in the internal demand for rigid conformity to the Kim Il-song orthodoxy. Indeed, the junior Kim might even try to outdo his father in order to prove the legitimacy of his political succession. With "politics and ideology in command," then, he would be very likely to attack and smash "bourgeois and revisionist tendencies," like Calvinists rooting out original sin.

Kim Chong-il would certainly remain loyal to his father's lifelong goal to reunify Korea under Communist control. This is the elder Kim's supreme goal, the mission in which he has never ceased to believe, the most deeply felt of his purposes. Chong-il might even have a compulsion to prove himself a worthy successor by attempting to achieve something his father had not. Under his leadership, therefore, North Korea's commitment to an eventual Communist takeover of South Korea would remain a perpetual threat to the peace and stability of the Korean peninsula.

In this connection, it should be remembered that Kim Chong-il is not a battle-scarred revolutionary; rather, he is a revolutionary grown up in an extremely comfortable greenhouse. As the beloved son of the DPRK dictator, he has lived in an artificial world where he is praised, flattered, and patronized. Having lived for four decades in an ego-gratifying political atmosphere, he may be even more narrow and impatient, more rigid and doctrinaire, and less informed and objective about the outside world than is his father. Such leaders often miscalculate, and the junior Kim is certainly capable of the most perilous adventures.

Though there is no immediate danger that the post-Kim Il-song regime will thrash about and muddle into a chaotic bog, the continuation of the old hard-line policy based on discipline, austerity, and sacrifice would be likely to present hazards for the new Kim Chong-il regime and could lead to popular discontent or unrest, especially among technocrats. (Historically, revolutionary puritanism and fanaticism rarely outlast one generation. And Kim Il-song's ideology will fade with him.) With the elder Kim's one-man dictatorship gone, moreover, his heir may be vulnerable to challenges by dissident factions and/or popular pressures for reforms.

The most serious challenge to Kim Chong-il's leadership in the post-Kim Il-song era, if any, would probably come from technocrats. It is possible that this challenge may be supported by professional, young army officers. A pragmatic (actually revisionist) coalition of technocrats and military professionals would strive for the repudiation of the orthodox policy line of Kim Il-song and its immediate replacement with other policies better adapted to the dull but efficient rationality of modern industrial society. These moderate elements are likely to be less fearful and more self-assertive than were Kim Il-song's old, close comrades-in-arms, whose lives were under constant threat from the paranoid dictator. They would advocate making a sober effort to redirect their country through a series of pragmatic reforms for domestic tranquility, bureaucratic normalcy, economic efficiency and affluence, and flexibility and moderation in foreign affairs.

In the face of this challenge, Kim Chong-il will have two options: to meet his technocratic and military dissidents halfway for compromise and accommodation, or to crush them once and for all. There seems little doubt that he would settle for the latter course of action.

First, the very logic of Kim Chong-il's succession instantly negates any possibility of compromise and accommodation between the contending groups. Furthermore, the junior Kim and his inner power circle of *chuch'e*-oriented fanatics of the younger generation will tend to be extremely self-righteous, rigid, and intransigent in their mentality and actions, for they have been raised under strict indoctrination in the most autocratic, closed society of North Korea. Accordingly, they are the kind of people who only know one thing—a war game to get what they want in the rough-and-tumble arena of North Korean politics—and they are not trained and experienced in the art of compromise and negotiation.

It is against this background that the death of Kim Il-song and Kim Chong-il's succession could trigger a brief but potentially dangerous period of internal turmoil in North Korea. No one can confidently predict in which direction this internal power struggle between the two contending factions would go; it could go either way, for anything can happen in politics. But it is important not to underestimate the entrenched power base of the Kim clan. Nor is there a guarantee—and it will be foolhardy to expect—that the moderate elements would easily win the power struggle and take over the leadership of the Pyongyang regime, in the same fashion as Hua Guofeng defeated the Gang of Four immediately after Mao's death. The coalition of technocrats and professional military officers could win only if the North Korean military establishment would support them or maintain a posture of benevolent neutrality—a highly improbable eventuality in view of the fact that loyal Kimilsongists continue to control the DPRK military forces.

If—and this is a big if—the power struggle could result in eventually placing more moderate elements in charge of the DPRK regime, both the United States and South Korea should not miss an opportunity to reassure Pyongyang that they would not take advantage of the internal political turmoil in North Korea. They should also signal their willingness to resolve issues that have stalled a formal peace on the Korean peninsula for nearly forty years. The messages or signals have to be delivered subtly so that the besieged Kim Chong-il faction would not be able to use them as political and propaganda ammunition to demolish its moderate opponents.

Indeed, peace in the East Asian region would be served far better if North Korea evolved into an independent, Yugoslav-type Communist state than if it relapsed into the reclusive, paranoid mind-set of the early Kim Il-song years.

There is an obstacle to that favorable scenario in which North Korea's moderate elements, the United States, South Korea, and, above all, the Far Eastern region would all benefit: if the internal power struggle develops unfavorably for the ruling Kim Chong-il faction, it could be a new cause of instability and even war on the fractious Korean peninsula. Unable to resolve mounting internal disturbances and convulsions in his favor and thus forced to make domestic reforms that discard his father's long-cherished political orthodoxy, Kim Chong-il would be tempted, or even prompted, to divert attention from domestic to external affairs by manufacturing a major crisis along the constantly tense DMZ in the Korean peninsula. By doing so, he may believe that he could unify his country and people behind his leadership and destroy his moderate opponents as the "capitalist enemies of the people," "anti-party turncoats," "foreign-worshipping flunkeyists," or some other convenient pretext, in the midst of wartime hysteria.

NOTES

1. Kim Il-song's keynote speech delivered at the Sixth KWP Congress on October 10, 1980, in *Foreign Broadcast Information Service*, Asia and Pacific, October 15, 1980, p. D25.

2. *Wall Street Journal*, August 21, 1980.

3. David Rees, *North Korea: Undermining the Truce*, The Institute for the Study of Conflict, no. 69 (London, March 1976), p. 6.

Bibliography

KOREAN-LANGUAGE SOURCES

BOOKS

An, Chang-su, and Pak, In-su. *Chuch'e-ae Songka* [The Song of the *Chuch'e* Idea]. Pyongyang: Samhaksa, 1977.

Baik, Pong. *Minjogui Taeyang, Kim Il-song Janggun* [General Kim Il-song, the Sun of the Nation]. Pyongyang: Inmin Ch'ulpansa, 1969.

Chogukui Jayu Dokrip gwa Inmin ui Haebang rul wilhayo [For the Freedom and Independence of the Fatherland and the Liberation of the People]. Pyongyang: Inmin Ch'ulpansa, 1968.

Choi, Myung-hak. *Maumsoge bichin Taiyan* [The Sun Mirrored in the Heart]. Pyongyang: Samhaksa, 1967.

Choson Chungang Yongam 1950, 1953, 1961, 1962, 1976 [Korean Central Yearbook 1950, 1953, 1961, 1962, 1976]. Pyongyang: Choson Chungang T'ongsinsa, 1950, 1953, 1961, 1962, 1976.

Choson Nodong-dang, Chungang Wiwonhoe Chiksok Tang Yoksa Yonguso [Party History Study Center, Central Committee, KWP]. *Hangil Palchisan Ch'amgaja dul ui Hoesanggi* [Recollection of the Participants in the Anti-Japanese Partisan Warfare]. 9 vols. Pyongyang: Choson Nodong-dang Ch'ulpansa, 1959–1961.

_____. *Inmin dul sokeso* [Among the People]. 3 vols. Pyongyang: Choson Nodong-dang Ch'ulpansa, 1962.

_____. *Choson Nodong-dang Yoksa Kyojae* [Teaching Materials on the History of the Korean Workers' Party]. Pyongyang: Choson Nodong-dang Ch'ulpansa, 1964.

_____. *Kim Il-song Tongjiui Hyokmyong Hwaltong Yakryok* [A Brief

Account of Comrade Kim Il-song's Revolutionary Activities].
Pyongyang: Choson Nodong-dang Ch'ulpansa, 1969.

_____. *Pulgul ui Panil Hyokmyong T'usa Kim Hyong-jik Sonsaeng*
[Mister Kim Hyong-jik, the Indomitable Anti-Japanese Revolutionary Figher]. Pyongyang: Choson Nodong-dang Ch'ulpansa, 1969.

Choson Nodong-dang, Chungang Wiwonhoe Sonjon Sondong-bu [Propa-
ganda and Agitation Department, Central Committee, KWP]. *Kim
Il-song Changgun ui Yakjon* [A Short Biography of General Kim Il-
song]. Pyongyang: Choson Nodong-dang Ch'ulpansa, 1952.

Choson Sahoe Chuui Nodong Chongnyon Tongmaeng Chungang Wiwon-
hoe [Central Committee, Korean Socialist Working Youth League].
Widaehan Suryong ul tara pae-u-ja [Let Us Learn from the Great
Leader]. 3 vols. Pyongyang, 1968–1969. Reprinted by Choson
Chongnyonsa, Tokyo, 1968–1970, 3 vols.

Chuch'e Sasang e Kichohan Sahoejuui, Kongsanjuui Konsol Iron [Theory
of Socialist and Communist Construction Based on the *Chuch'e* Idea].
Pyongyang: Inmin Ch'ulpansa, 1975.

Chuch'esidai e Inyom [The Principles of the *Chuch'e* Era]. Pyongyang:
Samhaksa, 1981.

Han, Byung-chun. *Kim Il-song Dongjiui Hyokmyong Hwaldong Yakryok*
[A Short History of Comrade Kim Il-song's Revolutionary Activities].
Pyongyang: Inmin Ch'ulpansa, 1970.

Han, Chae-dok. *Kim Il-song ul Kobal handa* [I Indict Kim Il-song]. Seoul:
Naewoe Munhwasa, 1965.

Han, Im-hyok. *Kim Il-song Tongji Uihan Choson Kongsandang Ch'ang-
gon* [The Founding of the Korean Communist Party by Kim
Il-song]. Pyongyang: Choson Nodong-dang Ch'ulpansa, 1961.

Hangil Mujang T'ujaeng Chonjokji Tapsadan [The Exploration Team on
the Vestigial Remains of the Anti-Japanese Armed Struggle Area].
Hangil Mujang T'ujaeng Chonjokji rul ch'ajaso [Visiting the Vestigial
Remains of the Anti-Japanese Armed Struggle Area]. Pyongyang:
Choson Nodong-dang Ch'ulpansa, 1960.

Hong, Chong-in. *Hyokmyongui Widaehan Suryong* [The Great Leader of
Revolution]. Pyongyang: Inmin Ch'ulpansa, 1969.

Hong, Ki-mun, and others. *Suryongnim e Pumaneso* [In the Bosom of the
Supreme Leader]. Pyongyang: Inmin Ch'ulpansa, 1977.

Inryu e Songka [The Song of the Mankind]. Pyongyang: Samhaksa, 1981.

Kang, In-duck, ed. *Kongsanjuui wa T'ongil Chonson* [Communism and
United Front]. Seoul: Tong Asea Yonguso, 1980.

Kang, Min. *Sachonman Choson Inminui Gyongai hanun Suryong* [Kim Il-
song, the Great Respected Leader of the Forty Million Korean
People]. Pyongyang: Minzyok Ch'ulpansa, 1967.

Kang, Sung-nam. *Saisidairul Sunotnun Widaehan Yongdo* [The Grand
Chronicle Crocheted on the New Age]. Pyongyang: Taeyangsa,
1969.

Kim, Chang-sun. *Pukhan Sibonyonsa: 1945 nyon 8 wol–1961 nyon 1 wol*
[Fifteen-Year History of North Korea: From August 1945 to January
1961]. Seoul: Chimungkak, 1961.

Kim, Chul-dong. *Sachonmanui Moksori* [The Songs of the Forty Million
Korean People]. Pyongyang: Hyanghaksa, 1978.

Kim, Il-song. *Kim Il-song Sonjip* [Selected Works of Kim Il-song]. 6 vols.
Pyongyang: Choson Nodong-dang Ch'ulpansa, 1960–1966.

———. *Kim Il-song Chojak Sonjip* [Selected Writings of Kim Il-song]. 7
vols. Pyongyang: Choson Nodong-dang Ch'ulpansa, 1967–1978.

———. *Kim Il-song Chojakchip* [Collected Works of Kim Il-song]. 5 vols.
Pyongyang: Choson Nodong-dang Ch'ulpansa, 1979–1980.

Kim Il-song Tongji ui Chungyo Munhonjip [Important Documents of Kim
Il-song]. 3 vols. Pyongyang: Sahoekwahaksa, 1971.

Kim, Jun-yop and Kim, Chang-sun. *Hanguk Kongsanjuui Undongsa, Cheil
Kwon* [The History of the Korean Communist Movement, vol. 1].
Seoul: Korea University Press, 1967.

Koh, Kum-chul. *Jogui pumeso* [In the Bosom of the Fatherland]. Pyongyang:
Moonyesa, 1968.

———. *Kim Il-song Tongjinun Choson Hyokmyongui Widaehan
Suryongimyo Sege Hyokmongui Tagwolhan Yongdojaui isida* [Kim
Il-song, the Great Leader of the Korean Revolution and One of the
Outstanding Leaders of the World Revolution]. Pyongyang: Inmin
Ch'ulpansa, 1969.

Na, Yung-yi. *Choson Minjok Haebang Tuchangsa* [The History of the
Korean People's Liberation Struggle]. Pyongyang: Choson Nodong-
dang Ch'ulpansa, 1958.

Nam, Hyuk. *Sachonman Inminui Taiyang* [The Sun of the Forty Million
Korean People]. Pyongyang: Minjyok Ch'ulpansa, 1967.

Nam, In-hyok. *Widaehan Suryong Kim Il-song Tongchi ui Yongdo mit'ae
Sungilhan Kyonghom* [The Experience of National Liberation and
People's Democratic Revolution Under the Leadership of the Great
Leader Kim Il-song]. Pyongyang: Humanistic Sciences Press, 1972.

National Unification Board. *Nampukhan Gyongje Hyonsan Bikyo* [Compar-
ison of the Economic Conditions of South and North Korea]. Seoul,
1980.

———. *Pukhan Nyonpyo* [North Korean Chronology]. 2 vols. Seoul, 1980.

Oh, Young-jin. *Sso Goonjung hahei Bukhan: Hahna ei Jeungun* [North Korea Under Soviet Occupation: An Eyewitness]. Seoul: Joongang
Moonhwa-sa, 1952.

Pukhan Ch'onggam 1945-1968 (General Survey of North Korea, 1945-1968]. Seoul: Kongsankwon Munjeyonguso, 1968.
Pukhan Yoram [Survey of North Korea]. Seoul: Ministry of Public Information, 1968.
Sachonmanui Taiyang [The Sun of the Forty Million Korean People]. Pyongyang: Dundaesa, 1969.
Shin, Seung-bok. *Hangil Palchisan Chamgaja dului Hoesanggi* [The Memoirs of the Anti-Japanese Guerrilla War by the Participants]. 10 vols. Pyongyang: Inmin Ch'ulpansa, 1970.
_____. *Inmindul sogeso* [Among the People]. Pyongyang: Inmin Ch'ulpansa, 1970.
_____. *Suryongui pumsogeso* [In the Bosom of the Great Leader]. Pyongyang: Inmin Ch'ulpansa, 1970.
Song, Sung-chil. *Choson Inmin ui Widaehan Suryong Kim Il-song Tongji ui Hyongmyongjok Kajong* [The Revolutionary Family of Comrade Kim Il-song, the Great Leader of the Korean People]. Pyongyang: Inmin Ch'ulpansa, 1969.
Yang, Ho-min. *Pukhan ui Ideorogi wa Chongchi* [The Ideology and Politics of North Korea]. Seoul: Korea University Press, 1967.
Yi, Chae-suk. *Kangchonui Yongjang* [Iron-Willed Brilliant Commander]. Pyongyang: Hyanghaksa, 1969.
Yi, Na-yong. *Choson Minjok Haebang T'ujaengsa* [A History of the Korean People's Struggle for Emancipation]. Pyongyang: Choson Nodong-dang Ch'ulpansa, 1958.
Yi, Yung-duk. *Kim Il-song Dongjiui Widaehan Chuch'e Sasang* [Comrade Kim Il-song's Great *Chuch'e* Idea]. Pyongyang: Inmin Ch'ulpansa, 1969.
Yim, Chun-chu. *Hangil Muchang T'uchaeng Shiki rul Hoesang* [Recollecting the Period of the Anti-Japanese Armed Struggle]. Pyongyang: Choson Nodong-dang Ch'ulpansa, 1960.

EDITORIALS AND ARTICLES IN *NODONG SINMUN* AND *KULLOJA*

"At the Central Committee Meeting of the KWP." *Nodong Sinmun,* December 15, 1956.
"Blood Ties with the Masses Is the Source of the Boundless Might of Our Party." *Nodong Sinmun,* February 3, 1981.
Choe, Hyon. "Arming of the Entire People and Fortification of the Entire Country." *Kulloja,* no. 12 (1966).
Ch'oe, Yong-kon. "The Great Leader Kim Il-song Is the Originator of Our Party's Revolutionary Tradition." *Nodong Sinmun,* April 1, 1972.

Chong, Kwan-yong. "The Glorious Victory of the Party's Economic Line."
    Nodong Sinmun, August 4, 1967.
Chong, Pyong-gap. "The People's Army of Korea Is a Trustworthy Protec-
    tor and Defender of the Revolution." *Kulloja,* February 25, 1967.
"The *Chuch'e* Idea Is the Great Guiding Ideology of Revolution Based on
    the Demands of a New Era and the Experience in the Revolutionary
    Struggle." *Nodong Sinmun,* May 31, 1982.
"The *Chuch'e* Idea Is a Great Ideology Which Has Elucidated Afresh the
    Basic Principles of Social Movement and Revolutionary Move-
    ment." *Nodong Sinmun,* June 7, 1982.
"The *Chuch'e* Torch Will Ablaze Forever." *Nodong Sinmun,* May 9, 1982.
"Comradeship." *Nodong Sinmun,* January 26, 1981.
"Firm Establishment of *Chuch'e* Is a Definite Guarantee for Splendid
    Achievement of Revolutionary Tasks." *Nodong Sinmun,* July 1,
    1981.
"For a Correct Understanding of *Chuch'e.*" *Nodong Sinmun,* July 21, 1956.
"For an Effective Fulfillment of the Economic Plan for 1957." *Nodong Sin-
    mun.* December 16, 1956.
"For the Victory of Marxism-Leninism." *Nodong Sinmun,* December 7,
    1960.
"The Glorious Armed Forces Which Created a Model of Loyalty to the Party
    and Its Leader." *Nodong Sinmun,* July 13, 1981.
"The Glorious KWP Inheriting and Developing the Brilliant Tradition of
    the Anti-Japanese Revolution." *Nodong Sinmun,* February 9, 1980.
"Great Leadership Enhacing the Revolution and Construction to New
    Heights Through Brave Operation." *Nodong Sinmun,* April 28, 1981.
"Great March." *Nodong Sinmun,* June 18, 1981.
"Great Programmatic Work Indicating the Way to Brilliantly Accomplish
    Our Cause Under the Banner of the *Chuch'e* Idea." *Nodong Sinmun,*
    October 20, 1980.
"Historic Works Representing Programmatic Banner in Enhancing Party
    Militant Power and Leadership." *Nodong Sinmun,* December 18,
    1980.
"The Immense Glory and Happiness of Our People Led by the Great
    Leader." *Kulloja,* April 1974.
"Independence and Proletarian Internationalism." *Kulloja,* July 1, 1969.
"It Is the Unshakable Revolutionary Will and Faith of Our People to Remain
    Loyal to the Great Leader Forever." *Nodong Sinmun,* February 18
    and 19, 1976.
Kim, Il-song. "On Some Theoretical Problems of Socialist Economy."
    Nodong Sinmun, March 1, 1969.
_____. "Summary Report of the Work of the Central Committee of the

Fifth Congress of the Korean Workers' Party." *Nodong Sinmun,* November 3, 1970.

Kim Il. "Concerning the Six-Year Plan (1971–1976) for the Development of the People's Economy of the DPRK." *Nodong Sinmun,* November 10, 1970.

Kim, Yong-chu. "The Respected Leader Kim Il-song Is the Great Man of Thought and the Great Theorist in Our Times." *Nodong Sinmun,* April 13, 1972.

Kim, Yong-nam. "It Is a Most Glorious Task for Our People to Carry Out the Revolutionary Cause to the End, Holding High the Party Leadership." *Nodong Sinmun,* September 22, 1980.

"The Leading Principles of the *Chuch'e* Idea Are Powerful Revolutionary Weapons Leading the Cause of Independence to Victory." *Nodong Sinmun,* June 28, 1982.

"Let Us Defend Our Independence!" *Nodong Sinmun,* August 12, 1966.

"Let Us Defend the Socialist Camp." *Nodong Sinmun,* October 28, 1963.

"Let Us Firmly Establish the Revolutionary Traits to Unconditionally Carry Out the Party's Decisions and Directives Throughout the Entire Party *Nodong Sinmun,* December 1, 1980.

"Let Us Firmly Establish the Revolutionary Traits to Unconditionally Carry Out the Party's Decisions and Directives Throughout the Entire Party." *Nodong Sinmun,* December 1, 1980.

"Let Us Further Increase the Militant Power of Party Organizations."*Nodong Sinmun,* December 29, 1980.

"Let Us Glorify Forever, Generation After Generation, the Great Revolutionary Achievements Attained by the Respected and Beloved Leader Comrade Kim Il-song." *Nodong Sinmun,* April 15, 1980.

"Let Us Make an All-Out Advance to Implement the Directives of the Sixth Congress." *Nodong Sinmun,* January 9, 1981.

"Let Us More Firmly Arm Ourselves with the *Chuch'e* Idea of Our Party." *Nodong Sinmun,* May 3, 1982.

"Let Us Protect the Socialist Camp." *Nodong Sinmun,* October 28, 1980.

"Let Us Realize the Great Ideology for National Unity Established in the Flame of Our Anti-Japanese Struggle." *Nodong Sinmun,* May 5, 1981.

"Let Us Resolutely Safeguard the Glorious Revolutionary Tradition of Our Party and Brilliantly Inherit and Develop It." *Nodong Sinmun,* November 8, 1980.

"Let Us Thoroughly Implement the Party's Leadership in the Revolution and Construction." *Nodong Sinmun,* December 19, 1980.

"Let Us the Whole Party and the Whole People Complete the Revolutionary Cause to the End by Firmly Uniting Around the Party and the Leader." *Nodong Sinmun,* October 21, 1980.

"Loyalty All the Way Through the Anti-Japanese Revolution." *Nodong Sinmun*, January 25, 1981.

"Loyalty to the Party and the Leader Is the Basic Trait of *Chuch'e*-type Communist Revolutionaries." *Nodong Sinmun*, October 5 and 6, 1980.

"Modeling the Whole Society on the *Chuch'e* Idea Is the Great Task of Our Revolution." *Nodong Sinmun*, November 24, 1980.

"The Nonaligned Movement Is the Anti-War, Peace Force." *Nodong Sinmun*, September 17, 1980.

O, Chin-u. "The Workers' Party of Korea Is the Great Guide Leading the Revolutionary Cause Along One Road of Victory Under the Banner of the *Chuch'e* Idea." *Nodong Sinmun*, September 3, 1980.

_____. "The Future Path of Our Revolution Under the Leadership of the Great Leader Kim Il-song Is Endlessly Bright." *Nodong Sinmun*, February 26, 1982.

O, Paek-yong. "Respected and Beloved Comrade Kim Il-song Is the Great Leader Who Laid a Solid Foundation for the Founding of Our Party." *Nodong Sinmun*, September 2, 1980.

O, Tong-uk. "The Concept of Self-Identity and Our Scientific and Technological Development." *Kulloja*, July 30, 1968.

"On the Brilliant Road of Building a *Chuch'e*-type Literature and Art." *Nodong Sinmun*, September 5, 1980.

"On the Road to the Flower Garden in Which the Revolutionary Art Films Are Blooming in Accordance with the Party's Guidance." *Nodong Sinmun*, July 24 and 25, 1980.

"Our Musical Art Brilliantly Flourishing and Developing in Conformity with the Demand of the Times and Popular Masses." *Nodong Sinmun*, December 29, 1980.

"Our Party Is the Banner of Guidance Pioneering the Future Path of Communism Under the Slogan of Imbuing the Entire Society with the *Chuch'e* Idea." *Nodong Sinmun*, August 20, 1980.

"Our People Will Continue to Advance Upholding the Banner of Nonalignment, the Banner of Independence." *Nodong Sinmun*, August 24, 1980.

"Party Organizations Should Victoriously Support the General Advance of the New Year." *Nodong Sinmun*, January 7, 1981.

"The People Praise Their Leader." *Nodong Sinmun*, December 22, 1980.

"To Protect and Complete the Revolutionary Task Launched by the Great Leader Is the Firm Resolve and the Revolutionary Creed of Our Party." *Kulloja*, February 1977.

"The Respected and Beloved Leader Comrade Kim Il-song Is a Great Ideological Theoretician and Man of Action." *Nodong Sinmun*, April 11, 1982.

"Respected and Beloved Leader Comrade Kim Il-song Is the Great Leader Directing the Cause of *Chuch'e* to Shining Victory." *Nodong Sinmun*, November 19, 1980.

"The Respected and Beloved Leader Comrade Kim Il-song Is the Great Leader Who Brilliantly Pioneered Our People's Fate." *Nodong Sinmun*, April 10, 1981.

"The Revolutionary Conviction." *Nodong Sinmun*, April 13, 1981.

"Revolutionary Morale Prevailing Among the Anti-Japanese Revolutionary Rank and File." *Nodong Sinmun*, June 28, 1981.

"The Revolutionary Task of Our People Under the Wise Leadership of the Great Leader Comrade Kim Il-song Is Invincible." *Kulloja*, April 15, 1969.

Sin, Tong-sop. "Further Development of the Machine Industry Is Urgent." *Kulloja*, March 15, 1969.

Song, Pok-ki. "The Central Problem in Chemicalizing the National Economy." *Kulloja*, November 30, 1967.

"Steel-Strong Unity and Cohesion of the Whole Party Is a Firm Guarantee for Accomplishing the Cause of *Chuch'e*." December 22, 1980.

"The Three-Revolution Team Is a Powerful Revolutionary Guidance." *Nodong Sinmun*, July 23, 1981.

"Under the Invincible Banner of Proletarian Internationalism." *Kulloja*, November 25, 1956.

"Voices Echoing from Distant Places." *Nodong Sinmun*, September 12, 1980.

"We Must Arm Our Society with the Idea of *Chuch'e* to Fulfill Our Historical Revolution." *Kulloja*, February 1977.

Yi, Chong-ok. "The KWP Is the Great Guide Leading the Republic Along the Road of Prosperity and Grandeur." *Nodong Sinmun*, September 15, 1980.

Yim, Chun-chu. "The Respected and Beloved Comrade Kim Il-song Is the Great Leader Who Has Glorified Our People as a Prestigious and Independent Nation." *Nodong Sinmun*, March 16, 1982.

OTHER JOURNAL AND MAGAZINE ARTICLES

An, Yong. "Better Quality Control in Production Needed." *Minchu Choson*, July 19, 1968.

Choe, Tok-sun. "The Present Situation of Our Country's Metals Industries and Prospect." *Kyongje Konsol*, June 1965.

Chon, Kwan-u. "New Test in Korean Historiography." *Sasange*, May 1966.

"The Great Leader Comrade Kim Il-song Is the Founder and Leader of the First State of Proletarian Dictatorship in Our Country." *Minchu Choson*, January 10, 1972.

Han, Sol-ya. "General Kim Il-song as Seen by a Writer." *Minsong*, January–February 1947.

Koo, Sang. "After Meeting with a Soviet-Korean Professor." *The Dong-A Ilbo*, June 30, 1982.

Lee, Chol-chu. "The North Korean Communist Party." *Sin Tong A*, May 1965.

――――. "The Fate of North Korean State Artists." *Sasange*, August 1965.

"Let Us Live Eternally as Kimilsongists." *Hyongmyong Choson*, February 16, 1982.

Pak, Tong-un. "Search for Unification Policy—North-South Unification as the Key to Solution of Korean Problems." *Sasange*, March 1964.

"The Path Followed by the Korean Historical Academic World Since the August 15 Liberation." *Yoksa Kwahak*, no. 4 (1960).

So, Nam-won. "The Fabrication of North Korean Economic Statistics." *Sin Tong A*, August 1965.

――――. "Twenty Years of North Korean Economic Transformation: Kim Il-song and 'The Flying Horse Movement' Economy." *Sasange*, August 1965.

NORTH KOREAN BROADCASTS MONITORED

(Clandestine) Voice of the Revolutionary Party for Reunification, In Korea, to South Korea, April 14, 1980. "VRRP Cites Seminars on Kim Il-song's Successor." *Foreign Broadcast Information Service*, Asia and Pacific, April 14, 1980, p. D1.

――――. "The Sun Ray of Guidance Which Is Brilliantly Carrying Out the Cause of Guidance." *Foreign Broadcast Information Service*, Asia and Pacific, April 30, 1980, pp. D12–D14.

――――. "Inheriting the Leader's Revolutionary Cause Is an Important Question Concerning the Future of the Revolution." *Foreign Broadcast Information Service*, Asia and Pacific, June 9, 1980, pp. D6–D8.

――――. Panel Discussion on the 'Glorious Party Center.'" *Foreign Broadcast Information Service*, Asia and Pacific, June 30, 1980, pp. D11–D12.

――――. "Discussion on the Successor to the Leader." *Foreign Broadcast Information Service*, Asia and Pacific, July 10, 1980, pp. D4–D7.

――――. " 'Ray of Guidance' Feature on Succession to the Leader." *Foreign Broadcast Information Service*, Asia and Pacific, July 11, 1980, pp. D5–D7.

――――. "Roundtable Discussion on the Successor to the Leader." *Foreign Broadcast Information Service*, Asia and Pacific, July 14, 1980, pp. D1–D3.

――――. "Orthodoxy of a *Chuch'e*-type Successor." *Foreign Broadcast*

Information Service, Asia and Pacific, July 17, 1980, pp. D1–D3.

_____. "The Revolutionary Cause of *Chuch'e* Is the Most Glorious Revolutionary Cause in History." *Foreign Broadcast Information Service*, Asia and Pacific, August 4, 1980, pp. D11–D12.

_____. "Unattributed Talk." *Foreign Broadcast Information Service*, Asia and Pacific, August 8, 1980, pp. D1–D2.

_____. "Dialogue Between Two Unidentified Speakers." *Foreign Broadcast Information Service*, Asia and Pacific, October 14, 1980, pp. D33–D36.

_____. " 'Ray of Guidance' Program: The True Meaning of Solving the Question of the Successor to the Leader." *Foreign Broadcast Information Service*, Asia and Pacific, November 18, 1980, pp. D8–D9.

ENGLISH-LANGUAGE SOURCES

BOOKS

Acheson, Dean. *The Korean War.* New York: W. W. Norton, 1971.

Lord Acton (John Emerich Edmund Dalberg-Acton). *Essays on Freedom and Power.* Selected, and with an Introduction, by Gertrude Himmelfarb. Prefaced by Herman Finer. Boston: Beacon Press, 1948.

Baik, Bong. *Kim Il-song Biography: From Birth to Triumphant Return to Homeland.* 3 vols. New York: The Guardian, 1969.

Barnds, William, ed. *The Two Koreas in East Asian Affairs,* New York: New York University Press, 1976.

Berger, Carl. *The Korea Knot: A Military-Political History.* Philadelphia: University of Pennsylvania Press, 1967.

Brief History of the Revolutionary Activities of Comrade Kim Il-song. Pyongyang: Foreign Languages Publishing House, 1969.

Brun, Ellen, and Hersh, Jacques. *Socialist Korea.* New York and London: Monthly Review Press, 1976.

Cho, Soon-sung. *Korea in World Politics, 1940–1950.* Berkeley: University of California Press, 1970.

Chuch'e: The Speeches and Writings of Kim Il-song. New York: Grossman Publishers, 1972.

Chung, Chin O. *Pyongyang Between Peking and Moscow: North Korea's Involvement in the Sino-Soviet Dispute, 1958–1975.* University, Alabama: University of Alabama Press, 1978.

Chung, Henry. *The Russians Came to Korea.* Washington, D.C.: Korean Pacific Press, 1947.

Chung, Joseph S. *The North Korean Economy: Structure and Development.* Stanford, Calif.: Hoover Institution Press, 1974.

Clough, Ralph N. *Deterrence and Defense in Korea: The Role of United States Forces.* Washington, D.C.: Brookings Institution, 1976.

Democratic People's Republic of Korea. *The Third Congress of the Workers' Party of Korea: Documents and Materials, April 23-29, 1956.* Pyongyang: Foreign Languages Publishing House, 1956.

————. *Documents on the Eighth Session of the Second Supreme People's Republic of Korea.* Pyongyang: Foreign Languages Publishing House, 1960.

————. *Democratic People's Republic of Korea.* Pyongyang: Foreign Languages Publishing House, 1958.

————. *Education and Culture in the Democratic People's Republic of Korea, 1945-1960.* Pyongyang: Foreign Languages Publishing House, 1960.

————. *Documents of the Fourth Congress of the Workers' Party of Korea.* Pyongyang: Foreign Languages Publishing House, 1961.

————. *Facts About Korea.* Pyongyang: Foreign Language Publishing House, 1961.

Djilas, Milovan. *The New Class.* New York: Praeger, 1957.

Freedman, R. O. *Economic Warfare in the Communist Bloc.* New York: Praeger, 1970.

Fundamentals of Marxism-Leninism. Moscow: Foreign Languages Publishing House, 1963.

Ginsburgs, George, and Kim, Roy U. T. *Calendar of Diplomatic Affairs of the Democratic People's Republic of Korea, 1945-1975.* Moorestown, N. J.: Symposia Press, 1977.

Henderson, Gregory. *Korea: The Politics of the Vortex.* Cambridge, Mass.: Harvard University Press, 1968.

Hoxha, Enver. *Reflections on China.* 2 vols. Tirana, Albania: The "8" Nentori Publishing House, 1979.

Hwang, In K. *The Neutralized Unification of Korea.* Cambridge, Mass.: Schenkman, 1980.

International Institute for Strategic Studies. *The Military Balance, 1979-1980.* London, 1980.

————. *The Military Balance, 1981-1982.* London, 1982.

Japanese Defense Agency. *Defense of Japan 1979.* Tokyo, 1979.

Jo, Yung-hwan, ed. *Korea's Response to the West.* Kalamazoo, Mich.: The Korean Research and Publications, 1971.

Khrushchev, Nikita S. *Khrushchev Remembers.* Translated and edited by Strobe Talbott. Boston: Little, Brown and Co., 1970.

Kim, C. I. Eugene, and Kim, Han-kyo. *Korea and the Politics of Imperialism.* Berkeley and Los Angeles: University of California Press, 1968.

Kim, Hak Joon. *The Unification Policy of South and North: A Comparative*

Study. Seoul: Seoul National University Press, 1977.

Kim, Ilpyong J. *Communist Politics in North Korea*. New York: Praeger, 1975.

Kim, Il-song. *Selected Works*. 5 vols. Pyongyang: Foreign Languages Publishing House, 1965–1972.

———. *On Some Theoretical Problems of the Socialist Economy*. Pyongyang: Foreign Languages Publishing House, 1969.

———. *Report on Work of Central Committee to the Fifth Congress Workers' Party of Korea*. London: Africa-Magazine Ltd., 1971.

———. *Revolution and Socialist Construction*. New York: International Publishers, 1971.

———. *On Some Problems of Our Party's Chuch'e Idea and the Government of the Republic's Internal and External Policies. Answers to the Questions Raised by Journalists of the Japanese Newspaper Mainichi Shimbun, September 17, 1972*. Pyongyang: Foreign Languages Publishing House, 1972.

———. *For the Independent Peaceful Reunification of Korea*. New York: International Publishers, 1975.

Kim, Se-jin, ed. *Korean Unification: Some Source Materials with an Introduction*. Seoul: Research Center for Peace and Unification, 1976.

———. *Problems of Korean Unification*. Seoul: Research Center for Peace and Unification, 1976.

———. *Politics of Korean Reunification*. Seoul: Research Center for Peace and Unification, 1977.

Kim, Se-jin, and Cho, Chang-hyun, eds. *Government and Politics of Korea*. Silver Spring, Md.: Research Institute on Korean Affairs, 1972.

———. *Korea: A Divided Nation*. Silver Spring, Md.: The Research Institute on Korean Affairs, 1976.

Kim, Se-jin, and Chung, Chong-shik, eds. *Korean Unification: Source Materials with an Introduction*. Seoul: Research Center for Peace Unification, 1976–1979.

Kiyosaki, Wayne S. *North Korea's Foreign Relations: The Politics of Accommodation, 1945–1975*. New York: Praeger, 1976.

Koh, Byung Chol. *The Foreign Policy of North Korea*. New York: Praeger, 1969.

Köhler, Heinz. *Economic Integration in the Soviet Bloc*. New York: Praeger, 1965.

Kolarz, Walter. *The Peoples of the Soviet Far East*. New York: Praeger, 1954

Leckie, Robert. *Conflict: The History of the Korean War, 1950–1953*. New York: Avon Books, 1962.

Lee, Chong-sik. *The Politics of Korean Nationalism*. Berkeley and Los

Angeles: University of California, 1963.

_____. *Materials on Korean Communism, 1945-1947.* Honolulu: Center for Korean Studies, University of Hawaii, 1977.

Lenin, Vladimir. *Selected Works.* Vol. II. New York: International Publishers, 1943.

Marx, Karl. *A Contribution to the Critique of Political Economy.* Translated and edited by Nahum Isaac Stone. Chicago: Charles Kerr and Co., 1918.

McCormack, Gavin, and Sheldon, Mark, eds. *Korea and South, The Deepening Crisis.* New York: Monthly Review Press, 1978.

Nahm, Andrew C. *North Korea: Her Past, Reality, and Impression.* Kalamazoo, Mich.: Center for Korean Studies, Western Michigan University, 1978.

Nam, Koon Woo. *The North Korean Communist Leadership 1945-1965.* University, Alabama: University of Alabama Press, 1974.

Nodong Sinmun, Editorial Department. *Self-Reliance and Independent National Economic Construction,* June 12, 1963. Peking: Foreign Languages Press, 1963.

Paige, Glenn D. *The Korean Decision.* New York: The Free Press, 1968.

_____. *The Korean People's Democratic Republic.* Stanford, Calif.: Hoover Institution Press, 1968.

Pearson, Roger, ed. *Korea in the World Today.* Washington, D.C.: Council on American Affairs, 1976.

Plekhanov, G. V. *The Role of Individuals in History.* Translated by J. Fineberg. Moscow: Foreign Languages Publishing House, 1946.

Rees, David. *Korea: The Limited War.* New York: St. Martin's Press, 1964.

Research Center for Peace and Unification. *North Korean Political System in Present Perspective.* Seoul, 1976.

Rudolph, Philip. *North Korea's Political and Economic Structure.* New York: Institute of Pacific Relations, 1959.

Sabine, George, and Thorson, Thomas. *A History of Political Theory,* 4th ed. Hinsdale, Ill.: Drysdale, 1973.

Salisbury, Harrison. *To Peking and Beyond: A Report on New Asia.* New York: Quadrangle Books, 1973.

Scalapino, Robert A., ed. *North Korea Today.* New York: Praeger, 1963.

_____. *The Communist Revolution in Asia.* Englewood Cliffs, N.J.: Prentice-Hall, 1969.

Scalapino, Robert A., and Lee, Chong-sik. *Communism in Korea.* 2 vols. Berkeley and Los Angeles: University of California Press, 1972.

Selected Works of Mao Zedong. Vol. 3. Beijing: Foreign Languages Press, 1955.

Seligman, Edwin R. A. *The Economic Interpretation of History.* New York:

Columbia University Press, 1902.

———. *The Economic Interpretation of History.* 2d ed., rev. New York: Gordian Press, 1966.

Shinn, Rinn-sup, and others. *Area Handbook for North Korea.* For the Department of Army, published by U.S. Government Printing Office, Washington, D.C., 1969.

Silberman, Bernard S. *Japan and Korea: A Critical Bibliography.* Tucson, Ariz.: University of Arizona Press, 1962.

Simons, Robert R. *The Strained Alliance: Peking, Pyongyang, and Moscow and the Politics of the Korean Civil War.* New York: The Free Press, 1975.

Solomon, Richard H., ed. *Asian Security in the 1980s: Problems of Politics for a Time of Transition.* Santa Monica, Calif.: Rand Corporation, 1979.

Suh, Dae-Sook. *The Korean Communist Movement 1918–1948.* Princeton: Princeton University Press, 1967.

———. *Documents of Korean Communism.* Princeton: Princeton University Press, 1971.

———. *Korean Communism, 1945–1980.* Honolulu: University Press of Hawaii, 1981.

Tucker, Robert C., ed. *The Marx-Engels Reader.* New York: W.W. Norton, 1972.

———. *The Lenin Anthology,* New York: W.W. Norton, 1975.

Weber, Max. *The Theory of Social and Economic Organization.* Translated by A. M. Henderson and Talcott Parsons; edited with an introduction by Talcott Parsons. Glencoe, Ill.: The Free Press, 1947.

———. *Essays in Sociology.* Edited by H. H. Gerth and C. Wright Mill. New York: Oxford University Press, 1958.

Yim, Yong Soon. *Two Koreas' Unification Policy and Strategy.* Occasional Papers/Reprints Series in Contemporary Asian Studies, no. 9. School of Law, University of Maryland, 1978.

ARTICLES

An, Tai Sung. "North Korea: Democratic People's Republic of Korea." In *1973–1982 Yearbooks on International Communist Affairs,* edited by Richard F. Staar. Stanford, Calif.: Hoover Institution Press, 1973–1982.

———. "New Winds in Pyongyang?" *Problems of Communism,* July–August 1966, pp. 68–71.

———. "North Korea: From Dictatorship to Dynasty." *Asian Affairs,* January–February 1977, pp. 172–83.

———. "All the President's Man." *Far Eastern Economic Review,* August 12, 1977, pp. 29–30.

_____. "The Heir Not So Apparent." *Far Eastern Economic Review*, July 7, 1978, pp. 27–28.

_____. "Dynastic Succession in the Communist State: A Profile of North Korea." *Korea and World Affairs*, Summer 1979, pp. 235–59.

Atta, Dale Van, and Nations, Richard. "Kim's Build-up to Blitzkrieg." *Far Eastern Economic Review*, March 5, 1982, p. 28.

Bradbury, John. "Sino-Soviet Competition in North Korea." *China Quarterly*, April–June 1961, pp. 15–28.

Chanda, Nayan. "The Ice Is Broken But the Chill Lingers On." *Far Eastern Economic Review*, March 5, 1982, pp. 32–34.

Cho, Chang-hyun. "The System of Local Government of North Korea." *Journal of Korean Affairs*, October 1971, pp. 12–21.

Cho, In-suk. "North Korean Economy." *Korean Journal of International Studies*, no. 1 (1975–1976): 23–40.

Ch'oe, Yong-ho. "Reinterpreting Traditional History in North Korea." *Journal of Asian Studies*, May 1981, pp. 525–38.

Choi, Chang-yoon. "The Sino-Soviet Conflict and Its Impact on the Korean Peninsula." *Korea and World Affairs*, Summer 1980, pp. 280–300.

_____. "Korea: Security and Strategic Issues." *Asian Survey*, November 1980, pp. 1123–39.

Chon, Tuk-Chu. "Is the 'Korean Confederation' Practicable? A Comparative Analysis of the East German Concept and the North Korean Concept of a Confederation." *Korea and World Affairs*, Summer 1980, pp. 349–62.

Chung, Chin O. "The Central Government and Power Structure of North Korea." *Journal of Korean Affairs*, October 1971, pp. 2–11.

Chung, Joseph S. "The Six-Year Plan (1971–1976) of North Korea: Targets, Problems and Prospects." *Journal of Korean Affairs*, July 1971, pp. 15–26.

_____. "North Korea's Economic System and the New Constitution." *Journal of Korean Affairs*, April 1973, pp. 28–34.

_____. "Economic Performance and Economic System: The North Korean Case." *Korea and World Affairs*, Spring 1977, pp. 67–86.

Clippinger, Morgan E. "Kim Chong-il in the North Korean Mass Media: A Study of Semi-Esoteric Communication," *Asian Survey*, March 1981, pp. 289–309.

Cumings, Bruce. "Kim's Korean Communism." *Problems of Communism*, March–April 1974, pp. 27–41.

Fallaci, Oriana. "Deng: Cleaning up Mao's 'Feudal Mistakes.'" *Washington Post*, August 31, 1980, p. D4 (Outlook Section).

Gayn, Mark. "The Cult of Kim." *New York Times Sunday Magazine*, October 1, 1972, pp. 16–17, 20–34.

Ha, Ang-ch'on. "The Chollima Movement Is the Central Line of the Korean

Workers' Party in the Socialist Construction." *Kyo-no Chosen*, May 1961, pp. 1–21.

Ha, Young Sun, "Nuclearization of Small States and World Order: The Case of Korea." *Asian Survey*, November 1978, pp. 1134–51.

Han, Jae-duk. "Communist Life in North Korea." *Korea Journal*, November 1963, pp. 1–13.

Hunter, Helen-Louise. "North Korea and the Myth of Equidistance." *Korea and World Affairs*, Summer 1980, pp. 268–79.

Kang, Shik-kwang. "Unification Policy in the 1980s: Adapting to Changing Conditions." *Korea and World Affairs*, Spring 1981, pp. 120–38.

Kang, Young-hoon. "The Men Around Kim Il-song." *Communist Affairs*, May–June 1966, pp. 22–26.

Kihl, Young-Whan. "North Korea: A Reevaluation." *Current History*, April 1982, pp. 155–59, 180–82.

Kim, Alexander J. "The 'Peak of Socialism' in North Korea: The Five- and Seven-Year Plans." *Asian Survey*, May 1965, pp. 255–69.

Kim, Cae-one. "Economic Interchanges Between South and North Korea." *Korea and World Affairs*, Spring 1981, pp. 77–106.

Kim, Chang-sun. "North Korea's Unification Strategy." *Korean Signal*, October–December 1975, pp. 29–33.

Kim, Gahb-chol. "The Shaping and Functioning of North Korea's Governing Ideology." *Vantage Point*, July 1981, pp. 1–10; and August 1981, pp. 1–10.

Kim, Gyo-hwan. "The Ideology of Three Revolutions." *Vantage Point*, June 1981, pp. 1–11.

Kim, Hak Joon. "The Origin and Evolution of the South-North Korean Division." *Problems of Korean Unification*, 1976, pp. 9–66.

_____. "Present and Future of the South-North Talks: As Viewed from Korea." *Korea and World Affairs*, Summer 1979, pp. 209–22.

Kim, Ilpyong J. "The Mobilization System in North Korean Politics." *Journal of Korean Affairs*, April 1972, pp. 3–15.

_____. "Approach to Economic Development." *Problems in Communism*, January–February 1973, pp. 44–54.

Kim, Il-song. "Report on the Work of the Central Committee to the Fifth Congress of the Workers' Party of Korea." *Pyongyang Times*, November 3, 1970, pp. 1–23.

Kim, Jae Dok. "Strategic Transition in North Korea's Unification Policy." *Vantage Point*, March 1981, pp. 1–13; and April 1981, pp. 1–11.

Kim, Myong Chol. "Biography of an Infant Prodigy." *Far Eastern Economic Review*, March 5, 1982, pp. 30–32.

Kim, Roy U. T. "Sino-North Korean Relations." *Asian Survey*, August 1968, pp. 708–22.

Kim, Young C. "The Democratic People's Republic of Korea in 1975." *Asian Survey*, January 1976, pp. 89–93.

_____. "North Korea 1979: National Unification and Economic Development." *Asian Survey*, January 1980, pp. 53–62.

_____. "North Korea in 1980: The Son Also Rises." *Asian Survey*, January 1981, pp. 112–24.

Koh, B. C. "North Korea: Profile of a Garrison State." *Problems of Communism*, January–February 1969, pp. 18–27.

_____. "Ideology and Political Control in North Korea." *Journal of Politics*, August 1970, pp. 655–74.

_____. "Chuch'esong in Korean Politics." *Studies in Comparative Communism*, Spring–Summer 1974, pp. 83–106.

_____. "The Battle Without Victors: The Korean Question in the U.N. General Assembly." *Journal of Korean Affairs*, January 1976, pp. 43–63.

_____. "Inter-Korean Relations: Seoul's Perspective." *Asian Survey*, November 1980, pp. 1108–22.

Kun, Joseph. "North Korea: Between Moscow and Peking." *China Quarterly*, July–September 1967, pp. 48–58.

Lee, Byoung-young. "Comparison of the Economic Power Between South and North Korea." *Korea and World Affairs*, Fall 1980, pp. 448–65.

Lee, Chong-sik. "The Korean Communists and Yenan." *China Quarterly*, January–March 1962, pp. 182–92.

_____. "The Socialist Revolution in the North Korean Countryside." *Asian Survey*, October 1962, pp. 9–22.

_____. "Politics in North Korea: Pre-Korean War Stage." *China Quarterly*, April–June 1963, pp. 3–16.

_____. "Witch Hunt Among the Guerrillas: The Min-sheng-T'uan Incident." *China Quarterly*, April–June 1966, pp. 107–117.

Lee, Dong-Bok. "North Korea and Its Succession Issue." *Korea and World Affairs*, Spring 1977, pp. 48–66.

_____. "Present and Future of Inter-Korean Relations: The January 12 Proposal and the Sixth Congress of the KWP." *Korea and World Affairs*, Spring 1981, pp. 36–52.

_____. "North Korea After the Sixth KWP Congress." *Korea and World Affairs*, Fall 1981, pp. 415–40.

Lee, Hong-youn. "Structure and Prospect of North Korean Trade." *Vantage Point*, September 1981, pp. 1–12.

Lee, Kang-sok. "Sources of Kim Il-song's Juche Ideology—with Reference to Maoist Thoughts—." *Vantage Point*, November 1981, pp. 1–11.

Lee, Pong S. "An Estimate of North Korea's National Income." *Asian Survey*, June 1972, pp. 518–26.

_____. "North Korean Economy in the Seventies." *Journal of Korean Affairs*, October 1974, pp. 3–17.

Lee, So-haeng. "Ideological Education in North Korea." *Vantage Point*, September 1980, pp. 1–10.

Lee, Young Ho. "Military Balance and Peace in the Korean Peninsula." *Asian Survey*, August 1981, pp. 852–64.

Lewis, John. "North Korea Starts to Put Its House in Order." *Far Eastern Economic Review*, August 17, 1979, pp. 42–44.

Moak, Samuel K. "North Korea's Agricultural Policies in Collectivization." *Journal of Korean Affairs*, January 1974, pp. 23–36.

Niksch, Larry A. "U.S. Troop Withdrawal from South Korea: Past Shortcomings and Future Prospects." *Asian Survey*, March 1981, pp. 325–43.

Oh, Ki-song. "An Analysis of Recent North Korean Propaganda Material." *Journal of Korean Affairs*, January 1972, pp. 25–41.

Omori, Minoru. "Mao's Worst Crisis." *New Republic*, January 28, 1967, pp. 18–19.

"On Personality Cult and Other Questions." *Beijing Review*, December 29, 1980, pp. 13–15.

Paek, Hwang-gi. "Armament Industry of North Korea." *Vantage Point*, March 1982, pp. 1–10; and April 1982, pp. 1–10.

Paige, Glenn D. "North Korea and the Emulation of Russian and Chinese Behavior." In *Communist Strategies in Asia: A Comparative Analysis of Governments and Practice*, edited by A. Doak Barnett. New York: Praeger, 1963, pp. 228–61.

Paige, Glenn D., and Lee, Dong-jun. "The Post-War Politics of Communist Korea." *China Quarterly*, April–June 1963, pp. 17–29.

Park, Hal Il. "A Diagnosis of the Proposal of the South-North Federation of Korea." *Unification Policy Quarterly* II, no. 2 (1976): 69–71.

Park, Tong-whan. "The Korean Arms Race: Implications in the International Politics of Northeast Asia." *Asian Survey*, June 1980, pp. 648–60.

Pfeffer, Richard M. "Serving the People and Continuing the Revolution." *China Quarterly*, October–December 1972, pp. 620–53.

Porter, Gareth. "Time to Talk with North Korea." *Foreign Policy*, Spring 1979, pp. 52–73.

"Power Should Not Be Concentrated in the Hands of Individuals." *Beijing Review*, November 3, 1980, pp. 15–17.

Rhee, Sang Woo. "Overriding Strategy Versus Subversion Tactics: A Comparative Study on South and North Korean Unification Strategies." *Unification Policy Quarterly* II, no. 4 (1976):40–65.

Richardson, Ron. "New Push for a New Kim." *Far Eastern Economic Re-*

view, April 24, 1981, pp. 32–33.

———. "The Heir More Apparent." *Far Eastern Economic Review*, February 19, 1982, pp. 16–17.

Robinson, Joan. "Korean Miracle." *Monthly Review*, January 1965, pp. 544–49.

Rummel, Rudolf F. "Korea and the Correlation of Forces Toward War." *Korea and World Affairs*, Spring 1981, pp. 18–35.

Scalapino, Robert A. "Foreign Policy of North Korea." *China Quarterly*, April–June 1963, pp. 30–50.

———. "Current Dynamics of the Korean Peninsula." *Problems of Communism*, November–December 1981, pp. 16–31.

Scalapino, Robert A., and Lee, Chong-sik. "The Origins of the Korean Communist Movement." *Journal of Asian Studies*, November 1960, pp. 9–31; and February 1961, pp. 149–67.

Scott Stokes, Henry. "Competition Between the Two Koreas Pays Off in Greater Prosperity for Both." *New York Times*, August 11, 1980, p. 10.

Sharkey, John. "The 1st Marxist Monarchy." *Washington Post*, October 1978, p. D2 (Outlook Section).

Shim, Jae Hoon. "Watching the Son's Rise with Suspicion." *Far Eastern Economic Review*, March 5, 1982, pp. 30–31.

Shinn, Rinn-sup. "Changing Perspectives in North Korea: Foreign and Reunification Policies." *Problems of Communism*, January–February 1973, pp. 55–71.

———. "North Korea in 1981: First Year for De Facto Successor Kim Jong-il." *Asian Survey*, January 1982, pp. 99–106.

Snow, Edgar. "Snow and Mao." *Kansas City Star*, September 28, 1969.

———. "A Conversation with Mao Tse-tung." *Life* (Magazine), April 30, 1971.

Tucker, Robert C. "The Theory of Charismatic Leadership." *Daedalus*, Summer 1968, pp. 731–56.

———. "The Rise of Stalin's Personality Cult." *American Historical Review*, April 1979, pp. 347–66.

White, Gordon. "North Korean *Chuch'e*: The Political Economy of Independence." *Bulletin of Concerned Asian Scholars*, April–June 1975, pp. 44–54.

Yang, Sung Chul. "The Kim Il-song Cult in North Korea." *Korea and World Affairs*, Spring 1980, pp. 161–86.

Yim, Yong Soon. "The Unification Strategy of North Korea: Adroit Diplomacy or Fishing in Troubled Waters." *Korea and World Affairs*, Winter 1977, pp. 440–65.

———. "The Prospect of Peaceful Unification of Korea in the 1980s: The Inter-Korean Internal Political Perspective." *Korea and World Affairs,* Spring 1980, pp. 187–208.

———. "North Korean Strategic Doctrine in the East Asian Regional System." *Korea and World Affairs,* Summer 1981, pp. 177–202.

Yoon, Leoyong Tae. "Rationality of South-North Nonaggression Pact." *Unification Policy Quarterly* 2, no. 2 (1976):45–47.

Zagoria, Donald S., and Kim, Young-kun. "North Korea and the Major Powers." *Asian Survey,* December 1975, pp. 1107–35.

JAPANESE-LANGUAGE SOURCES

Arai, Seidai. "Kitachosen no Naisei to Gaiko" [Politics and Diplomacy of North Korea]. *Kukusai Mondai,* July 1967, pp. 18–25.

Chosen Keizai Nenpo [Korean Economic Yearbook]. Tokyo: Kaisosha, 1939.

Gekkan Chosen Shiro [Monthly of Korean Materials]. Tokyo: Chosen Mondai Kenkyusho, 1972.

Han, Sol-ya. *Hero General Kim Il-song.* Tokyo: Chosen Shinbosha, 1962.

Hayashi, Takehiko. *Kita Chosen to Minami Chosen* [North Korea and South Korea]. Tokyo: Saimaru Shuhankai, 1971.

Kim Nichi Sei Chosaku-shu [Collected Works of Kim Il-song]. Tokyo: Miraisha, 1970.

"Kita Chosen no Seijikeizai" [North Korean Political and Economic Conditions]. *Chosa Geppo,* July 1965, pp. 11–27.

Nakayasu, Yosaku. *Kankoku Dokuhon* [Korean Reader]. 4 vols. Tokyo: Jijo Tsushinsha, 1963.

Senji, Tsuboe. *Hokusen no Kaiho Junen* [Ten-Year History of North Korea]. Tokyo: Mikkan Rodo Sushinsha, 1955.

Toitsu Chosen Nenkan, 1967–1968 [One Korea Yearbook, 1967–1968]. Tokyo: Toitsu Chosen Shimbunsha, 1967.

U.S. GOVERNMENT SOURCES

Arms Control and Disarmament Agency. *World Military Expenditures and Arms Transfers, 1967–1976.* Washington, D.C.: July 1978.

Central Intelligence Agency, National Foreign Assessment Center. *Korea: The Economic Race Between the North and the South* (a research paper). ER 78-10008, January 1978.

———. *Directory of Officials of the Democratic People's Republic of Korea* (a reference aid). CR80-11041, March 1980.

Congress, Senate, Committee on Foreign Relations, *U.S. Troop Withdraw-*

al from the Republic of Korea, January 9, 1978. Washington, D.C.: U.S. Government Printing Office, 1978.

Department of Army. *Area Handbook for North Korea.* Washington, D.C.: U.S. Government Printing Office, 1969.

_____. *Communist North Korea: A Bibliographic Survey.* Washington, D.C.: U.S. Government Printing Office, 1971.

Department of the Interior. *Minerals Yearbook 1949.* Washington, D.C.: U.S. Government Printing Office, 1951.

Department of State. *Korea Economic Mission.* Washington, D.C.: U.S. Government Printing Office, June 1947.

_____. *North Korea: A Case Study in the Techniques of Takeover.* Washington, D.C.: U.S. Government Printing Office, 1961.

_____. *The Record on Korean Unification 1945–1960.* Washington, D.C.: U.S. Government Printing Office, 1961.

The Korean Conundrum: A Conversation with Kim Il-song. Report of a study mission to South Korea, Japan, the People's Republic of China, and North Korea, July 12–21, 1980, to the House Committee on Foreign Affairs. Washington, D.C.: U.S. Government Printing Office, August 1981.

OTHER SOURCES

Asahi Shimbun (Tokyo)
Asian Forum (Washington, D.C.)
Beijing Review (Beijing)
Daily Mail (London)
Dong-A Ilbo (Seoul)
Economist (London)
Far Eastern Economic Review (Hong Kong)
Far Eastern Economic Yearbooks, 1970–1982 (Hong Kong)
Foreign Broadcast Information Service, Daily Reports, Asia and Pacific (Springfield, Va.)
Frankfurter Allgemeine Zeitung (Frankfurt, West Germany)
Hoc Tap (Hanoi)
Hongqui (Beijing)
Indian Express (Bombay and New Delhi)
Japan Quarterly (Tokyo)
Japan Times (Tokyo)
Journal of Asian Studies (Ann Arbor, Mich.)
Kita Chosen Kenkyu (Tokyo)
Korea Herald (Seoul)
Korea Today (Pyongyang)

Le Monde (Paris)
Los Angeles Times (Los Angeles)
Mainichi Shimbun (Tokyo)
Ming Pao Daily (Hong Kong)
New York Times (New York)
North Korea News (Seoul)
Pacific Affairs (British Columbia, Canada)
Pravda (Moscow)
Pyongyang Times (Pyongyang)
Sankei Shimbun (Tokyo)
Studies on Chinese Communism (Taipei)
Ta Kung Pao (Hong Kong)
Tong-il Ilbo (Tokyo)
Washington Post (Washington, D.C.)
1980 World Bank Atlas
Yomiuri Shimbun (Tokyo)
Zenei (Tokyo)

Index

About the Author

TAI SUNG AN is Everett E. Nuttle Professor of Political Science and Chairman of the Department of Political Science and International Studies at Washington College in Chestertown, Maryland. Professor An is the author of *Mao Tse-tung's Cultural Revolution, The Sino-Soviet Territorial Dispute, The Lin Piao Affair,* and *A Political Handbook of North Korea* (forthcoming). He is the author of numerous articles published in leading journals, the recipient of the Lindback Award for Distinguished Teaching at Washington College.